The cry went up when the men were positioned. Shells exploded along the crest and the site was so close that the flattened men could hear the rounds leave the tube. After the sixth mortar round hit, small-arms fire ranged in on Beach from rearward along the ridge. His men became fully occupied in defending their ground.

Sgt. Tyrone Adderly, leading First Squad, Third Platoon, was in the position directly north of the bridge and facing west. Beach had no way to re-enforce him because his group was pinned. Adderly could see dark forms moving off both flanks and across his rear. He whispered to his people, "Hug the dirt. Don't fire. They may miss us." It was the best policy....

The charge against gun No. 3 was repulsed. Smokey the Bear came over and began dropping flares. At last Beach and Captain Whalen were having a running dialogue and Whalen knew for the first time where all the riflemen were positioned. The enemy had bunched around gun No. 6.

"Turn those guns around and let them have it," Whalen said to the crews on No. 3 and No. 5.

➤

"The best writer of our time on men in war is General S.L.A. Marshall."
—Hollis Alpert, *Saturday Review*

➤

BATTLES IN THE MONSOON

Also by S.L.A. Marshall

Bird

Published by
WARNER BOOKS

BATTLES IN THE MONSOON

S.L.A. MARSHALL

WARNER BOOKS

A Warner Communications Company

WARNER BOOKS EDITION

This Warner Books Edition is published by arrangement with
The Battery Press, Inc. P.O. Box 3107, Uptown Station,
Nashville, Tennessee 37219

Cover photo: U.S. Army

Warner Books, Inc.
666 Fifth Avenue
New York, N.Y. 10103

 A Warner Communications Company

Printed in the United States of America
First Warner Books Printing: May, 1989

10 9 8 7 6 5 4 3 2 1

Dedication

With Love
to
Cindy
Crew
Kathy
Sukey
Robbie
Bruce
Mikelle
H.W.O.K.
All Other Kinnards
and Their Friends

Contents

Foreword

My third trip to South Vietnam, which ran from early May into July, 1966, while resulting from numerous pressures, personal and professional, being put upon me, was directed toward one narrow objective, herewith easily defined.

I wanted to know for my own good how the United States Army was coping with the extraordinary conditions of irregular warfare, much of it in dense jungle, all of it in an unfavorable environment that, as to climate, terrain and emotional adjustment to a small ally being almost wholly strange to our way of life as to our military customs and outlook, was certain to put unusual stress upon troops.

If I could find out for myself, what was to be learned might also hold something of interest, and possible value, for the American people and perhaps for the military establishment.

Covering a war, determining how any army operates in the field, has never seemed to me to be a very difficult task. It does not so much require the mastery of a complex technique as the willingness to get on one line and hold with it till the job is finished. This any competent reporter is able to do; the failure or reluctance to abide by the rule is simply proof of incompetence. Further, I cannot honestly say that such a commitment may only be insured by large resources of enterprise, imagination and fortitude. The work may seem strenuous as one describes it. The strain is not felt in the doing. The discovery, as well as the drive that comes from the work itself, more than compensates for all the small hazards, worries and exertions. At age sixty-six there is also a bonus that comes out of proving to one's self that one can still do it.

There are various ways of covering field operations, and the business has not come up with any new and important secrets or formulae since the Crimean War. Furthermore, there is no great difficulty in establishing a dependable datum plane for an exacting analysis of field operations that will serve the professional needs of fighting forces. How to do it has been well and frequently spelled out since World War II.

The magic of communications in the modern world and the proliferating of news-gathering and information-disseminating services within the general society and as adjuncts of the bureaucracy are as extravagantly impressive as any wonder of the age. Think for a minute! Here is Telestar out in space distributing the phenomena of our day around the world at the speed of light. The USIA, a relatively new thing in our national life, is deployed around the globe at the expense of the taxpayer with the mission of clarifying the world view on our most important affairs. In Saigon there are 350 correspondents supposedly assigned to making the war and its issues understandable to people everywhere, a group thrice the size of the press gallery in the Korean War.

Yet despite all of this elaboration, the struggle in Vietnam is the most wretchedly reported war in the fane of our history since old Zach Taylor fought at Buena Vista. Never before have men and women in such numbers contributed so little to so many.

No American living, though he be a military scholar or only an armchair expert, may begin to understand how the war is being fought by the forces of the United States from what he is told over the air, or by what he reads, or from what all government agencies have to say on this subject. He may carefully read every weekly news magazine, subscribe to every press service, and listen to every pronouncement by the national spokesmen, and he will still not get it. The outpouring simply compounds his unavoidable state of confusion.

Nothing intelligent is written of tactics, of new problems encountered and either solved or contended with, of the working field relationship between U.S. forces and the Vietnamese (a wholly new thing in military experience), of the logistical Gordian knots peculiar to this strange war, or of how average American youths, city-bred, brave and endure the privations of jungle campaigning. We get wisps of such stories, but nothing comprehensive.

Example: We are told that the American soldier in Vietnam is a "new breed" of fighter and that his combat morale is high beyond any prior measure. But wherein is he different? From what magic arises this new *élan*, when some senators behave like poltroons and treason by a rabble is tolerated and given a different name? About the answers, we may only wonder, though getting at the truth could conceivably contribute to the future well-being of the United States.

Example: It is still regarded as a monstrous blunder by the United States military that so much money was wasted beginning in July, 1965. Fleets of ships went forth laden with military supply. There were no ports to receive them. So they idled offshore for weeks in some instances while the demurrage piled high. Still not understood is that the wastage resulted from a command decision deliberately made by Gen. William C. Westmoreland, as courageous and right-minded a decision as any military chief was ever called to make. In July, 1965, the war was at the point of being lost; it could be saved only by deploying U.S. troops inland as fast as they arrived, despite the lack of base facilities. The one solution for the seemingly insoluble problem was to treat the ships as floating warehouses and to hell with the demurrage. If troops could go to battle with only "hot cargo" items—ammunition, medicines and rations—getting along without toothpaste, extra clothing, toilet paper, cigarets and all manner of PX supply, the taxpayer ought to be able to take his part of the rap.

The body of my case, however, lies in this book. The battles of which I write were hardly reported as such to the American people. There are some reporters such as Ward Just and Charley Black of Columbus, Ga., who dig in with the combat line, show after show. Invariably those who do are themselves former fighters. I saw no other correspondents in the battle areas. There was the exception when one incident mainly—the dramatic action of Captain Carpenter— brought them forward in platoons to give him the national spotlight. The reader may judge whether the incident was so uniquely meritorious, either as a tale of heroism or a feat of arms, that all else within the frame of the campaign should have been treated as without significance. Carpenter was himself nauseated by this gross concentration on the fleeting and sensational to the exclusion of nearly everything that mattered. So as I see it, we have over and over again in Vietnam the melancholy tale of Pork Chop Hill, which became a famous fight by accident, the press having ignored it wholly. There was nothing great about it until Gregory Peck won it. I can never be sure of the public taste. But if the United States Army along the combat line has such little importance to our society that the press, in virtually ignoring it, is merely catering to the whims of readership, we have slipped more than a little bit. The thought makes it no easier for me to take seriously the young man who calls himself a war correspondent when he spends his time chasing after riots in Saigon.

For some part of the failure of the press corps in Vietnam in earlier years the government bureaucracy, including the military, was indeed responsible. Its general attitude was suppressive and repressive, made so in part by the secrecy of the Diem regime and the shaky military juntas that immediately followed. Either awkwardness or sheer ignorance, on the part of those who make our policy, strained unduly the relations between press corps and officialdom. The problem could have been somewhat ameliorated had the Pentagon's director of public information been capable of understanding it. Since he was not, the more prominent members of the press corps sharpened their hatchets against government policy and were awarded Pulitzer prizes for their efforts.

There is no such condition today. American correspondents are given freer access to the battle fronts and bases, with readier and more agreeable facilities for moving about, than they were ever accorded before in any war. The commanders give them warmer welcome and take them into confidence more fully than in times past.

With all these advantages, and with the exception of perhaps a dozen or so press correspondents, the only members of the corps who consistently work the front are the TV reporters and camera crews. They accept the risk gamely enough. If they have one fault seriously calling for repair it is that they concentrate on the gore, the shock, the horror and the agony disproportionately. The war, as it is dished up to the American family in the living room every evening, is the modern equivalent of *All Quiet on the Western Front*, which had not one undertone of humor, light and warmth. War is not like that.

Why the newsmen do not get with it is the mystery. Some of them would doubtless be willing. Possibly, under the influence of the managing editor's desk, the majority prefer the pursuit of the day-to-day sensation, any story that may add to tension, doubt and divisiveness at home, any subject that may whet controversy.

One who has worked this vineyard through the larger part of a greatly rewarding lifetime cannot be unmindful of the full weight of these pressures on men and women afield in a strange country who have families, bills to meet and reputations to make, and on their superiors in a sometimes comfortable front office who have daily and hourly decisions to make, attempting to distinguish between the important and the unimportant—what makes big news today and what is relatively trivial in the scheme of things.

There are sufficient reasons why they should be more perplexed, if not more distracted, than ever before. My home state has a governor ever ready to be interviewed on how the war in Vietnam should be conducted, though he knows nothing about military operations and is little informed about main problems in foreign policy. His qualifications for high office are as they may be. But in his readiness to shape public thinking on the problems faced by the nation in Southeast Asia, he is the average American VIP—his willingness to sound an opinion invariably outruns his supply of information. Possibly it is because we are fighting an undeclared war that there is little or no restraint exercised by those individuals who feel that taking a position which may be politically popular is the sensible and rightful way to dispose of the issues.

With the latter I am not concerned in this book, though I have repeatedly and unequivocally put my position in the clear. I went to South Vietnam simply because I wished to know how the United States Army was coping with its problems.

In December, 1965, I wrote a syndicated column analyzing the campaign of the First Cavalry Division beyond Plei Me and into the Ia Drang Valley. It was not highly favorable, and was in fact injudicious, since I had reached conclusions out of three magazine articles supposedly interpreting the operation to the American people. Shortly I received a letter in mild reproof from my old comrade, Maj. Gen. H.W.O. Kinnard, commanding the division, who suggested that I better come and have a look for myself.

In December, then, I began keeping my calendar clear for the months of May, June and July, 1966. The particular reason for choosing this quarter was that it coincided with the beginning of the monsoon season. The period of inclement weather seemed certain to tax American resources inordinately and provide the critical test of the U.S. Army's power to contend under the most adverse circumstances.

During the interim, other pressures—one of them of an official nature—were put on me to proceed with the mission. They were, in one sense, immaterial. If it was all right with my wife, Cate Marshall, then I would go. Throughout our marriage she has been a trooper. Six or seven times she has packed me on not more than one hour's notice to go on a comparable adventure, which makes life very easy for me.

This time we had months to think it over. She hesitated only because she wished to be sure that there might be something worth gaining, other than for ourselves. The latter never seems to bother her a great deal.

I follow but two rules of thumb in doing this kind of work. The first is that I will stay with one division or its equivalent for at least thirty days running. Only so can I arrive at a set of criteria by which I can judge operations throughout the Army as a whole: it is a period of learning for me. The second rule is that I will never try to cover the whole show, but within the limited sector that I have chosen, I will do whatever is required to complete the reconstruction of going operations. This time I chose the II Corps Zone as my laboratory because Harry Kinnard was there when I started, and so was most of the action.

Many old friends, such as Kinnard, Jack Norton, Dave Hackworth, Swede Larsen, Ted Mataxis, Sergeant Major McCullough and Sergeant Hernandez, were there to help and encourage me, thus lightening the task beyond common understanding. The many new friends I met along the way, for example, Generals Will Pearson, Jack Wright and Glenn Walker, Colonels Beatty and Becker, Hank Emerson, Jack Hennessey, Hal Moore, and many, many others, including Sergeants Kirby and Koebbe and Private Dolby, gave me the assistance which made the work possible. To them all I feel deep obligation. The pity is that I cannot complete the list, for I would have to name hundreds of men. My twin hopes are that they will understand my failure to mention them and that what comes out will be worthy of their confidence and trust.

It should go almost without saying that to General Westmoreland and his staff, his deputy, Gen. John Heintges, and his public affairs assistants, I am more than all else indebted because they made certain that the path was cleared for me all the way along the line. Looking back, I am aware of my good fortune. What could have been difficult was made simple because of their consideration. Within the military, our own or any other, I have never been vouchsafed a more wide-open opportunity, made particularly pleasurable because of their company. Beyond being great warriors, these are enjoyable companions.

Cate Marshall has had to go through the labor of book bearing with me, which inflicts more anguish and strain on the party of the second part than any other kind of labor and bearing in our family. She does the manuscript, edits the notes and sits as critic; there is no other reader or judge. For whatever is in error she is therefore responsible, meaning that the Army, the government and the author are free of blame absolutely. For taking this great load off my mind I simply ask blessings on her.

S.L.A. Marshall

Dherran Dhoun
Birmingham, Michigan

BOOK 1

Crazy Horse

Out of Rumor and Hunger

Their plan had been set the night before. They would ford the river under cover of dark and start climbing the first hill to get well within the forest growth before dawn cracked.

That way they hoped to escape surveillance from the heights beyond. It necessitated a jumpoff at 0400, much too early for the cooks to be up and about. So the patrol stayed with it, though it meant starting the uphill grind on an empty stomach.

Here was one of those little breaks that so frequently determine the course of a battle and alter the face of war itself. It was just one of those things, one of those bells that sometimes ring.

Absolutely no one of the Civilian Irregular Defense Group in the remote fort at the head of the Vinh Thanh Valley could foresee that, not the early start, but going forth hungry made all the difference that would lead to an astounding success.

No one at Camp Radcliff, the not-distant defensive base where the First Cavalry Division had fashioned a seventeen-kilometer-long barrier around Hon Kon Mountain, could anticipate that the appetite of a small patrol, unconnected with the division, was about to give new direction to its forces, opening to undreamed opportunity.

Though located within a twelve-minute ride of one another by chopper, the two camps were almost poles apart. There was no direct line of communication from one to the other. They could not converse even by radio, though messages could be relayed through the Special Forces "B" Team at center of An Khe village.

The big camp was as modern as the next second, relatively comfortable, and so strongly secured by its fields of wire and circle of watchtowers, backed up by the enclosed guns and fighting aviation, as to be beyond danger of serious challenge. Its people could bucket about with impunity almost anywhere in the near neighborhood.

The C.I.D.G. fort at the head of the next valley to the northeast of the giant hedgehog was a relic, a patchwork of ill-sited trenches, with fighting bunkers and underground sleeping quarters in no definable or describable relationship to one another, but simply thrown together around the no longer serviceable concrete walls of an old French redoubt.

There was nothing good about this souped-up ruin, except its people and the fact that it was sited on a rounded knoll overlooking the flat bed of the Song Con River. The surrounding field of wire, with bunkers sited to pour out enfilading machine-gun fire, gave the two Montagnard companies garrisoning it a tenuous hold on security. They are mercenaries paid by the United States. Their wives and children move where they do and, in the event of attack on the base camp, share the risks. Shed no tears for them; they act far happier than most American families.

Being in American service, they are advised by Special Forces soldiers. But to keep everything squared away in this politically complex partnership, they are rated as civilians, though they fight in jungle suits. Further to assuage the pains of sovereignty, there is a Vietnamese detachment on station with them to interpret, keep a finger in administration, and if need be, fight.

As to why the patrol set forth in the darkest hour of 14 May, 1966, seeking it hardly knew what, the initial cause was ugly rumor later compounded by dark suspicion.

Across the Song Con from the fort are five small villages

all having the same name. So they are called Vinh Phuc One, Two, Three, Four and Five, to keep from confusing the postman, should he come knocking. There are also five Vinh Thanh villages, distinguished from each other in that fashion. It is a quaint local custom, adding spice to this chronicle. In early May the story began circulating from one Vinh Phuc to another that the C.I.D.G. camp would be knocked over in mid-month. A helpful citizen bore the tidings to the parties of the second part, to whose ears it sounded like a tale that the enemy dearly wanted someone to believe. Anyhow, it prompted Capt. Frederick A. Tinsetta to redouble his intelligence effort, which is to say he posted a reward of 1,000 piasters for capture of a VC prisoner, or about $5. at the going rate. He did not expect much of that.

Through roundabout channels the rumor at last reached Lieut. Col. Bobby Lang, G-2 of the cavalry division. He sifted it and concluded tentatively that if the enemy wanted such a notion bruited about, it was to draw a relief column of the division via the road to the head of the Vinh Thanh Valley, there to sandbag it. As a first undertaking, the cavalrymen had purged that area of Viet Cong in the early autumn of 1965, then renamed it Happy Valley, which is easier to spell than Vinh Thanh.

Tinsetta and the other people at the fort, figuring that they were right under the gun, couldn't hold still on Lang's assumption and, moreover, did not know about it. They ran a patrol over the river and through the trees in the early morning of 8 May. By luck it snared one jungle prowler who, getting a bullet through his right heel, was no longer in shape to run off. He freely admitted being a local VC, at which point the No. 1 most wanted man was returned to the fort, hobbling. Being shot in the foot, he ran off at the mouth, and without being punched around, but warming to the friendly game of conversation, he boasted that his company, minus himself naturally, was about to join a well-armed battalion from the outside and have a go against the Vinh Thanh camp.

"Two of our platoons are right up there," he said, pointing to the peak directly north across the valley. It is the same mountain that, dominating the old French fort, though being nameless, was subsequently christened "Hereford" by a cow-minded Texan serving on the cavalry division staff. It is one way to cross beef cattle with history.

The POW rambled on, though Tinsetta, having already heard more than enough, was saying to the others, "From here out, there must be patrolling every day and ambushing at night." So there was, more or less. No one came forth to claim the 1,000 piasters.

Colonel Lang also got the report, via the grapevine, and again picked up his ears. This soldier smells out things like a beagle. But as with all intelligence in the Vietnam war, what one thinks one sniffs in the first place is never exactly or in general what one finds. Mice pop up where elephants are hunted expectantly, and vice versa.

Lang strongly recommended that a B-52 strike be put on the cap of the big peak and spread to the north along the backbone of the mass. He will never have a more inspired hunch in his career, which should be long and productive. If shortly after he was less sure that such strength was present as to justify the big clobber, that weakening may be laid to professional training. G-2's become accustomed to thinking "yes" on Monday and "no" on Tuesday.

At any rate, the Air Force turned down Lang's request. A small tactical air strike was substituted for the big bang; it covered only a small part of the area and missed the key ground. The eight tac aircraft went in with half loads. What is known from subsequent POW interrogations is that, had the B-52's laid it on as requested, they would have wiped out at least one NVA regimental headquarters.

That is not to say that the decision worked out adversely. The strike might have turned enemy ambitions for the moment, but his main forces would have remained in these mountains and no battle would have developed.

By now the prickling at the C.I.D.G. camp had begun to interest Gen. Jack Norton at Division, Gen. Harry Kinnard at Corps and General Westmoreland at MAC-V.

There is this about intelligence flow in the Vietnam war. The small bits of information may be more fuzzy and less susceptible to arrangement in a meaningful pattern than ever before. But what happens, and what is to be said of it, resounds more clearly and loudly at all levels of command. The G-2's are better communicators than the old school, and what they pick up gets fuller circulation quickly despite grievous technical handicaps.

It was just at this time that I flew with Kinnard to see Norton and we got the first inkling that something of promise might be astir around Vinh Thanh that would switch operations in a wholly different direction. Already on schedule was a Corps operation code-named Sam Houston, due to begin on 22 May, that might have to be modified or canceled. These two old friends talked of whether the cavalry division could afford to get involved in a campaign in the high mountains. The situation remaining obscure, the question remained tabled.

The few people at the old French fort were still concerned with the immediate threat to their future, unaware that what they did and what might come of it was enlisting the interest of everyone above them.

So the patrol of 15 May began as strictly a local affair with a few men doing what they thought best in the interests of the people right around them. No sense of doing anything big-time, no feeling of being sons of destiny, weighted them as they prepared to winnow the jungle with a hand rake. The better reason for taking a closer look at them now is that they will reappear much later in the drama.

The patrol of thirty men was the I & R (intelligence and reconnaissance) platoon of the ninety-man-strong Son Hai Company. These mountain men were far off their native heath. Members of the H Re tribe, they come from Quang Ngai village. The youngest among them was a fifte-year-old medic. The adult males are stalwart, keen of mind and given to sobriety. Hard fighters, skilled at tracking, they are acutely sensitive to every sound of the jungle through which they slip noiselessly. Wholly friendly to people they like, utterly rude to those they don't, they had thrown in with the Americans unreservedly.

Theirs was the only company of H Re in the district.

They had been at the Vinh Thanh fort only ten days and did not know the mountains due north of it. That already there was full confidence in them among the Special Forces soldiers was due to their impressive record.

In August, 1965, Son Hai Company had withstood full-scale siege by the Viet Cong for seven days in the outpost at Kanak fifteen miles west of Vinh Thanh. Some months following the repulse, the post was closed down as being too exposed.

From January till May, 1966, Son Hai Company stood guard over Mang Yang Pass, twenty miles west of An Khe. Their task was to keep open Route No. 19 so that military traffic could travel the highway between the sea and the bases on the Kontum Plateau. It was next the Mang Yang Pass that French Mobile Group 100 was annihilated on 24 June, 1954, in one of the great disasters of that war. The company had come through its long-drawn vigil at the Pass, as through its ordeal by fire at Kanak, without losing one man through desertion.

By dark the patrol crossed the flood-swollen main channel of the Song Con in assault boats, then splashed across the sand bars and waded through the shallower waters of the tributary that joins the main river just above the fort. The movement was due northeast and they went double time, alternately jogging and walking. For more than one mile in front of them the land sloped upward treelessly, without ravines or creases. They rushed, feeling they had to be sure of closing to within the first draw, where the jungle growth began, before first light broke.

They moved single file, with a point of one squad thirty paces to the fore. This scout element was formed wholly of the mountain men. Sgt. David C. Freeman, of Baltimore, Md., the medic and the youngest of the two Special Forces soldiers going along, was midway of the column. Sgt. Burton R. Adams was next the rear. Following him was the radioman, though Adams did the talking, and last the leader of Son Hai Company, Dimh Ghim, who was simply addressed as "Commander."

In their rucksacks they carried cold boiled rice and meat

sauce for flavoring. Some time later it would have to suffice for the missed breakfast.

By 0600 they came to the draw between the two villages, Vinh Phuc Four and Five. It was just in time. There the well-beaten trace they had been following from the valley bottom split toward the two settlements. There was no track pointing forward into the bush. So they plunged on into a growth that thickened rapidly and rose even higher, there being nothing else to do. Only they spread out a little more to brighten the chance that someone would find a portal or passageway. These things were done silently.

Luck unbelievable—their first of the day—smiled on them within five minutes of entering the bush, as they toiled up the steepening slope. One scout fairly stumbled out of the tangled foliage and into a jungle trail, well beaten down but not more than one meter wide, so that automatically they formed in file column again. Though the trail led almost due east, which was not the direction they had intended taking, they decided to follow along.

It was far tougher going than they had known on their earlier foray. The trail did not follow the drainage line but looped upward toward the crest of a long ridge finger. Such was the overhang of twisted bamboo and tangled vine that the lead scout could rarely see the trail for more than five or six meters ahead. There was no thought of putting out flankers. The jungle was too dense, much time would be lost, and besides, they would make excessive noise working through the trees.

They continued the tortuous ascent for lack of any good alternative. At best they moved forward at the slow pace of a death march, for they had to go bent over and head down, so low was the green and matted roof above them. At worst they went to their hands and knees, crawling along, and for the same reason. There was room for nothing else between the sharp roots that they kneed and the foliated mass pressing them down. Over how much distance did this cramped maneuver extend? They reckoned it to be more than one mile.

Three hours of it, and they were dead beat. At least the

Americans so felt. Also hunger pangs were now hurting more than the pain of the trail to the depletion of their energy.

It was at exactly 0900 that Dimh Ghim, on the advice of Adams, passed the whispered word up the column that they would take a break for food. They had been resting at the turn of each hour for ten minutes. This time they would take fifteen minutes.

Some of the mountain men had brought along tins of sardines, preferring that admixture with the cold rice to the meat sauce. So they proceeded to their feast in utter silence, no clanging of utensils, no words being spoken. And they ate with relish.

On that stern discipline among these warrior primitives the wheel of fortune suddenly pivoted. That, combined with the nigh incredible coincidence that at the same moment they had taken a food break, a patrol of North Vietnamese regulars had fallen out for repast on a trail not more than forty yards away. They had been moving downhill, probably to scout toward the Vinh Thanh fort.

Of the existence of the other trail, as of the near presence of the enemy, the patrol was in those first few moments wholly ignorant. Concerned with their food, their thoughts were otherwise as blank as if they were quite alone on the mountain. Man hungering is much like man wounded; he is gripped by one main interest that tends to numb his senses. Moreover, the totally soundless diner has yet to be born.

Freeman thought he heard a twig snapping somewhere but could not be sure of the direction, and as he bent to his meal, gave it no further thought.

What made all the difference was that while the mountain men ate with relish, the careless enemy dined with gusto. Over the lushly grown space between, despite the diffusion caused by the jungle mass which thwarted accurate direction finding, the sounds of men talking and of objects being moved about began to cut through and to register. When that happened the patrol, having just started, ceased eating and picked up arms. The fatigue was suddenly gone.

Hai, the interpreter up front, had been the first to hear.

He motioned with his fingers, and the members of the point instantly froze in position. He whispered to the others, "I think I hear Chinese being spoken."

That word was passed back from man to man. By the time it reached Freeman, he, Adams and Dimh Ghim had heard the sounds also. And they thought they had the direction. It came from about even with the column but from some way down the same fold in the ridge. So there had to be another trail there. But they could not be sure of the distance.

Dimh Ghim was all excitement. He wanted to face the patrol right and in a single line advance it through the jungle in headlong assault on the enemy. Such, invariably, was his disposition, in this instance overriding the hard reality that the bush looked impenetrable and his people carried only machetes.

Adams restrained him from giving the order. Freeman, too, having backed downtrail to join them, argued against it.

It was elementary logic.

"If they are a large force, they will stay there, catch us when we are tired and scattered, and we will be slaughtered. If they are small, they will hear us hacking through and will get away."

Adams then supplied the only sensible procedure.

He said, "That trail is so close it must intersect this one. So we push on upward, find the meeting, and drop down on them."

Dimh Ghim nodded. The word was passed upward along the column. They were moving again in less than one minute, if anything quieter than ever before. The talking and laughter from the other camp must have drowned out such sound as their climbing made, for the camp stayed unwarned.

Again luck smiled. Not more than three minutes after they had resumed march, they came to a fork where a second trail branched off in the direction they wished to take.

Downhill, they followed it not more than 100 feet. There the one trail split in three. The red earth was equally packed on all of them. The trackers found no fresh footprints pointing along any. Here was the trilemma; the one trail that counted was undeterminable.

All doubts were resolved in an instant of decision, put forward by Freeman, supported by Adams, pronounced by Dimh Ghim. That is the usual way of military decisions in moments of high crisis. Someone says, "Do it this way," others chime in, and from consensus the outright risk is accepted.

Freeman would take one squad and go the left trail, Adams another squad and move via the center path. Dimh Ghim would go only with the mountain men down the trail on the right, along which contact was reckoned least likely. If any of the three ran into something too big for one squad, he would back away without a fight. Should it look too strong for the whole patrol, he would return, try to collect the others, and they would all get out. Worrying Adams and Freeman above all else about the division of force was the likelihood that Dimh Ghim would start a fight, no matter what he found.

Going downhill, this time all three elements hurried as they had not done before. These trails were wider, the overhang higher. They fairly trotted along.

Freeman, on the left, moved not more than 100 meters, from which point the path dropped off sharply into a rock-walled ravine. He knew then that he must be on the wrong path and would not bag the game; the terrain lying ahead would have blocked out the sounds. He descended a short distance, then called a halt and paused, uncertain what to do next.

Adams, on the central trail, moved several hundred meters till he was at last certain that he was well beyond the ground where the patrol had fallen out for breakfast. There was no point in continuing. Either the enemy group had pushed on or else he had drawn the wrong alley. So he motioned for the squad to hold up while he thought things out.

Those waits, left and center, were broken by a volley of fire that rang through the jungle. It came off the right, from where Dimh Ghim and his people had to be. And the firing went on and on. To the ears of Adams and Freeman there was just one comforting thing about the volleying. It was all U.S. carbine fire mixed with the more staccato bark of the Browning Automatic Rifle.

Already wound up by an excitement that may explode when triggered by the unexpected, even the steadiest hand may do that momentarily which is wholly irrational. There was Freeman with his machete out, striking wildly at the bush in a vain try to cut through on the shortest line to Dimh Ghim. He laughed aloud that he could do anything so foolish.

Then he charged uphill to the intersection, his squad following. They got there just in time to meet Adams and his people returning. Winded, as they turned into the far trail, they slowed their pace a little; and besides, the fire had stopped.

Getting to Dimh Ghim, they found he had the situation well in hand. His squad had already split into fire teams that were guarding both ways along the trail.

Between these two groups, spaced thirty or so yards apart, were the bodies of five North Vietnam regulars at the upper end, and lower down, eighteen rucksacks laid out on either side of the trail, five of them soaked with fresh blood.

But these were the least significant details.

Dimh Ghim and his men had come down on the rear of an enemy platoon while its people were still fallen out beside the trail.

They had approached undetected and had their weapons set before they volleyed.

The eighteen rucksacks bespoke the size of the force.

With the five dead, it counted twenty-three.

They had killed every man they could see and possibly a few who were hidden from sight by the vines and shadows. But despite larger numbers that, startled, had stampeded downhill, leaving their arms and all of their packs, without firing an answering shot, it was still a bulls-eye—the perfect hit.

The body closest to Freeman and Adams, as they took stock of the prizes, was that of the NV lieutenant, who had brought up the rear. A brass-buckled canvas belt was the only emolument of his one-time authority. The four dead, right next him, were his immediate subordinates.

Dimh Ghim had done most of the killing with the BAR. Later he had blown his whistle for the other two groups to come to him, though in the rush no one had heard that sound.

Between the NV lieutenant and the four dead men beside him, that fire had bagged everything that truly counted.

In a tin box on the shoulders of the third body down the line was an instrument that Freeman at once recognized as a universal mortar sight, of Chinese make.

In the rucksack on the second body were a compass and binoculars.

Beside the fourth body was a cloth satchel containing a quadrant.

It was the find on the lieutenant's corpse which tied in these pieces of loot to events almost ready to unfold. He had been a walking repository of classified material until Dimh's bullet cut him down.

In his pack was a manual, along with a firing table for the 120 mm mortar. There was also a memorandum, reading that the unit should be ready to attack not later than 1600 on 19 May. A hand-drawn map, neatly and accurately drafted, showed mortar firing positions, ammo supply points, observation points and the trail network winding between the mountain and the riverbank opposite Vinh Thanh. With the firing table were azimuths, ranges and coordinates, all with reference to that same target. The church steeple in Vinh Thanh—of possible use as an OP—was marked for destruction. It was more than enough to remove all doubt.

In their exuberance the mountain men had formed a perimeter and were busy firing around the circle. There was always the chance that another enemy might stumble into a bullet. Busy with their consulting, Adams and Freeman let them go on for a while. It added little jeopardy.

Freeman, pointing to the mountain, said, "It looks like there's a battalion up there."

Adams answered: "With a one-twenty mortar, it will not be VC."

By 1100 the search of the vicinity had been completed. Both Americans now worried that their own camp might be immediately threatened. The date on the paper was not conclusive. There was no time to be wasted.

There was one more go at the other rucksacks, which yielded another find. Besides a battery roster and a notebook carried by one of the squad leaders, which gave the strength of the unit, the names and job positions in a two-tube battery with fifteen rounds per gun, there was also an unposted letter which was to go to higher authority. It explained that the reason no more ammunition had been brought forward was that the unit was 50 per cent down with malaria.

Then Adams radioed full information to the Vinh Thanh camp. His first words to Captain Tinsetta were: "We got good stuff." From there the news was sped to Maj. Raymond L. George, chief of the Special Forces B Team at An Khe. He got it at once to Col. Bobby Lang, the cavalry division G-2. General Norton passed it up the line to General Kinnard at Corps, whence it was made a kernel for the daily intelligence grind-out at MAC-V, Saigon.

Having no notion that their report was spiralling, Adams and Freeman gathered their people together. Paired riflemen had been sent out to look uptrail and down while the radio conversation went on. Now they moved down the same trail that the enemy had taken, headed for the closest LZ (landing zone) in the bottoms. They had already told George they would go that way, and since nothing in the terrain they had traversed looked good for a landing, they named the one LZ they knew.

It took them three and one-half hours to reach it, though they had gone only three kilometers. So they had been moving almost constantly for the greater part of eleven hours. The pad had room for only one chopper to come in, but they had no thought that it would carry them out. The Huey already waiting for their arrival had been sent up-valley by Colonel Lang to bring all their prizes back to Camp Radcliff for complete examination.

Of souvenirs, the patrol had kept only the belt from the dead lieutenant and the North Vietnam money found on the bodies, which had been divided among the mountain men. The rucksacks, the shovels, sealed bandages, ponchos and hammocks they had left on the trail. They were too heavy to carry; to bury them would kill too much time.

So they turned about and started for the high ground again, over another trail farther to the north. According to assignment, they were to be out for another three days, prowling the jungle. If supply ran short, they were to find the likeliest spot, then food and ammo would be flown to them. All of this was normal; it was SOP.

Adams said, "Here we go again." It was a dead-pan look. Freeman replied, "Sorry about that."

That part of the adventure had ended happily, the main problem arising from it had been passed upward to other hands, including Major George's, and they would go on to other things. It was no time for sergeants to worry about the follow-through.

Back at the base camp on the Song Con, life continued its abnormal rounds. Some of the women walked about bare-breasted, as is the custom. Mothers fed their babes in the gun pits or wherever there was handy shade, fearing to bed them down unattended in the sleeping bunkers. The rats inhabiting this jungle of a fort ran to two pounds and were mighty fierce.

Such was the pestilence that there had been a campaign to knock them off with rat poison. But that had backfired. The natives around Vinh Thanh rate the flesh of rats a delicacy. The rats, eating the poison, raced to the riverbank to get water and there died. The neighbors picked them up, ate them, then had to be rushed to the dispensary for an emetic, stomach pump and other first-aid. So that had to be stopped. Four mountain men, who were rated fighters, had just been detailed to duty as full-time rat trappers.

But there was a cleaner, if somewhat less tangible, hope for the future. A mother mongoose had jumped from a hole next the trench outwork surrounding the fort, and mistaking it for a rat, a sentry had gunned her down. Her three young were taken inside the fort and were being bottle-fed with TLC by Freeman and the other Americans, who nursed the cheerful thought they might grow up as rat hunters instead of snake killers.

Apart from the rats, it was a cleanly place, and sweet-smelling, despite the tumble down look of the fort. The works were set firmly on a mound of decomposed granite, still solid enough that there was no dust about, soft enough that the trench banks could be cut true and straight against the downpour of the monsoon. Inside the CP bunker there was always cold beer and Coke in the freezer, which was more than the big camp at An Khe could boast. The SF soldier is very good that way.

The patrol's prizes got back to Colonel Lang in late afternoon of 15 May. He studied the documents for several hours. On the hand-drawn map the trails done in red ink not only pointed west toward the C.I.D.G. camp but east toward Soui Ca Valley, the flat land beyond the mountains; there was the key to the enemy routes in and out of the prospective fighting zone. The paper pinpointing the intended main targets, such as the church and the fort, and specifying their distance from the mysterious battery, showed not one of them to be more than 4290 meters away, the optimum range of the 120 mm mortar.

Adding these things, Lang concluded that the evidence was real enough: the big mortars must be on the mountain somewhere, and with them at least one North Vietnam battalion. For the moment he had ceased to think big. The mortar sight bothered him; it had a strange pin. So he put in a phone call to Major Brown, the MAC-V expert on enemy matériel, who, on arriving from Saigon, confirmed that it was a universal sight, which fact Freeman, the SF medic, had guessed at first look.

The stuff was spread before General Norton that night. The well-worn and balky headquarters generator having gone out, as happened several times nightly, he examined the prizes by flashlight.

Several matters were on his mind. Most of the division's infantry numbers were briefly resting and re-outfitting after two wearing campaigns. Four months before, the division had helped re-establish the Special Forces outpost at the head of Happy Valley. The main idea was to have it serve as bait to lure the Viet Cong so that the division could stage a big zap.

But now that the trap was working, the thing wasn't as easy as that. Once Special Forces and the mercenary companies became seated at the fort, the upper valley had become their TAOR, or tactical area of responsibility. If the division were to participate, it had to be by their invitation.

Nor was it Norton's prerogative, really, to determine whether elements of the division should be committed. That right was reposed in Col. John J. Hennessey, commander of the First Brigade. All that happened in the sector of countryside extending northeast of the base camp fell within his zone of responsibility. He must decide whether or not to commit troops to the upper valley in the event of a call for help.

For the time Hennessey, though fully alerted to developments and straining for a fight, was puzzling over the question: With what? One of his battalions was committed to barrier defense at Camp Radcliff. A second was on long patrol protecting the security of Route No. 19, the main traffic artery from the coast running through An Khe to Kontum and the far border. Two companies of the third battalion (2/8th) were earmarked to deal with what came forth in upper Happy Valley, if it proved more than a false alarm.

Norton remained doubtful. In this strange war not more than 10 per cent of intelligence worked out. It could be another wild-goose chase. Yet if there were big mortars somewhere around the other valley, it would be better to go after them now than take a chance that they would be moved up to shell Camp Radcliff.

Lang, the G-2, had the last thought of the night and talked it over with Hennessey.

First Brigade had been looking for a low-grade operation

of company size in enemy country, with small risk. Lang had recommended a sweep around Deo Mang pass, the defile between the base camp and the port of Qui Nhon. Once the VC grip there was as a vise; now the enemy most of the time let it alone. The reason for this odd assignment was that one company of the 8th had a brand-new captain and first sergeant, who needed a little conditioning.

The captain had asked for a rifle company, having tired of being a division of PIO. The sergeant was a much-loved figure, having been all along the factotum of Division Headquarters Mess, where home cooking was not missed. He, too, wanted some fighting.

"I was thinking," said Lang, "instead of sending them to the Pass tomorrow, we might let them sweep that peak above the C.I.D.G. camp."

Hennessey reflected.

Then he asked, "If I get into this thing tomorrow, can I keep from being too heavily committed?"—one of the more unpleasant possibilities in war that a soldier hesitates to dismiss.

Lang replied, "Yes, you will get some sound training, without being too tied up."

So it became agreed, as it was later done, an inspiration of which nothing better can be said than that it seemed to look good at the time. At the top level of the cavalry division there was still no firm belief that the hills so close to home base were loaded with big game.

Bravo's Training Grind

Deciding where Bravo Company should be set down amid the mountains was no large guessing game for Lieut. Col. John Hemphill.

Rather, as with the designation of that unit to blaze the new trail, it was pretty much Hobson's choice.

How the C.I.D.G. patrol had walked and what it had discovered together but pointed in one direction—toward the high peak directly across the Song Con River from the old fort.

On that mountain there was only one spot where two helicopters might land together, without someone first having to blast a shaft through the jungle roof and clear it of timber.

Halfway up the spine of the mountain, resting on it as conspicuously as a large mole on the bridge of a man's nose, was a glacis overgrown with tall elephant grass. This break in the jungle cover was plain to be seen from the floor of the valley, and Hemphill, by reconnoitering the mountain from a Huey, confirmed that it would serve the purpose. He also observed that there was no other place to go.

It was named Landing Zone Hereford that morning before anything larger than a crow had alighted there. Stockmen familiar with the Highland Hereford breed might agree that the designation had this appropriateness, if none other.

Capt. John D. coleman of Bravo Company was having his first go at leading a rifle company. 1st Sgt. Ronald A. Koebbe, an ebulliently cheerful professional from Cincinnati, had come to the job that day. Every platoon sergeant was without experience at fighting in Vietnam.

Still, this greenness at the top levels, matching that of the mountain, did not make them more skittish or wary. Having only the vaguest knowledge of the intelligence developments which had led to their orders, they thought of the outing as a training exercise.

"That was our pitch to the men," said S/Sgt. Henry L. Roach, of First Platoon. "We were testing our resupply—seeing if the new canvas water bag, that can be folded and tied, would work out better than our old jerry cans."

Though the problem may sound more simple than grave, water supply is a critical factor in Vietnam operations. Each soldier afield drinks more than two gallons daily. In the same time he will take as many as six salt tablets to guard against heat exhaustion. Canteens and water bags have to be refilled from the fairly cool and ubiquitous highland streams. An iodine pill is then dropped into the container. Each rifleman carries a bottle of pills taped to his canteen.

The company counted only 126 men present for duty, thirty-one of its people being in hospital with malaria. For a unit thus light, facing a strenuous mountain climb and in no real anticipation of a fight, Bravo (2/8th) certainly went well loaded. Every man carried at least twenty magazines, or 400 bullets for his M-16. There were 1000 rounds apiece for the six machine guns. All hands had a minimum of two, but most of them carried four hand grenades. There were two M-79 grenade launchers per squad, with fifty rounds for each weapon. Also they carried food for six meals, in C rations. For the one 81 mm mortar that was carried along there were twenty-six rounds. This last was useless weight. The mortar crew never found a spot where they could fire the tube without hitting the jungle mass in the immediate foreground.

At 1015 on 16 May they were lifted from the base camp at An Khe by the first serial of six choppers. Coleman and Koebbe were the first men off the lead Huey as it descended onto Hereford. The ship did not touch earth. They jumped into the elephant grass from five or six feet up, as did all who followed them. By 1250 the rear of Bravo Company closed on the landing zone; its van was by then in movement toward the top of the peak.

Already, without a shot being fired, four men had been lost to the company. Two of them had keeled over on the LZ—downed by malaria. The others, in jumping free, had come down on pungi sticks and had had their legs ripped open by these ever-present and nastiest of the enemy's strange devices. Hundreds of the sharpened bamboo stakes had been set amid the elephant grass; saving the company heavy loss was the torrential rain of the evening before, turning the clay setting to mud, so that when men brushed the sticks, they toppled over. A Huey was flagged down and the four casualties were evacuated.

Winding upward along the spine of the ridge from the landing zone was a trail. They saw the opening in the jungle wall, which began right at the upper edge of the small clearing. The path was about eight feet wide and well beaten down: the bower of bush and vine above it was so low that they could not walk erect. By 1315 most of them were strung out, toiling upward, somewhere along this trail. Sergeant Roach was still on the LZ with First Platoon; the four casualties had been among his people, and another man was down with a wrenched ankle.

Coleman had told Koebbe to tag along near the rear of the column. With Koebbe were Special Forces Sgt. Fred Wells, from the Vinh Thanh detachment, a Vietnamese interpreter, Trinh Duc Phuc, and an intelligence sergeant, Anh Bgyen Duc. All had volunteered to come along. Coleman was afraid that if the Vietnamese moved too far front, the two Asiatics might get shot by his men in mistake for Viet Cong.

At the head of the column was the Third Platoon, led by 2nd Lieut. Nichol E. Haney. The one-squad point was about halfway to the cap of the mountain and the time was around

1415 when Haney got on radio to tell him, "There's commo wire running alongside this trail."

Coleman said, "Roll it up and bring it back."

Haney replied, "I can't; it's too damned heavy."

Neither of them felt particular alarm at the discovery or reflected for any time on what it might mean. After all, they were green at the game.

Hennessey, on getting the news, was a little more jolted. He had flown up to LZ Savoy, next the fort, to be in closer touch with the maneuver. He knew that the enemy usually used commo wire to link a battalion with higher headquarters, but below that level used it very rarely.

Colonel Lang, the division G-2 back at the base camp, read the same report with mixed feelings. The division frequently ran into enemy wire during fighting operations, sometimes as much as twelve to fifteen kilometers of it. Not just the larger formations, but the mortar, recoilless and heavy weapons companies of the NVA strung wire and used telephones. The wire might signify only that the 120 mm mortars were indeed on the mountain. On the other hand, he had never known the Viet Cong or the NVA, if bent only on a one-night bivouac or hit-and-run mission, to string wire.

The evidence being, if not in conflict, at least unsatisfactory, he would have to think things out longer. It irked him that the last patrol had missed taking a prisoner. He might then have more to go on.

The company column slogged on up the slope, free of such painful broodings, oppressed mostly by the inescapable burden of heat. The gloom of the jungle seemed to ease it not at all. The air was still, dank and stifling. They were already sopped through with sweat before the rain came down hard around 1440.

The column had stretched out still more. Haney, the younger man, was setting a faster pace than Coleman with the headquarters group or than SFC Howard V. Rowe, with the Second Platoon somewhere in between them.

Koebbe and his people came even with where the commo wire started. Beside the trail were six small bamboo huts. Running along its center were three booby traps that Haney's scouts had seen in time—long pits bedded with pungi sticks and lidded with a bamboo mat covered with forest duff.

They had pressed on and upward, going not more than 100 meters, when Koebbe heard the sounds of fire. There was no warning alteration in the atmosphere right around him. His men were panting and stumbling; they had marched about 1300 meters uphill from the LZ, and to all of them it seemed "more like three miles." Muffled by the thick forest, the noise of engagement barely reached them. Faint it was, yet very distinct.

Koebbe said to his men, "We've hit something."

Roach and the men of First Platoon on the landing zone had heard none of this.

These things had happened. Coleman and the men with him had reached the summit without a shot being fired. Haney and the Third Platoon ahead of them were actually going downhill where the trail wound along the top of the rearward slope of the mountain.

Strung out as were the two leading platoons, the men with Coleman were on the crown of the mountain, and Haney's people were approaching the first knob lower down and to the north, but were still crossing the saddle. Close as were the platoons, they could not see one another.

That's when the first shots rang. They came from Haney's men; at first the men farther down the column heard only M-16 fire. It was centered on six enemy soldiers moving the same way on the trail with their backs turned. Four were gunned down.

Silence followed the volley. The tension that had gripped Coleman, Koebbe and the others to the rear slowly eased off.

Haney spoke on radio to Coleman: "I've got my Victor Charley."

"Good," said Coleman. "You better hold up right there."

Koebbe and his group tried to go faster, but they were now reeling from fatigue. Pulling at the vines and bamboo to help steady themselves, they reached the top of the mountain wholly spent.

Again came sounds of fire from forward of them, this

time mixed—friendly and enemy—the AK47 and the sharper crack of the M-16, and automatic weapons joining the chorus. It went on and on without break or variation.

Haney was on radio to Coleman. "We're pinned down; I've already lost three men."

"What's your estimate?"

"They've got a re-enforced platoon."

He was back on again in a few seconds. "They're about to overrun me; I've got to maneuver."

But he broke off without saying which way he would move, an omission that doubled Coleman's doubt about what to do next, though he had already decided the company was going in a pretty bad direction.

Things were not quite as bad as Haney had reported. There being open space to one side where the trail widened in crossing the saddle, he had put out a flank guard—three men with a machine gun.

This detail had vanished with the first enemy volley. The skirmishers had come from the woods right next them. Firing as they rushed, they cut down the three-man guard, grabbed the gun and moved on toward the platoon. One American, unwounded, rolled downslope a way and by a circuitous route finally returned to the company lines unhurt. PFC David Ruth, the gunner, was knocked down by a bullet that shattered his right arm. The assistant gunner, PFC John W. Teague, was stunned but not mortally hurt by a bullet that clipped his scalp. On falling, Ruth smeared blood all over his face. Within five minutes the enemy doubled back on the pair. Ruth played dead. The enemy rolled him, picked his pockets, took his M-16, his pack and other gear, but otherwise left him alone. Teague stirred, and so they shot him dead.

None of this the main body yet knew. Sensing the strength against him, Haney was already backing toward its position on the higher ground. This was his "maneuver."

Coleman's main impression from the din rising on the lower slope was that he was hearing "one hell of a torrent of fire." Koebbe thought it was "getting louder and louder"; but then it was coming closer, as Haney fell back. Sergeant

Rowe said to S/Sgt. Jerry E. McCullough, leader of his Second Squad, "I think we are just about to get it—right here."

Where they stood, still waiting uncertainly for whatever might develop, they were in dense jungle that topped off at about fifty feet. It was no position. Tangled bamboo and vine clump, along with the timber, limited horizon to a few yards at best and split the command. For rudimentary cover the mountaintop was strewn with boulders and not a few fallen trees, some bulking as high as a man. Of better promise were the root structures of the many standing banyans that had scooped up the earth and left convenient hollows. Of these slight advantages, however, the men were not yet thinking.

One of Koebbe's men had toppled from heat exhaustion in the interval. He was helped back toward the LZ, with two comrades to guard him, one carrying an M-79. This was the last attempted getaway of the day. Going downtrail they were ambushed. Their bodies were not found, and they are still marked missing. The M-79 showed up later in the fight—in enemy hands.

McCullough got low and curled himself up in the roots of one of the larger trees. Down the slope, on his side of the peak, not many yards away, he heard a "lot of men chattering." It sounded like Chinese. He told himself that these were enemy prisoners and Third Platoon must be bringing them in.

Haney and his men, in point of fact, at about that moment were backing into the ground where the main body waited. In the latter there was still no clear sense, much less a fixed feeling, about the gathering precariousness of the situation.

Koebbe felt, more than heard, some movement down the slope to his left. He looked that way. Twenty yards off was the back of a kneeling enemy machine gunner, and the gun was firing in the wrong direction. Koebbe fired and yelled at the same time. His men, already spreading out fast and going to earth, got the signal, and much of the fire power of one platoon bore on that one target. Koebbe said, "That one worked,'' then glanced about to find that no one was listening.

Koebbe ran to the body—found it shredded to a bloody pulp. In one pocket, untouched, was a map of the C.I.D.G. camp. The dead man wore khakis and an NVA hat. That jarred Koebbe—this first notice that the company was not fighting Viet Cong locals.

As he darted back upslope, bearing two long-wicked concussion grenades that the dead man had carried, fire broke out all around the position except on its rear, around the trail whence they had come. The bullets fairly screamed overhead and some few struck earth around the rim of their ground. But most of the fire seemed casually aimed.

McCullough's aberration was over. He saw enemy skirmishers moving directly toward him from his left front—about twenty-five of them. That's when he and Lieut. David D. Bradshaw, alongside him, began pouring fire from their M-16s. Standing not thirty feet from McCullough, on a knoll, was the largest Asiatic he had ever seen, obviously an officer, who towered head and shoulders above the others. He stood there in the clear ''directing traffic,'' waving his arms, showing his men where to move in.

McCullough shot him. He dropped, arose, and continued waving his arms. McCullough fired again, with exactly the same result. After the third bullet he lay quiet. The volleying from the top, with others joining McCullough and Bradshaw, quickly beat off that rush and killed most of the rushers.

By this time Sergeant Roach's platoon had come up to the company and had fallen alongside Sergeant Rowe's people. The pressure subsided only momentarily. Snipers worked forward into the rock-strewn ground to their right. PFC Stephen Thomas, Rowe's RTO, took a bullet in the back of his leg. McCullough got one through his back, in the left side, out the right. That is the way most wounds go in the Vietnam war. Bullets. In the head. Or in the rump or small of the back.

The air heated swiftly on the right where Coleman lay. One group of NVA skirmishers, having swung that way, crawled up close. The bullet swarm thickened around them, though Coleman saw nothing until one enemy soldier jumped up not fifteen feet in front of him and stood there pumping automatic fire into his ground. That made it a little too personal. For the first time Coleman fired an M-16 in anger—and missed. The artillery forward observer, Lieut. Carl V. Hunt, Jr., Second Battalion, 19th Field, gunned this blighter down. It was seconds too late: one burst of the fire had riddled and killed Hunt's radio operator, lying beside him.

McCullough, a former dash man who had broken a few records, was so greatly suffering that he retained no further impressions of the battle. Coleman was disgusted with himself that, given a fair mark, he had bobbled.

Coleman was already in radio contact with Hemphill and Hennessey. Hemphill was overhead in a Huey; Hennessey was monitoring the conversation from LZ Savoy in the valley. One question was salient in both of their minds: What are we up against?

Coleman answered, "I'd say a re-enforced platoon."

In later conversations with them he repeated this same estimate, even, as in the first instance, he simply passed along, though not automatically, what Haney had told him after the first contact.

Making little sense then, it made less later. The people around Rowe had beaten off the best part of a platoon, and the ring of force was growing and tightening. The company was spread out over seventy meters' length of crest. None of its ground was being left unscathed.

Fortunately Hemphill and Hennessey took the estimate with a grain of salt, but with no argument, making allowances for Coleman because of his greenness. Another rifle company was already on the way to LZ Hereford and the top of the mountain.

The pressure was still on Coleman's ground. He saw three of his riflemen lying just a few yards to his front, non-engaged. A few feet down the slope and to their left, two NVA riflemen were firing on him.

He yelled to the men, "Get with it and fire left!"

They didn't. Then from Coleman's right a grenade arced and fell just beyond the three drones, thrown by one of their own friends.

Coleman yelled, "Watch it! You'll kill our people!"

He was wrong about it. The grenade blew, killing the two enemy, missing the three Americans.

It was about then that Coleman began to think about his position as a whole and reflect on what he had to do. The company was spread over too much ground, and not one thing was tied in with another.

Rowe and the others were already worrying about that. The time was about 1700, and dark would soon come swiftly to the jungle floor. Rowe and some men near him had started shrinking the deployment, crawling rearward a few feet whenever the fire lifted. Coleman got Bradshaw on the RT and told him to bring part of his platoon over to the right of the CP position and "get in tight."

Shortly all of his platoon leaders were within shouting distance of him. Haney he had not seen since his fallback, but after the contraction he could hear Haney sing out, "We gotta get closer!" Coleman did not think so quite yet. He would have one more trial of strength with them to test whether those monkeys were as hopped up as they seemed.

Sgt. Picardo May and Pvt. Gerald Harvey had just come up from the LZ, where they had gone on an escort mission. May, Coleman had been told, was rated as a potential malingerer because he always developed "low back pain" when a fight was imminent. Harvey was facing charges for having used his fists on a superior. Coleman told them both to go and take up forward ground in Haney's sector.

They went willingly enough—and then they pressed too hard. Within less than a minute Harvey was back—holding his guts. They had been shot through, and he soon died. May had been shot dead by the same sniper. The sudden deaths shook Coleman to the marrow.

Haney came crawling back.

He said, "We better get wholly on defensive and stay that way."

Coleman asked, "How many men you got on the line down the slope?"

"About one squad."

"Are they wounded? Can we get them back?"

"They're dead; you don't send live men out to get dead ones."

On these words, from the second lieutenant to the captain, the decision would be made. There would be no more threshing about. They would get tight and try to hold.

There came in another call from Battalion, Major Jayne, the Executive speaking, with nothing more important to impart than that some help was on the way.

Coleman got on radio to Koebbe, told him he wanted to contact the position all around the roughly oval-shaped perimeter. Then there was something else; he would like it very much if Koebbe, with the Special Forces sergeant and the "two interpreters," would move in right next the CP.

As reorganized, the position became roughly an ellipse, rather pointed at both ends on the high ground, 150 feet long by 75 feet wide, with both of its sides a little downslope. The rain still came, not beating down, but dripping and dribbling from the forest top.

Koebbe and the other three men crawled along to Coleman; the CP was on the far end of the perimeter side that overlooked the valley. They settled down amid the far-spreading roots of a large banyan tree, so that despite the protruding roots, the four individuals were pretty much in line.

Fifteen feet in front of them and downslope, a large fallen mahogany spread at an angle across their front. Two of Coleman's riflemen—the two greatest jokers in the unit—had already deployed next the tree, so that its trunk bumped their helmets. They were engaged in hot argument, but as that was habitual with them, no one listened.

Sergeant Wells, of Special Forces, was bothered about the whole deal. Koebbe heard him speaking on radio to Captain Tinsetta at the C.I.D.G. camp. He was saying, "You better send us some Montagnards. We know here how Custer felt. It's the same kind of situation."

There was time for those words and not much more. They had lain there not more than two minutes.

From down the slope a machine gun, silent until now, opened fire directly on their line, traversing rapidly.

Koebbe felt bark from the banyan root splinter off and slash his cheek. He sang out, "There's a close one."

Wells was on his left; Trinh Duc Phuc, the interpreter, and Anh Ngyen Duc, the intelligence sergeant, were on his right.

They returned no answer.

Then he shook Wells, saying, "I heard you get through to the base camp."

There was no response. Wells had taken a bullet through the top of his skull.

Then he shook Trinh and Anh. They, too, were dead. They had been killed in exactly the same way.

Koebbe decided to stay right where he was and duck still lower, on the theory that lightning does not strike twice in the same place. Like most riflemen, he was superstitious. And the Indian Sign was working. The machine gun did not traverse again along his line.

The banyan roots where Koebbe lay looked better to Coleman than his own more exposed ground. So he moved over and got next the roots on the other side of the tree. Strange thoughts were running through the big man's head. As he sat there, with his rump next the trunk and his flanks somewhat covered by the buttress-like roots, he worried most about the size of his feet; they looked perfectly enormous and there was no way that he could make them less or give them any protection. Natural as rain, such fixations as this come to men under fire and help ease the strain from larger worries.

The two jokers downslope, Spec. 4 Jorge H. Hernandez and Sgt. Rodriguez Gonzales, were debating much larger tactical matters. Hernandez is a thirty-eight-year-old Cuban, born in Havana, Gonzales a year younger California Mexican. Though they had a Damon and Pythias friendship, their impact on the company was more of the Laurel and Hardy variety. Hernandez is an unconscious humorist, a big bear of a man whose every word and gesture borders on the ridiculous. Gonzales is the tailor-made straight man.

They were down low, next the fallen tree. There was air space on its under side—a slot at least six inches deep, between the bark and the earth, through which they could peer down the slope. Gonzales wanted to get the gunner who had knocked off the three men next to Koebbe. The hassle with Hernandez was about how to fire.

It would have to be through the slot. From atop the dead tree their M-16s wouldn't bear on the downslope. The question was whether to fire in bursts or fire one round at a time, through the slot.

Gonzales, a paratrooper, said, "Give them bursts."

Hernandez, who had been long a rifleman with the 2nd Infantry Division, said, "One shot."

Gonzales said, "No, bursts."

From Hernandez: "You crazy, Gonzalo, like all air-borne fellas. Fire bursts, you geeve poseeshon away. Then what we do? No, Gonzalo, don't be like all air-borne, boolsheet, just boolsheet. Use the cabeza."

So went the wrangle, back and forth, till Hernandez ran out of wind, and Gonzales simply pushed him aside. The slot was only about six feet across and they were confined to the cramped space directly back of it by the rimrock on either side.

Gonzales fired two long bursts—both full clips.

The bullet consensus was immediately with Hernandez' side of the argument.

The same machine gun opened fire on their tree.

At first too high, and biting into the wood, within a few seconds it had dropped to the slot, to range back and forth across it.

Neither man fired back. Next the tree the two put on a horizontal dance, bodies swinging back and forth. Gonzales' legs on top of Hernandez, the latter repaying him in kind, as they swung to and fro like pendulums.

Then Gonzales got wedged on top of Hernandez and pressed him down with dead weight. Hernandez felt something go wrong with his lower left leg and was certain the leg had been shot off at the knee. Agonized, he reached down to feel the bloody stump. There wasn't any; the leg had simply gone to sleep.

This sort of act cannot run on indefinitely. Koebbe called out to Gonzales, "What in hell is all that racket down there?" He couldn't see the fire dancing along the slot from his position among the banyan roots.

Gonzales started to reply. Then a hand grenade rolled through the slot and exploded at arm's length from him. Breaking unevenly, it threw a dozen shards into Gonzales' right side. He reeled backward and flopped between the two dead Vietnamese.

Hernandez stayed on. The machine gun opened fire on the tree again, throwing not less than 200 rounds. This time, alone, Hernandez resumed the horizontal dance from side to side, trying to escape the line of fire. He was lucky for only the first half minute.

Then he got two bullets. One creased the calf of his right leg quite evenly, the other cut the left in the same place.

Stung by the pain, he knew he was either dying or about to die. The thought didn't unstring him. He fell apart because he remembered in that moment the red flannel sack in his pocket containing $150 in bills. He had stored in out of three paydays. If he died in this hole, his wife, Maria, and his three kids would never get the money.

Koebbe took a bullet in his leg at about the same instant in which the thought of his pending loss panicked Hernandez. The bulky Cuban jumped up the slope, made a flying leap for the banyan tree and came down directly atop Koebbe with all his weight.

That impact drove Koebbe's chest down against the banyan roots, breaking four ribs. He couldn't gasp; all wind was gone from him; he felt himself blacking out and feared he was dying, though he wasn't sure from what cause.

As Hernandez went into his dive, another bullet cracked him through the legs, though to the wound he gave no slightest heed.

Hernandez was clutching at Koebbe and crying, "First

Sarge, First Sarge. Here's one-fifty dollar. You must put in company safe, see my wife get it.''

Koebbe was still breathless.

Two minutes passed before his head cleared enough to let him sputter a few words.

He gasped, ''You big damn fool—for chrissake, Hernandez, you damn near killed me. . . . I ain't no bank . . . If you wanta live . . . get over there by Gonzales.''

Koebbe cocked his arm and was ready to ''let Hernandez have it'' at that moment; then he realized he was bodily too weak. Even so, Hernandez pressed the little red bag into his hand before crawling over to get next Gonzales.

Before going to Gonzales, he had defended his action to Koebbe with great dignity, saying, ''Not my fault, First Sarge. Gonzales' fault. He give position away.'' Hernandez was crying as he lay down beside Gonzales. His friend, who was hurting no less, tried to say a few comforting words. It was no good. Hernandez was for the moment inconsolable— and still more perplexed. He could not remember whether the tears were because he had thought of his family suddenly or because he had hurt Koebbe and the first sergeant had told him off. A very strange man this Cuban, no no buffoon, but a character of characters, he is given to declaiming to his comrades under any circumstances: ''I love thees country. I love thees army, thees uniform, maybe to die in it.'' At least that bit from him does not sound funny to them and they crack no jokes about it.

Soon the two men resumed fire, and then the sniffling stopped, though not the argument. Hernandez got off one shot at a time. Gonzales let the whole clip go. Hernandez said mournfully, ''Gonzalo, we catcha hell, we catcha hell because of you.''

At about 2000, six gunships came over, having been called for by Lieutenant Hunt, the observer. These are Hueys carrying fourteen rockets apiece, with door-mounted M-60 machine guns. The first two rockets in the initial run exploded inside the perimeter, wounding one American. The cry, ''Medic, Medic!'' rose high. Hunt got them on radio in the nick of time as they came in for the second pass and made the adjustment. The rockets struck on both sides of the trail, 200 meters beyond them.

Then for a time the gunships continued circling and firing. The two misaimed rockets had struck very close to the big banyan.

Coleman called to Koebbe, "Don't you think we'd better move the CP? It's positively unhealthy around here."

Koebbe said, "Sir, I can't move the CP. I can't move myself. I can just barely breathe."

And so they stayed put.

Little more than one hour later, Captain Cummings and the lead platoon of Alpha Company reached the top of the peak and entered the perimeter. They had been on the trail from LZ Hereford more than two hours. Neither time nor the condition permitted shifting men about so as to apportion a separate sector to this re-enforcing element. Its men separately fitted in as splices around the oval already held by Bravo Company.

Coleman all along had felt futile as to himself. This was not leading, as he understood the word. A captain should move about and rally his men. But on that hill that night there was no way to do it. If he tried, he would be killed, while doing no good. So far his main contribution had been to help regulate the supporting artillery fire, and even there his role was only that of a relay. Haney, from farther down the slope, was observing the shells and passing the word along. The doubts were soul-sapping.

Alpha Company's moving into position, and his part in it, doubled his self-questioning. He had become little more than a cop at an intersection, showing people where and when to go. His chief function was that of being around. It is all rather ridiculous, he told himself.

But something of consequence *had* happened. With the arrival of the re-enforcement, the enemy had seemed to draw off. The fire against the position had abated, was more intermittent, and was coming over greater distance and hitting, for the most part, high in the trees. That stirred hope that things would be better in the morning.

Still Coleman was taking no chances on that. He circulated instruction that Bravo Company would stage a *"mad minute"* when first light broke and checked it out with Cummings. In this exercise by the defense, all hands fire all weapons around the perimeter and keep the blast going for sixty seconds, the central idea being that if the enemy is preparing to charge as the darkest hour ends, the shock fire will turn him about.

Though the trail to the rear stayed open, the enemy not having pinched in between the perimeter and LZ Hereford, there was no thought in any of them that it might be better for the two companies to pull stakes and slip down the mountain. Yet all hands sensed by now that they were embattled by at least one battalion. They reacted as if there had been no escape route. The subject stayed unmentioned. This was their fight and there was no option but to see it through.

Their foreground now obviously held less of danger. Still they did not post outguards some distance down the slope to give warning if the enemy came on again or send patrols to probe for his presence. Each squad had brought two claymore mines to the top of the mountain; they did not plant the mines while the lull permitted. The reason why: they were too tired to think of these things.

There were no sleeping bags and no sleep worthy of the word. A few men had been killed. That was enough to keep all others wakeful, uneasy and wondering what would come next. They spoke little, and then mostly in whispers. The truth was that the full-scale, unexpected attack had shocked them, though for the most part they were worrying about what it would mean to themselves when morning came. Neither Koebbe nor Coleman moved about among the men. Koebbe was immobilized by his wounds and his crushed rib cage and was wheezing very badly. Coleman was dog-tired. A giant of a man, older than anyone else present, he was carrying excess weight from his months as a desk soldier.

Nothing that he had heard beforehand had helped steel him for the situation in which he now found himself. Not expecting full-scale battle, he had even less anticipated having to meet a headlong assault. He knew that he had been wrong, quite wrong, in putting the estimate to higher command that he was fighting off a platoon-size attack, then persisting in it even after he, with a fair-sized company re-enforced, was being hit from front and both flanks. That he could come clean with himself about why he had done so in no way lessened his chagrin. It was his first time out as skipper of a rifle company; he was overanxious that his superiors should not feel he was acting "chicken." Yet the fact was that his shrugging had cost the company nothing.

Not less startled by the turn of events was Colonel Buchan, the division G-3. It had been his premise that the enemy would not stay in the area, doggedly contesting ground yard by yard, if the division made a play with major force from the start. Now he speculated that all resistance might be gone after the second or third day. And that would be just as well. The cavalry had never really operated before in such high mountains. Beyond Hereford lay a truly wild region, unroaded, inaccessible, and unknown to Americans.

Gen. Jack Norton was thinking along much the same lines. The question gnawed at him: Is the possible opportunity important enough to take on this terrain and throw away all our advantages? He thought it was "much like having to walk blindfolded into a morass." At the same time he was being pressed to send one of his brigades 100 miles to fight along the western border.

It was Hennessey's fight and Hennessey was the one heady optimist. If extended operations were upcoming, he would have to have more people, though he had been warned that he could expect no more resources, because of demands of other missions. That worry he put aside. He was certain that contact would be broken during the night and the enemy would be gone by dawn. But on turning in at 0200, he left instructions that he be called at 0530 so that he could be in the air over Hereford by 0610. More than all else, that was a technical precaution. The two companies atop the hill were operating under Lieut. Col. John Hemphill and they rightly belonged under Colonel Beard. He would make that shift at 0700 and so notified Beard.

At the position on top of the mountain fog settled in

several hours before midnight. Combined with the steady drizzle, it cut visibility to a few feet, though that made little difference. The tangled growth all about them was so dense that each man could feel of the company presence only the two or three soldiers lying closest him. Puff the Magic Dragon (a C-47) circled above them and dropped flares. It was vain waste. Throwing the peak in bold relief as seen from LZ Savoy, the brilliant light could not begin to penetrate the jungle roof. There were two levels of canopy here, one at twenty-five feet, the other at about fifty.

Cummings' company, on coming into the perimeter and settling among Coleman's men, so that the two units were pretty much intermingled, had troubled to cover the dead and the wounded with their ponchos. In the circumstances there had been no possibility of evacuating any of them downtrail to the LZ, and the men of Bravo had been too tired, too preoccupied with the fight, to think of covering them. All of the casualties were laid out around Koebbe— the squad of KIA's, the 17 WIA's. That made him feel no whit less like a wet dog with no place to shake. It was a little like being entombed alive. Roach, through a small hole in the jungle roof, at last could see one star shining. He thought to himself, ''It's like being at the bottom of the tallest flue.''

At 0200 Coleman lit two trip flares right at his CP, taking that risk so that Lieut. Col. Morris J. Brady's air artillery Hueys would have a mark on which to guide. (This is the Second Battalion of the 20th Artillery.) The flares burned for five minutes, putting the position in full glare. They came on, six helicopters, each carrying forty-eight rockets, the whole under the command of Maj. Roger J. Bartholomew of Charley Battery, as hot a pilot as the Army boasts. Coleman said, ''Charley ought to be within a hundred yards of me both east and west,'' putting this over the radio. The strikes came in just that close. The people strafing the slopes had seen the beacon clearly enough. The men in the jungle, though hearing the throb of the Hueys, caught not a glimpse of them. Still, it is a wonderful thing, the air artillery, and the uplift it gives to the spirit of beaten-down infantry. Most of the rockets are HE rounds. Against jungle, the ARA gets a lot of detonating that is high in the trees. That scares the people below. But it very seldom hurts anybody.

These were probably the longest hours that any of them would ever know. They stretched on and on like a bad dream, recalled later as something terrifying, but with no connection between one fleeting impression and another. Koebbe's hearing remained at attention, but he was dully aware that something was missing—the will to react to anything he heard or even to think upon it for longer than a fleeting instant.

Dark of early morning, and a great stillness was over the place. For two hours not a shot had been fired. The quiet was broken for Koebbe when he heard the crack of a bamboo somewhere downslope, as if it were being hacked through. He looked at his watch. The time was 0555. He dragged himself over the twenty-five feet of ground between the banyan tree and the CP to make sure that Coleman was wakeful. He was. Then he crawled back. It had taken ten minutes. Through most of that time Koebbe had heard an enemy machine gun firing, and the bullets were ripping through the foliage above him.

Sergeant Rowe and some of Cummings' men knew even more surely that the heat had not lifted. A few mortar rounds were being lobbed into their ground. Yet this sense of action imminent was not general. Minds drugged by fatigue, many present had no reaction, did not realize that this was enemy fire and could not tense to a fight already started.

When Coleman blew the whistle for the "mad minute," close-in rifle fire was already pressing one north-facing sector, while people on the other side of the perimeter did not know of it. They continued to believe that their fusillade caught the upward-creeping skirmishers off balance and precipitated the charge.

If the mad minute did not have the impact of a spoiling counter, it at least renewed the full-scale fight the second it lifted. As one of its ornaments, Coleman sent word to the squads to douse the slopes with violet smoke grenades. They did it at 0605.

Through the purple fog rising amid the grass-green bamboo Koebbe saw them coming—only four figures in khaki, twenty meters away and stalking straight toward him, working weapons as they advanced. Then in an instant they were clear of the ambient violet. He could hear Hernandez and Gonzales firing like wild from their position just above his right shoulder. The Cuban had quit being a one-shot soldier.

Koebbe opened fire with his M-16, got off two bullets. Then his right hand wouldn't work; he was puzzled that the finger on the trigger did not respond. The whole arm tingled. The palm tightened and he could not open it.

Then he noticed that his blouse was turning red.

Koebbe leaned back against the flukes of the great banyan, looked up at the far-spread branches of the tree, under which certain ones had taken root.

Then he weakly called, "Medic, medic."

He still had no idea whence the blood flowed. It was the right hand that had failed him, but the growing pain was around his left breast.

The medic came and stripped off the blouse.

A gout of blood spurted from Koebbe's left biceps. To his eye, that part of the arm looked like "so much raw liver." Working at top speed—for there were other cries for aid around the perimeter—the medic bandaged him. Koebbe started crawling toward the CP.

A few feet along, and he heard an M-79 round explode close enough to him that he got part of the concussion. (This was the same M-79 that the enemy had captured along the downtrail ambush during the night. Hernandez and Gonzales killed the firer. The weapon was recovered.)

Standing in a hole within five feet of Koebbe was a Negro soldier, Pvt. Morgan Blaylock. His nose gone, one eye torn from the socket, an ear almost separated from his head, the chin looking as if ready to drop from the face, Blaylock, though still conscious, did not cry out or whimper.

He stood utterly motionless during the ten minutes that the same medic swathed his whole head in bandages, except the mouth, and gave him a shot of morphine, while Koebbe looked on.

Koebbe continued his slow crawl. Watching Blaylock had done something for him. He realized that his own plight was not so bad and he was proud that one of his own men had set him such an unforgettable example.

Colonel Hennessey in his Huey was directly above the fight scene now, altitude 500 feet above the mountain. But it did him little good. All he could see was the roof of the jungle, and this just barely, because of the pre-dawn mist. On radio, Cummings of Alpha (1/12th) was doing most of the talking from below. The gist of what he said was: "We are getting heavy automatic and mortar fire. It is coming in from all directions. We need more ammunition." Hennessey reflected that this was Cummings' first fight also; there was little or nothing he could do to help him.

Hennessey continued to circle above the peak for so long as the fire fight lasted. He had already been on the radio to Colonel Beard: "About that change-over, forget it for a while; now is not the time." He was astonished by the intensity of the attack, judging by what Cummings had said, and the relatively few sounds of the battle that rose to his level. He guessed that the attack was a feint designed by the enemy to stall for time so that heavier forces might be moved forward. He sweated to get something in behind their spearhead to cut off the enemy line of withdrawal. He knew that the two companies on top of the mountain were in no shape to pursue. There were two platoons on LZ Hereford, but they had to stay there. Hereford was the only LZ through which the casualties could be moved out from and the ammunition moved onto the big mountain. He would still have to figure out how to get a battalion lifted as quickly as possible to northeast of the mountain to block the enemy.

During the twenty-five minutes of Koebbe's personal ordeal, the two companies had beaten off the attack, under varying degrees of direct pressure by fire, but not without hard loss, which also fell unevenly against one sector and another.

Bullets no longer flailed their ground. The enemy was in recoil, still firing, though the sounds grew fainter as the seconds passed. They knew then that they had won. There was no cheering.

Least of all was there any feeling of exultation in Third Squad, First Platoon. The guns at LZ Savoy had shelled the retreating enemy. Their last round, bursting short when it struck into the trees above the company, killed the leader, Sgt. Robert Padilla, instantly. Flattened beside him, PFC David Frantz, the squad's 18-year-old grenadier from Kankakee, Ill., broke into sobbing. He adored Padilla—"the guy always ready to listen to our troubles."

Captains Coleman and Cummings were standing in the clear at the CP when Koebbe got there. Collected around them already were fifty-four of their own wounded and the bodies of twenty men killed in action, not counting the two dead Vietnamese. All of the dead were laid out within a copse of bamboo.

The same thicket provided the poles by which the bodies could be carried down the mountain. The ponchos served as the beds of the improvised bamboo litters. They set about the task of organizing this lift before they did anything else.

Koebbe heard Coleman putting out the word to the platoons that elements of another battalion had put down on LZ Hereford and would soon be on top of the mountain. It still took the head of the relief column two hours to appear and begin the relief.

Men who had been in the fight set about to litter out the dead.

Coleman said, "Not on your life. Recheck every body to make certain. Be sure they are dead. Then carry out first those wounded who cannot walk."

The few remaining able-bodied men hoisted their heavy loads and went first down the trail. They were followed immediately by the walking wounded—the majority—many of them hobbling.

Coleman asked Koebbe, "Can you still fire?"

Koebbe replied, "Try me, sir."

It was a stall-stop-and-start movement all the way, because of the stress of hoisting the heavy loads in the litters across the fallen trees and over numerous boulders.

Halfway to Hereford, they heard one rifle shot. They saw grass and bush moving in front of them, but fortunately they withheld their fire. It was more of the relief force ascending the mountain and being a little too cautious about it.

Without seeing them, Koebbe at last sensed what was happening. He got on radio to the people below, saying, "You get off the trail. We're coming through." As he had ordered it, it was done, and the two columns hardly saw one another.

They were three hours making this journey. The first man Koebbe saw on LZ Hereford whom he knew was Brig. Gen. Jack Wright, the ADC of the cavalry, whose only frustration was that he had arrived a few hours too late.

The wounded were evacuated from the LZ in the Hueys during the early afternoon. The dead were cleared away from the LZ by 1600.

Regularly, at Camp Radcliff, the bugles blow retreat at five o'clock in the afternoon. By then, Koebbe, Blaylock and the other bed cases were at the base camp hospital within earshot of the music.

Bravo's relatively few whole-skinned soldiers, among them Rowe and Roach, were back in their tents just prior to mealtime. The few who were caught in the open when the bugles prefaced that "*To the colors*" was coming halted in place.

"It's Retreat," one soldier said to another.

So it was—and the first time in Bravo Company's last thirty-six hours that the word had been mentioned.

Almost Hill 766

In the same early hours of 17 May that Alpha and Bravo Companies awaited their trial by fire on the mountaintop, the operation, so gingerly and tentatively begun, mushroomed without taking form.

Of that dimensional change the decision-makers were themselves unaware, not being able to read the mind of the enemy. That dark side always bears on what develops.

More from hunch than from reasoned calculation, and because it was the prudent thing to do, General Norton yielded to control by the brigade commander, Colonel Hennessey, two more battalions, the First of the 5th and the Second of the 12th.

Charley Company of 1/12th had been in perimeter on LZ Hereford through most of the night, under mortar fire and harassed by snipers.

Hennessey had not worked with either of these battalions before. That did not especially bother him. The cavalry division is more free-wheeling about structure, and less constrained by organizational lines, than any in our past wars. The combat army in Vietnam is all inclined that way. Medley companies, ad hoc battalions and thrown-together brigades are the usual thing. And the mix seems to work just as well.

It was about 0815 on 17 May when Hennessey told Lieut. Col. William Ray, commanding 1/5th, to land on Hereford, get up to the action, assist in every way possible and attack to the east. He reckoned that what was left of an enemy battalion might still be there.

At the same time he alerted Lieut. Col. Otis Lynn to stand by with 2/12th. Lynn was already aloft in a Huey, ready to reconnoiter. Hennessey had picked out a place deep in the mountains well beyond LZ Hereford where he thought Lynn might get his men down, either by rappelling out of Hueys or by descending via rope ladders from a Chinook. Division troops had not done this kind of thing very often; it was too sticky and tricky for use, if there was any other way.

Trailed by Lynn, Hennessey flew on line to the narrow valley where he intended the battalion should put down. The Huey orbited directly above it. Hennessey said on radio, "That's the spot I mean."

Norton, up before dawn, was in the TOC (tactical operations center) 100 yards from his quarters when the report came in about the attack at daybreak. He said to his Chief of Staff, Col. George Beatty, Jr., as gentle a soldier as is to be found, "We ought to change that name." The move onto the mountain by Bravo Company of the day before had simply been demarked on the map by the word "Herford" (*sic*). He did not refer to the bad spelling; his idea was to call this little show "Base Plate." The connotation was that a relatively few of the enemy would be trapped and smashed against the mass of the one mountain.

However, anything remotely connected with the problem of base defense around An Khe is called part of "Operation Benning." Officially, so far as Saigon and MAC-V were concerned, the skirmishing around the Vinh Thanh Valley still came under that localized heading.

At 0730, with Colonels Buchan and Lang as passengers, while he handled the Huey, Norton took off for LZ Hereford to see things for himself. Alpha Company of 1/5th was still bringing in people to the same small spot. The division commander circled for twenty minutes before there was room to put down. As he did so, the downwash from the chopper riffled and flattened the elephant grass and Norton could see the surface littered with pathfinding equipment, mortars, jerry cans, rations and debris. "It looked like a junk yard."

As the Huey settled, Norton said to his co-pilot, W. O. Vaught, "Take this thing off!"

Vaught asked, "What? With only one pilot?"

Norton said, "You heard right."

Vaught left. It was in Norton's mind that he would work his way up the mountain to where the action was. But first he went looking for Capt. Nick Waddock, who commanded Alpha Company. They were old friends, since service together in Korea, though Norton had not seen Waddock in six years.

He found Waddock and company just beginning their move uptrail. Thereupon Norton, his aide, Captain Brennan, and Colonel Buchan attached themselves to one of Waddock's platoons and started marching.

Not more than 200 meters along, this column suddenly found itself amid Charley Company, 1/12th, which was supposed to be well ahead. The men had fallen out beside the trail, now choked with a glut of people.

Norton said to Waddock, "Nick, this isn't movement; it's acute constipation." Then he asked, "Why aren't the wounded being brought down?"

Someone standing by said, "The VC have interdicted the trail and no one can be brought down."

Though this information was altogether wrong, Norton, believing it, changed his mind. If the wounded could not be evacuated via the trail, the operation was in grave trouble. It was time for him to think about pouring on more artillery fire as well as the outlook for blasting out an LZ on top of the mountain.

Buchan said quietly to him, "I don't think we belong here."

Waddock was losing his temper. His people were all charged up and wanted to get on. He yelled to the men of

Charley Company: "You move on or you get out!" They pulled aside into the bush, and his column went on through.

Waddock's rear CP had remained on LZ Hereford. On his way out Norton said to the people there, "Get out your bayonets, bolos and anything you can cut with. Clear away all the grass anywhere around this LZ. After that, stack all equipment and litter along the edge of it."

Still, that wasn't enough. After Vaught had returned for him, he stopped at LZ Savoy, to which point Hennessey had moved his TOC—a capsulated headquarters shaped like a Quonset hut that can be lifted to the forward zone by a Flying Crane. There he talked with both Hennessey and Hemphill.

He said, "The discipline on that LZ isn't worth a damn. I want it kept cleared of people. Then I want all the elephant grass around it cut down. Nothing will be safe till it's done."

The words were firm and clear. The air was ripe with good intentions. Yet as too often happens, what is everyman's task becomes no man's task in particular. Sure, there was a cutting of the grass on Hereford. But it was done perfunctorily rather than thoroughly. The rank growth above, below and on the flanks of the cramped space where the Hueys put down was left untouched. And of that was to come much grief.

Hennessey was overloaded with other problems of a more technical kind that morning. Hemphill was about to turn command on the mountain over to Colonel Beard.

What Hennessey had intended for Colonel Lynn's battalion had not worked out as planned. According to the maneuver scheme, that force was to be dropped in the narrow valley to the northeast, climb the mountain beyond it, and there, atop Hill 766, go into a blocking position. There was a small clearing in the valley about 600 meters from the base of Hill 766. Ray's battalion, from the back slope of Hereford, was slated to push straight on toward Lynn's block and, hopefully, zap all enemy troops skulking between. A simple plan, neat rather than gaudy.

All things were right with it save one—the atmosphere.

The Hueys had to go in first to the clearing carrying the rappellers; the Chinooks, with their rope ladders, would become dead ducks if there were any shooters below, firing from blinds. But because of the altitude density and extreme heat, the choppers, on getting to the clearing, found that they could not hover. By midmorning Hennessey knew he couldn't make it that way. He scratched his head and bent over the map, then flew from Savoy in his Huey for another quick look.

To the south of the spot that he had reconned earlier lay another small tract of cleared space on low ground. Twelve hundred meters farther away from Hill 766 it looked feasible. Hennessey dubbed it "LZ Horse."

Then he got on radio to Lynn, saying, "Get your people in there as quickly as possible and carry out the original mission."

That meant going the extra distance to the base of Hill 766 through a rough countryside thickly covered with bamboo and clumps of forest, and still climbing the mountain. Like ten days in jail, it was easy to say, hard to do.

The Hueys went in first and the rappellers were ready with their ropes. Then the pilots, on taking a closer look at the ground, decided it was possible to land. They could do it, one chopper at a time. As each fire team unloaded, it scampered to a sector of the clearing, as signaled by the direction in which the Huey's nose was pointing, until at last LZ Horse was secured all around by one platoon of riflemen.

Then the Chinooks started coming in with the body of the battalion, carrying thirty men in each load. They shuttled back and forth eight times before the movement was complete. They were happy enough when they were told to move out; they realized that LZ Horse was on forbiddingly low ground, as did Hennessey. Hard hit by malaria, the battalion mustered only 290 men.

Capt. Joseph Russell Beeman, a thirty-one-year-old Philadelphian, was in command of Bravo Company. As they came in, Capt. Bruce Wilson, who had secured the LZ with the Reconnaissance Platoon, met him and said, "I think Lynn has news for you."

He had, indeed. Lynn told him to get moving with his company to the top of Hill 766. They pored over a map, but it was unsatisfactory. The hill was marked plainly enough, but the upper part of the mountain mass northeast of them could not be seen from where they stood, due less to accident of ground than to low-hanging clouds and a fog that blanked out most of the sub-ridges. The rain was coming down hard.

It bothered Beeman that he could not see the objective. He said, "That could be any distance away."

Then he picked up the map and started. Second Platoon led off, followed by Third, Weapons and First, in that order. The company strength was ninety-two. Their crunch toward the high ground was overlong and wearying, and afterward they could not remember much about it, except how the mud sucked at their boots and how frequently men slipped and fell headlong. They knew that if they kept going straight, they were bound to hit the right mountain. The map showed no high ground in between. They kept straight.

That the battalion had found a cleared space of sufficient size that first the Hueys and then the Chinooks had been accommodated astonished Hennessey and surprised the G-2, Colonel Lang. Operations pretty much pivoted around the availability of LZs. Knowing that, the enemy routinely sought to deny use of any limited flat space by fixing it with poles that would knock out the rotor blades, fallen timber and pungi sticks to snag troops as they jumped to deploy, or else by close-guarding it; the other alternative, if the flat was too far-spread for staking, was to fight shy of the vicinity. All things at LZ Horse had been negative. That implied VC and NVA were nowhere about. An intelligence deduction from a neat tactical gambit, it inclined Lang philosophically to accept the distilled wisdom of the centuries as once put by the Sphinx to the Anzac soldier: "Don't expect too much!" Hennessey, too, reckoned he had gone fishing in a mud flat. General Kinnard at Corps, a soldier not given to vulgarisms, wrote a note in his diary: "I wonder what the little bastards are up to."

They were up to where Beeman and company were heading. Of that the captain had no advance warning as the column came to a steep rise and started its climb. He was certain this had to be Hill 766. But there was no way to check on its height save to scale it. Upward from 200 feet above his head, the mass of the mountain was concealed by storm cloud that was still lowering.

A shallow draw confronted him, a narrow path winding unevenly up its center, flanked by a rushing stream. The trees bore down on stream and trail from both sides. This was the natural way to go and the column took it.

The route, to use Beeman's words, was "steep-sided as the outer walls of Moby Dick," not as smooth, but possibly as slippery. There was no gravel for footing. The clay was a mushy ooze. Loose rock gave way beneath their feet, unpinned by rivulets draining via the path. Continuing to slip and tumble back on one another, they learned finally that there was only one way to get ahead. By clinging to the vines and grasping at the bamboo edging the trail, they could grip and go upward a few inches at a time.

In one hour, in this fashion, they had advanced all of 150 meters, and it was coming late afternoon. As yet Beeman was unused to Vietnam's brief summer twilight, and he was loath to make plans, there being no point till he got to the top of the mountain.

Nothing left to the company was dry except its powder. At the foot of the mountain the men had waded a torrent, almost three feet deep and twice that in breadth. Pausing for a breather, Beeman wondered if it made sense to continue.

He got his answer. Right then the front of the column drew fire—not much; he could hear the crackle of three or four rifles, and the bullets whistled harmlessly overhead.

Still, the direct upward climb was not renewed, except by the Third Platoon. Second Platoon was directed to attempt maneuvering leftward along the same level, thereafter to hook upward and to the right, looking for the enemy's open flank.

Beeman went along with this element, thinking as he did so that he had been silly to bring the heavy weapons platoon along; their stuff was unsuited to the problem, the jungle being too thick.

Without drawing fire again, they surmounted a considerable bulge in the earth that later proved to be the military crest of the hill. The gloom thickened, but there was still light enough to see a few things; the real difficulty was with the heavy shadows; Beeman felt that he was proceeding half-blind. First and Weapons Platoon had followed behind Second.

They got unscathed to the top of a prominent knob, possibly because, while they maneuvered, Third Platoon had laid on heavy fire upslope. That might have diverted enemy attention.

Then Beeman tried to send his force out, still circling northwest to get on the other side of the mountain. The move was stopped dead by a hail of fire, out of which the captain counted the chatterings of at least three machine guns and still more automatic rifles. (Much later, seventy-two foxholes and bunkers were checked out on this portion of the hill.) Beeman saw three of his men fall, could not tell whether they were wounded or dead. Then bullets began splashing the mud right next to him. He thought he heard a mortar fire. Ten meters back, the way he had come, was a wide-spreading banyan tree. On passing, he had noted a well-dug enemy firing pit nestled next its roots on the downside.

That would be the place, and now was the time. Dark was coming on fast. He made a jump for the hole; that was to be his CP for the duration of the night. On radio he called Weapons Platoon, saying, "You move the casualties down to the valley. Get them on the far side of the creek. Set up a defense and stay there with your weapons."

Third Platoon's leader, SFC Leroy F. Pope, got him on radio straight afterward. This was his message: "I've lost three men. We're pinned down by rifles and machine guns. There's no chance to advance on this line."

Beeman said, "Back away till you get in defilade. Then swing around and come in behind me."

He had already called in artillery to plaster the crown of the hill. Helping him was the forward observer, Lieut. Bryant T. Collins, who squatted just outside the hole behind the banyan tree. The supporting batteries—one from the 17th, the other from the 19th Battalion—were based at LZ Cobra in Vinh Thanh Valley. And they were good at their business. According to the coordinates given them by Collins, they had it right this time—the stuff should be breaking all along the crest of Hill 766.

It wasn't so. Beeman knew it wasn't so; and so did Collins. No shellfire of any kind was exploding into the cloud-bound crest above them. They would be able to hear it, if not see it, though the cap lay another 150 meters on.

"We're not getting it!" Beeman protested.

Collins repeated the words.

Somewhat more than a mile away at the battalion base in the valley, Lynn was monitoring these conversations. His ground was no bed of roses, either. Mortar shells were exploding into it, and his S-3, Maj. Gene Fox, had just been hit.

Hennessey had just dropped in on LZ Horse.

He was about to shove off afoot for Beeman's position.

He wanted to see firsthand how the fight was going.

"If they can't hear those shells," said Lynn, "they've got to be on the wrong mountain."

"Wrong mountain?" echoed Hennessey. "Well, if this isn't the craziest damned horse I ever rode!"

And wrong it was. Beeman was halfway up a subordinate ridge 600 meters short of Hill 766, connected with it by a flattish saddle. Beeman had not really blundered; this prominent terrain feature did not show on the map. The irony was that no enemy awaited them on the big mountain which dominated the area. Beeman had come to his donnybrook by going at a molehill.

This sad tale of trial and error was wafted to the base camp at An Khe and was good, not just for laughter, but for history. It changed the name of the game. Started as "Herford" (sic) and called "Base Plate" for one morning, the going fight evolved as Operation Crazy Horse, without protest from the 7th Cavalrymen present who begrudged not the fresh honors accorded the memory of a foe of yesterday.

In the II Corps zone, Vietnam, sweeps, or battles which develop therefrom, are named after distinguished Americans. (Like Crazy Horse?) Operational titles such as Killer and Masher are tabooed. The main idea is to make our aim seem less brutal, more genteel. It's the Madison Avenue approach to making bloodshed more acceptable. The net result will be the scrambling of history. Battles are not called such and remain unidentified by their place names.

On his anonymous hill Beeman was not doing any better. Pope of the Third Platoon, wounded twice in the back and once in the nose, passed the word to his men: "Keep flat and back away from the fire." It had just the wrong effect on one man.

Sgt. Kenneth W. Pickett, the NCO farthest forward, jumped to his feet, screaming, "No goddamned gook is big enough to make me crawl on my belly," and charged upslope toward the nearest machine gun.

A gun from higher up the hill felled him with three bullets in his head almost as his scream died. The same burst wounded Pvt. George J. Pfaff, Jr., behind him. Pfaff also got it in the head.

Beeman had the word from Pope via radio. Spurred by it, he told Collins, "Bring in artillery fire"—a nasty problem for Collins and the gunners. There were no dependable coordinates. Reckoning how the hill lay had to be done by-guess-and-by-God. Somehow they found it. The first four rounds exploded high in the canopy upslope, fifty feet above ground, doing no good. The fifth exploded directly into Beeman's position, wounding five men, including 1st Sgt. Ramon Aponte, who took a shard in his right shoulder. It was nobody's fault. The round, with a time-delay fuse, had ricocheted from a tree.

Beeman yelled, "Cut the arty!"

Aponte was four feet from him, right next Collins.

Now it was full dark. While an aid man worked over

Aponte, Beeman got out word to the company: "Time to dig in." They did—in a way. The mushy soil yielded to the spade readily enough; as fast as they dug, the holes filled with water.

At this point the enemy broke off fire.

Thereupon Beeman got on radio to the crew of his one 81 mm mortar, 400 meters from him in the valley: "Put fire directly in front of me as fast as you can." There came thirty-six rounds, exploding into the slope about thirty meters beyond the position.

Looking up at the fires, Beeman's men then for the first time during the fight saw, beyond the flashes, the enemy— thirty or forty dark forms that arose and were lost in an instant as they receded into a greater blackness. There wasn't time to bring one bullet-firing weapon to bear on them. But in that instant they noted one thing well. The forms were well-camouflaged. They looked like "so many trees moving."

In that moment it was Beeman's impression that all his fires had done them little hurt, though his pessimism was wrong.

The captain stayed awake through the night, regulating the mortar fires. Soaked through and chilled, there was no sleep for the men. Sgts. Jimmy Stewart and Aster Watts were killed by an ill-aimed rocket. Several other leaders were down with fever; twenty more malaria cases would be evacuated from LZ Horse the next day. But all hands had been told to stand to when 0530 came.

At 0605 Sgt. Oscar M. Harvey, leader of First Squad, First Platoon, walked along the foxhole line, checking his men on the extreme left flank of the company position.

He glanced left, then turned back toward Beeman, shouting, "Good God, watch out, here they come!"

An enemy platoon was bearing directly toward his open flank. Through the fog Harvey had seen them not more than thirty meters away. They had circled the back slope (Beeman had posted no outguards either to his flanks or front, though the enemy pullback had given him the opening) to take the line in enfilade.

As Harvey yelled, the charging skirmishers broke into a scream. They came on, hurling potato-masher grenades.

One machine gun in Harvey's ground cut a dozen of them down, forced the others to flatten, then jammed wholly. His second machine gun was smashed by a grenade before it could fire. The squad and its position were wiped out within thirty seconds—three men killed, three men wounded, all by grenades. Gunners Randolph C. Scott and Clarence W. Hagey had died on their weapons.

Though that left Beeman's spot behind the banyan tree wide open, this part of the attack had already slackened. Now the fire from two machine guns—a .50 AA HMG and a captured American M-60—was boring straight toward the CP from upslope, and splinters were flying from the banyan.

Beeman got Lieutenant Ryan, leading the mortar platoon, on the radio, saying, "Bring it in close, just as close as you can." Ryan did—so close that one white phosphorus round spilled over into the CP and blistered Beeman's right hand.

Thinking out loud, he asked, "Why in hell are there always so many more of them than of us?"

Just then Colonel Lynn called him on the radio to inquire, "Are you having a mad minute?"

For the first time Beeman laughed. "No," he replied, "but Charley sure is."

Then he added very seriously, "Colonel, I've got to have help. These VC keep coming. I don't have enough men."

Lynn promised to get part of Alpha Company started forward from LZ Horse just as fast as possible.

Three of Beeman's dead lay a few yards to right of him, a little upslope. Something drew his gaze in that direction, though at first he was not aware why. Then he saw it. One of the M-16 rifles in a dead man's hand was slowly rising, the motion being hardly perceptible.

An enemy skirmisher had crawled in among the American dead to get their weapons. Draped in vines and leaves, and hugging earth, he got that far undetected. As Beeman jumped up, so did the man, as if to turn. Beeman fired, once, twice, three times. Every bullet hit. The figure dropped, crumpling, and looking for all the world like a bush blown over.

Never before had Beeman consciously killed a man. He had his moment of satisfaction.

Sergeant Harvey, who while taking a grenade frag in the shoulder had escaped the ruin of his squad by running rightward to cry alarm, flopped down next to Beeman, behind one of the banyan flukes.

Beeman asked him, "Will you give me some cover while I pull this CP back? It's too hot here."

Harvey turned to do it. The machine gun cracked down before he could make another move. One bullet shattered his wrist. Beeman provided the covering fire while Harvey went to the rear.

2nd Lieut. Claiborne Randle, Jr., came along and went prone right where Harvey had been.

"You better get the hell out of here," said Beeman. "This place is no good."

Not more than a second later a bullet from the same gun drilled Randle through the right hand.

All of these things were reverberating up to the highest levels. Knowing now that Beeman was blocked and had his hands full, Hennessey changed Ray's order for 1/5th. This battalion, instead of continuing its overland sweep from Hereford, would be lifted to LZ Horse, then go on to Hill 766. Ray and his people were already in motion. Attached was a platoon from the 8th Engineer Battalion. Its task was to cut a shaft in the jungle atop Hill 766 large enough for two Hueys to funnel down and land side by side. Hennessey knew now that the proportions of the fight had become such that two LZs at Hereford and Horse were not enough. After the new LZ—called Milton—was in and secured, the rest of Ray's battalion was to sweep to the southeast, firing as it moved.

There was good reason for this order. Lynn's battalion in the valley was getting peppered. Snipers harassed the company guarding LZ Horse, which was again being mortared. The other company, on a sweep to the east, was fighting off hit-and-run skirmishers in the bush. Lynn was himself winged by a sniper on the LZ while trying to mount a Huey.

Too, Saigon had taken another look, and the battle at last had an official handle, not too fitting. It happened in this way: Maj. Charles L. Siler, the division PIO, called Lieut. Col. George Lewis at MAC-V to report progress. "We have three battalions committed and there are more than two hundred enemy dead in those hills," he said. A sudden light dawned on Lewis. "That can't be a piece of Benning," he said. "You got to have a name for it." Siler got on radio to Capt. Dudley Todemy at Hennessey's TOC. The story about Beeman climbing the wrong hill and Hennessey cracking wise was still making the rounds. Like a double play, it was tossed, Todemy to Siler to Lewis: "Call it Crazy Horse."

Applying do-it-yourself, Beeman got the jammed machine gun working again by about 0830; then, under its covering fire, he withdrew his CP to a safer spot thirty feet down the slope. Beeman knew a trick or two about firing the M-60; either you first ranged on the dirt and came up with it, or you missed. Soon afterward Lieut. David D. Porreca got up to him with the lead platoon of Alpha Company. Beeman was so happy he could have kissed him. He knew Porreca as a first-rate fighting man.

Porreca was sent north along the hillside, in extension of the line where Harvey's squad had been. By midmorning, with his men settled in, Porreca's flank looked solid enough. Lieut. John Murray arrived leading another platoon. Beeman sent him rightward to try on the same line where Pickett had been stopped the night before—bucking upward along the draw via which they had climbed. Though Murray's platoon first descended to the hill base, then crawled up carefully, low and well-spread, it was no go. The ground ahead was a beaten zone under the flails of two machine guns.

So Porreca's platoon was ordered to deploy to the left around the hill, Beeman's notion being that the move might lift the pressure from Murray.

"Crawl on your bellies," Beeman said, "and don't fire as you go."

They went, festooned all over with vines, branches and

bamboo sprouts. If not the neatest camouflage on the hill, it was the best they could do.

That was an inspired order in a propitious moment.

Porreca met an NVA platoon in full motion swinging around the hill to get on Beeman's rear. So pointed, he was directly on their flank. They came with two machine guns.

And it was Porreca personally who doomed them. Beeman saw his friend standing in the clear grenading. He yelled, "Take that, you sons-of-bitches!" His first bomb smashed the lead machine gun and killed four of the crew. Again he yelled, "Take that, you sons-of-bitches!" The second bomb got the second gun and four more crewmen. Along with some rifle fire from his men, that onslaught also killed the attack. Its survivors fled.

Followed by the platoon, Porreca came on back, aglow with satisfaction, saying only, "There's a lot of dead VC over yonder." His platoon had crawled past seven bodies before the fight began.

Beeman's hill began getting fire from an entirely new direction. To his practiced ears, the rattle of the machine guns and crack of the rifles sounded friendly; it felt not. Ray's people, in their sweep from Hill 766 to the southeast, were following orders and "shooting up the country." But their sense of direction was a bit wobbly and they were swinging too wide. Beeman called Battalion, saying, "Get them off my back." The word got to Hennessey and he told Ray, "Don't fire unless you are fired on."

Beeman sent Porreca to help Murray in the draw. It did not work. As Porreca's platoon got almost flank to flank with Murray's men, three more machine guns opened fire.

Porreca called Beeman on radio: "I have nine men wounded; no chance to push forward!"

Then Murray called: "I have five wounded. We're pinned. This fire is too heavy."

Beeman realized then that the position that barred the draw was being steadily re-enforced, probably by fresh people coming in from the east.

He told them both, "It's no use, pull back!"

Porreca replied, "That's impossible; if we stir, we're dead."

Murray said, "We can't do it."

Then Beeman heard mortar booming from the other side of the hill. Three shells came in just above the CP, which was saved by the canopy. The rounds exploded among the treetops.

Porreca has a good ear for mortar music. He called the FO, Collins, gave him a reckoning according to the sound, and Collins made a snap calculation. Unbelievable luck: the first 155 mm round to come in landed dead on target. The tube ceased to fire; its wrecked metal was found next day.

Then Porreca and Murray arranged it among themselves. Alternately the platoons would lay down a covering machine-gun fire. The platoon not so engaged would first withdraw its wounded. Then the other platoon would cover while the casualties were moved out. This done, they could all get away.

It worked. They did it without further loss.

After their retrograde, the able-bodied wheeled left to close in tight on Beeman's line. His Fourth Platoon—the weapons men—had spent the afternoon toting ammunition up the hill. Now they began double duty, carrying the casualties down.

The hour was about 1630. The jungle was darkening. Beeman saw Lieut. William C. Comme coming toward him with the rest of Alpha Company. Together they reshaped the position, going into a tight perimeter.

Water, cold canned chicken and cold boiled rice was brought up to them. It was the first food they had tasted in thirty-six hours. Nothing served them by the Army had ever tasted better.

Amid the meal there came a query from Battalion: "Do you want any C's sent up?"

The man was talking about C rations.

"Not on your life," said Beeman. "There are already too many VCs around."

As they completed their new diggings, trip flares and claymore mines were installed all around the outer line.

There were no fires that night, except that Beeman kept his one 81 mm mortar going. Its bursts danced in the upper woods all night. In the two days the one tube got off 783 rounds, an extraordinary performance.

Together Beeman and Comme laid on elaborate plans. When morning came, they would form in line and sweep right over the top. Elementary.

Soon after first light they started. There had been no artillery preparation. The day was bright and the sky clear. In the woods they found nothing but mangled flesh, torn arms and legs and heavy blood trails that carried over the crest and to the eastward.

Puzzled at first, they found no one-man positions. All the foxholes and bunkers had been filled with fresh earth. So they started digging. The first hole held the body of an NVA soldier. They kept at it. By noon they had uncovered ninety-three bodies—all buried in the fighting positions by the people who had fled the hill.

Their count of dead was as reported here. Twenty-seven of Beeman's men were wounded. The ratio—the loss rate—was still better than ten to one in their favor.

Beeman realized, a little late in the game, that he had done fairly well.

That did not quite end the campaign for Lynn's shrunken battalion, now counting less than 200 men. Lynn himself had gone to an aid station, had a bullet cut from his right arm, then returned to duty on LZ Horse.

Directly east of Hill 766 was a long stretch of lower ground, not so much a valley as a maze of rocky badland furrowed by innumerable ravines running in no particular direction. It looked to Hennessey like the sort of country the enemy would use for a supply base; he told Lynn to get in there and search it.

They spent a day, found a cache with thirteen tons of rice, two huts with large stores of arms and ammunition and a cave with several boxes of enemy uniforms.

There were no people.

Private Dolby

By the morning of 19 May, Colonel Hennessey had it figured out that he must be battling at least one North Vietnam regiment.

Any place he moved people within a ten-mile zone amid the mountains east of the Song Con River, whether north or south or toward the seacoast, they were being hit, not only with exceeding promptness, but by heavy numbers.

Viewed now in retrospect, his had to be a quite conservative reckoning. One regiment spreads mighty thin over more than fifty miles of territory. Either Hennessey was running in bad luck, or the unfriendlys had done a capital job of divining his chess game and where he would set the knights and the pawns.

What Hennessey did not yet know was that there were at least five battalions of the NVA within the battle zone, some of them, true enough, greatly crippled by malaria, but then there were also fighting elements of local Viet Cong.

Colonel Buchan, the division G-3, was also taking a new reading. The question intrigued him: Why were they making a stand-up fight of it? It was wholly unlike the enemy to move to contact unless all things were in his favor; the Americans believed this to be axiomatic. So Buchan tentatively concluded that they were hitting back because they had no other place to go. Within the month Third Brigade of First Cavalry Division had campaigned hard in the Bon Song area to the northeast with bloody success. Col. Hal Moore's forces had killed more than 400 VCs and NVAs. The ROK Tiger Division had made several sweeps to the eastward. The Vinh Thanh Valley was a barrier to westward of the mountains so long as the division stood ready to pounce if the C.I.D.G. camp got hit. It seemed probable that the highland fastness had long been used as a sanctuary—a rest sector—to which the Viet Cong retired to lick their wounds, train and re-equip. The supply stations now being uncovered suggested that. They had an old look.

General Kinnard flew up from Nha Trang that morning to talk things out with Jack Norton and to visit his old friend, Sergeant Koebbe, in hospital. Koebbe was sitting up and taking nourishment. But he failed to tell Kinnard how his ribs had been broken: they hurt him too much when he laughed.

The two generals saw eye to eye. The terrain being what it was, there was no choice but to move tactical units beyond what they both held to be the rule-of-thumb distance to insure ready artillery support and prompt re-enforcement.

Kinnard said, "It's not our kind of operation. Sorry about that. But keep pressing."

"At least it's going," said Norton, "and it's no dry well."

Fretting them more than all else was that not one enemy prisoner had been taken. The circumstances of the fight almost precluded it. Enemy wounded were dragged off before they could be dragged in. There had been no hand-to-hand fighting in the literal sense. Every fire fight had had the nature of a small siege with the Americans holding the ramparts.

That was too bad; it meant that intelligence had to walk blind. Lang was crying for prisoners, and within a short time everyone would be crying for prisoners. It was still a better kind of crying than was occurring on the campuses back home and in the U.S. Senate.

Hennessey was more preoccupied with how and where to

move companies than with that particular problem. He planned to exploit along two axes, with one battalion hitting on each, one going north, the other northeast. Colonel Broughton's men (1/8th) drew this last assignment.

They were destined to maneuver toward a speck on the map which half of the men of the division called "the Crow's Foot" and the other half called "the Eagle's Claw," to the confusion of ornithology more than cartography.

They might better have named it "Back-of-me-Hand." Place one flipper on the table and press, palm down. That is how the Crow's Foot area looks from above, where the mountains taper out and the lower ridge fingers reach toward the China Sea. There is a melancholy desolation about this fouled-up land. The earth is poor. The somewhat rounded fingers, and the flats between them, cannot even afford to support a jungle. The knuckles shine white in the sun, where they have not been cratered to reveal red earth underneath. In a countryside where most vistas are enchanting, and the bounty of still undeveloped valleys, made for farming, promises more for the future than all the projected plans of politicians, this is one of the more miserable regions.

The brunt of the next move, insofar as it concerned 1/8th, fell on 117 men of Bravo Company under Capt. Roy D. Martin. Here was no average skipper. Fairly tall, a little bulky, somewhat sober-sided, he was intense about his work. Broughton, who led the battalion, was somewhat awed by him. He said, "No other man knows more about how to get the Viet Cong; he's the best thing that's happened since Daniel Boone."

To know him is to get the feeling that he would be good almost anywhere. There are depths in him, and he makes no studied attempt to hide them. He has the quality that Scots call "innerliness."

They loaded up at An Khe aboard Hueys at 0700 on 21 May and about forty minutes later they were set down at LZ Horse. From that beaten-down pad, now carpeted with dust where the elephant grass had been, Martin and his Bravo Company took off under a broiling sun, striking north through a baked countryside. Four days earlier Captain Beeman and another Bravo Company, landing at the same place, had splashed north to a hot fight on a drenched hill. What had happened to them, however, went unsung. Martin's men did not know the extent of Beeman's fight or have any close-to-fact grasp of what had gone before that had led to their own commitment. That is something not tried by the Army in Vietnam, or attempted by any U.S. Army previously, or set as an ideal by any army at any time. Troops do not get told. The real reason isn't that command thinks it better to break the sad news to them gently; command rarely, if ever, knows where it has been, as to the "little picture." Command doesn't have time to garner the grain.

Five hundred meters north of LZ Horse, Bravo caught up with Charley Company of the same battalion, which under Capt. William Mosey had simply tarried there on the bank of a creek. Like Powder River, this string of water was more wide than deep. But it ran through rather flat country and there were packed trails on both sides of it. The plan was that the companies, moving abreast, would keep beating along this stream corridor, with Bravo sweeping the right bank and Charley the left. How far they would go would depend on what came of it. This was not jungle. There was lush grass along the stream. Both ways from it the valley flat was covered with low bush, not too dense to forbid a fairly broad deployment both ways from the trails. One aspect of nature baffling to the chance visitor in Vietnam is that marsh birds, or birds of any kind, are almost never seen in such a pleasant and seemingly inviting habitat. It is as if they had fled the land.

Bravo Company marched with a point of one fire team out front, twenty-five to fifty meters. It was followed by Second and First Platoons with a common front. Third Platoon was fifty meters back—the company reserve. Weapons Platoon, with the mortars, had been dropped at LZ Horse. The men spread out in packages of threes.

The day was hot but not humid. Even so, the loads were heavy enough. Each rifleman carried 450 rounds for the M-16 and two hand grenades. Each leader also carried two smoke grenades. (This is a tricky thing in the Vietnam fighting. The enemy also carries smoke in the same colors and is adept at using any one of them simultaneously to confuse the signal. So the meaning of a particular color has to be changed from day to day.) For each M-60 machine gun there were 1500 rounds. Two men in each squad lugged M-79 grenade launchers. The twenty-three rounds per weapon were distributed around to equalize the weight.

At 0930 the front moved up a small hill that latched onto the creek bank. The point came under the fire of six rifles, went flat and returned it. After a five-minute exchange the enemy broke off and vanished. It was probably an outpost or warning party. There had been no blood drawn by either side.

High noon, and they came to a bend where the creek trench turned sharply left from the line they had followed. By then Bravo had far outdistanced Charley Company. Martin held up and told his men to work over both banks of the stream thoroughly.

They did, and what they found made him feel that he had stopped movement just in time. Both banks were thoroughly organized with well-built permanent enemy works. On the right bank were log bunkers, six to eight feet deep with overhead covers of timber and packed earth. There were more bunkers across the creek where, within the bend, a rounded knoll nosed down to the stream.

Martin could smell it that the enemy had just pulled out and must be close at hand. He connected the departure with the brief exchange on the other hill earlier. There were quartering bunkers on the knoll in the bend. The leaves and grass laid out for beds were fresh and unflattened. Marks in the nearby trees showed where hammock hooks had just been yanked out. Bits of cooked rice on the bamboo tables were soft to the touch.

Martin put Second Platoon across the creek to hold the knoll until Charley Company came up. So passed another three hours. When Mosey arrived, Martin asked him to go into perimeter with his company in the bend and serve as general reserve while he attacked the hill mass just past the bend on his side of the creek.

Confronting Martin was a ridge with two prominent knobs and a fairly high saddle faced by a steep draw between them. Rightward of the ridge a tributary came out of the high ground to join the creek where it made the U-turn around the bend. With the ground short of that feeder stream, he did not have to be concerned. It was so flat and devoid of cover as obviously to be of little use to the enemy. Everything beyond that dividing line looked ominous.

There were tall trees on the ridge and within the draw. But it was not jungle. There was very little canopy and even less underbrush. Here was fairly clean forest. One could see into it in almost any direction for twenty-five or thirty meters.

This was his plan: Third Platoon would attack along the closest edge of the hill mass, advancing parallel with the small stream. Second Platoon, which was to be on the left, would cross the creek, swing to the left a little, and move up the draw. First Platoon, in the center, would give way a little to the right and then move up the same draw. If the two knobs were defended, First would take the right one, Second the left. Later they would link with Third Platoon on the far side of the ridge.

No softening-up fires by the artillery or the mortars at LZ Horse were asked for on any of these positions. They were available. The LZ was only 2600 meters away. An oversight, it was one time when Martin did not have the convictions of his courage.

So they started.

What Martin next knew of his battle was that, within 100 meters of the creek, First Platoon had been brought in check by the fire of several machine guns and not a few Chicom assault rifles, from the two knobs on right and left. Second Platoon reported that it was making "rapid progress." What he did not know, because he could not see it, was that Second Platoon, being the faster gun, had beaten First Platoon to the draw, worked its way up the same slot first without drawing fire, gone on to the far slope, and there been stopped by machine guns blazing away from its right flank.

Partly for topographical reasons, more largely because of what enemy bullets were doing to First Platoon, it was impossible for the people in the two positions to convey to Martin just how things had happened and what had to be done so that they might be of help to one another. Neither could imagine the other's situation.

Martin told Second Platoon: "Return to your original position [the creek bank] and I'll get an air strike on the force holding you up." They did it by turning left and coming all the way around the ridge, extracting themselves with little difficulty. Second Platoon's radio message to Martin had said: "The VC have slipped in behind us and that's why we're catching hell." What none of the parties in this involved situation understood was that the VC who supposedly had "slipped in behind" Second Platoon had been there all the time. They were the soldiers in fixed positions atop the two knobs who were beating First Platoon to earth. It was a trap: they had sprung it successfully, though most of them died in the end for so doing. The fire bands of the two machine guns crossed exactly where First Platoon was stopped next the trail. It was no accident.

Third Platoon, on the right flank, was having a field day while these misadventures occurred elsewhere. Lieut. Gerald East called Martin to say: "I've just killed eleven of them who were trying to swing around my right flank." That opening, to Martin, sounded as if it were worth exploiting. He asked Captain Mosey to give him help, and Mosey sent forth his Third Platoon to support Lieutenant East. Shortly a message came in from this re-enforcement: "We have just knocked off six more VC."

Sporadic rifle fire came in from a hill spur on Martin's right rear, that is, it came from the wrong direction against the CP. Mosey called his mortar platoon at LZ Horse, and with their 60's they put a blast on the spur.

All of these things were very small change. The enemy's gravity center was directly ahead of First Platoon. But one mischance after another had kept Martin from making that reading of his problem. He was not getting the information he so direly needed.

Sgt. Alonzo Peoples, a Negro soldier from Gaston, Ga., was at front of the leading squad when First Platoon started up through the center of the two-pronged ridge. There was a wide, well-trod path running up this draw in a fairly straight line. However, the platoon leader, Lieut. Robert H. Crum, told them not to take it. Though Second Platoon had already gone that way and was atop the ridge, Crum still feared an ambush. So they slipped upward through the trees on either side of it.

There had been no firing against Second Platoon.

First Platoon, with Peoples leading, got three-fourths of the way to the top.

Right then, from directly above them, an automatic rifle opened fire. Everybody went flat. The aim was way high. Nobody got hurt. Feeling sheepish, they arose to resume march.

Before they could step off, heavy fire—machine gun and rifle—came against them from front and both flanks. The sounds left no doubt: the fire was right on them; they had walked into an ambush.

Crum was the first man hit; a bullet had gone through his right shoulder.

PFC Michael G. Cryar, the point man, was on ahead, ten yards beyond Peoples' squad, all alone and flat next the trail. Peoples was busy with other things. Crum, who had been behind Peoples, sang out to Cryar, "Get ready to draw back. I'll cover you."

Crum stood up, fired quickly, yelled, "I got one." Then another bullet knocked him backward, and as he came down hard he yelled, "I'm hit."

Sergeant Peoples was also flat. From where he lay, just within the tree line, it was about twenty-five meters to the top of the ridge. He reckoned that one .50 caliber machine gun and two light machine guns were firing from there.

Peoples was firing his M-16 upslope and telling himself that he was doing no good with it. He could not see any of his squad, because of bushes and fallen timber. Then he heard Mayberry's voice.

PFC Russel Mayberry was a few yards off to Peoples' left. He had been firing grenades from an M-79 launcher. His voice rose to a scream: "One Three, One Three, come help me. I'm shot in the dick. That's where I got it."

Peoples yelled back, "That's all right. Nothing to worry about. Lay quiet. I'll come get you."

Peoples started crawling. Between him and Mayberry lay a fallen tree, three feet through. Peoples started to work his way over it. A splintered limb snagged him around the boot top. For perhaps one-half minute he hung suspended, leg high in air, struggling frantically. Then a bullet smashed through the suspended leg and the jolt freed him.

He crawled on and got to Mayberry.

Mayberry said, "Sarge, you're hit bad."

Peoples lowered Mayberry's pants, looked at the wound, and said, "Man, there's nothing wrong with your dick. You just got a little scratch in the groin. I'm hurt worse than you are."

Burned up, Peoples started crawling back to the squad, after first calling for an aid man to help Mayberry.

The .50 machine gun was still firing. The bullets seemed to be coming right at him. He lunged for the protection of a boulder, hit it with the top of his skull, and blacked out.

The medic, Spec. 4 Michael J. Jaworski, was working on Crum. PFC David Charles Dolby, age twenty, of Oaks, Pa., had called for him. Dolby is a soldier of almost perfect physique, proportioned like a professional fullback. Highly intelligent and vocal, he is one of those rarest of warriors—a man with keen imagination who at the same time, when under fire, seems to be wholly without fear.

Dolby was the platoon machine gunner. He had been in the Army ten months. Yet he was seeing the action with deeper understanding than any other man in the company.

Crum said to him, "Have them cease fire; pass the word along."

That seemed odd to Dolby. The enemy fire was still bearing down, though he could see only the muzzle flashes.

Still he did as ordered. As soon as the American fire slackened, the enemy fires seemed to double.

Crum, who was suffering badly, paid no heed.

Five meters to his left, flattened out, were Dolby's ammunition bearer and assistant gunner, PFC Kenneth Fernandez and PFC Michael E. Devoe. The only other man he could see was PFC Tommy Nettles. A grazing rifle fire kept all three men pinned, and none was firing.

Dolby took a chance on it.

He yelled to them, "Give me a covering fire. Try to get it on the machine guns. I'll get up there and try to knock out the position."

Crum said to him, "That can't be done and you know it."

Dolby took the thirty meters of sloped trail to the saddle as fast as he could run, carrying an M-16.

From atop the ridge he could see both machine-gun positions, one on either side of him, about seventy-five meters apart. Both were well camouflaged with great mats of foliage purposefully woven into a facsimile of live jungle growth. What gave them away was that a bank of red earth, thrown from the holes, glared alongside each pit.

Dolby jumped in behind a large banyan and, still standing, fired at the gun pit on the right. Then one more .50 caliber machine gun, from somewhere on his right rear, opened fire on the tree. Dolby jumped to the other side of it, then backed his way down the trail, firing upward as he went.

Crum had been hit again, this time by a .50 caliber bullet through his left arm. The arm had gone numb. That's what they told him, though Dolby did not see Crum; soldiers had dragged the lieutenant leftward away from the trail about thirty meters.

In the brief interval that he had been gone, Third Squad, which had been with Peoples behind the point, had taken more blows. Cryar was down with a wound. So was PFC Phillip B. Walz, shot in the back.

Walz was wholly despondent. He said to Dolby, "Everybody's hit. We're done for."

Without bothering to check the others, Dolby charged

back up the slope again, this time carrying an M-79 launcher that someone had dropped. On the second try he got only twenty meters. The fire of the heavy machine gun was beating back and forth across the trail, barring the way.

Again he backed toward the other men, firing.

Walz said, "We better cease fire and try to get out of this," and then added, "The lieutenant wants to see you."

Dolby found Crum lying behind a large tree, beside his RTO. The lieutenant, blood-drenched, was flat on his back. Dolby judged that he was already dying. Crum said to him, "Dolby, you're in charge. If you think you have to pull out, don't leave anybody behind."

His words laid their full weight on Dolby.

Peoples, who was also sprawled out within earshot, had regained consciousness, body immobilized, mind in a daze. The words made their impression, though in a strange way. He thought thereafter that he was the man who had told Dolby to take over the command. Dolby did not even see him during the fight.

The .30 caliber machine gun on the left of the enemy hill had zeroed in on the ground between the trail and the tree where Crum lay. Dolby had gone through the fire to get to him.

Four men of Third Squad, all of them wounded, lay amid the boulders in this beaten zone. All had dropped their weapons, Dolby noted, and were merely trying to escape the fire. The medic was trying to take care of them, while the bullets kicked up earth around him.

Nettles continued firing up to the moment when a sniper knocked him out. The bullet hit his rucksack. A cup and some C rations within it absorbed much of the shock; the bullet didn't get to him. But it drove these objects against the back of Nettles' neck with the accuracy of a rabbit punch and knocked him cold.

There remained fighting in the position only Devoe and Fernandez; both had been nicked by bullets. Dolby was the only man as yet unhit. The engagement had been going about one hour.

Very little of Third Platoon's ordeal was getting back to

Captain Martin. He knew that Crum's people were pinned, but he thought that some of them were still fighting. The RTO, PFC George Wallace, was reporting only what Crum gave him to say, and Crum, understandably, was talking little. Still early in the game, the diminution of the American fire in the center of the fight began to tell its own story. Wallace told the forward observer, Lieutenant Livengood, to bring in the artillery and call for an air strike.

Nettles regained consciousness and resumed firing. Dolby thought he was moving too far forward. He called to him, "You pull down a little bit and pass the word to any others up there."

Then he crawled over to Wallace to tell him, "Have the captain get some smoke fired on this ridge top." Almost before the words were out of his mouth, artillery shells began breaking along the crest. They were followed quickly by an ARA rocket strike against the same ground. They poured it on in salvos—twenty-four rockets at a time. The effect was only fairly good. Dolby though most of the stuff was hitting beyond the target area.

Telling Wallace what he was going to do, he charged up the hill a third time to put out green smoke and mark the enemy line of resistance. A strong wind whipping over the hill rolled the smoke right back on him. Dolby yelled to Wallace, "Tell them to disregard."

While these things were happening, Fernandez had crawled off a few yards to get behind a big tree; he was no longer firing.

Devoe was in the open on all fours. Dolby couldn't tell what he was doing. But he knew that he was moving into the line of fire of the .30 machine gun.

He yelled at him, "Get behind that tree on your right."

Thereupon Devoe seemed to freeze from fright and stopped dead-still.

That's when the burst caught him—one bullet in the mouth and two through the heart.

The force spun him into a roll fifteen yards down the slope, where the body came to rest midway between Fernandez and Dolby. They were flat. The dead man was sitting upright.

The worst of the enemy fire was coming from the flanks of the position above. The two killing guns then were slightly to the rear of the platoon survivors in the draw. That was the hell of it. Either the distant batteries had to knock these positions out, or there could be neither advance nor withdrawal. Dolby tried again and again to get the fires adjusted through the FO at the company CP. But they never came in right. So he knew he was whipped.

Counting himself and Wallace, there were only four men in any condition to continue. The others were dead or wounded, except Private First Class Rodriguez, who was missing.

Dolby called to Martin to ask, "What do you advise me?"

Martin said, "Stay where you are; help is on the way."

Fernandez crawled around the position to make sure the wounded were behind cover of rocks or trees, or to drag them there.

Then he started calling, "Rodriguez! Rodriguez!"

In this moment Cryar got hit again—a third bullet, this time through the brain.

It was getting dark. Rain began falling.

Second and Third Platoons and part of Charley Company got set for the last big push against the enemy position. Martin put it out to all units: "Fire a mad minute!"

The other platoons pulled trigger with a will.

No one around Dolby so much as raised his rifle.

As that rattle of musketry died, Crum got hit again, the bullet striking his side with such force that he was driven away from the tree and into the open.

Jaworski, the medic, who had spent most of the time trying to do something for the lieutenant, went to him and tried to apply mouth-to-mouth resuscitation.

With such strength as he had left, Crum tried to shove him off.

Then he mumbled eight words: "How are my men? How are my men?" and died.

Jaworski and Dolby looked but said nothing to one another.

Spec. 4 John R. Forte came up then. The mad minute and the sweep by the re-enforced line had dampered the fire from above. Not all the enemy had pulled out. A few bullets nipped at the trees. The machine guns had gone silent. The men capable of it felt it was time to rise and move about.

Forte said to Dolby, "I don't think I'd worry too much about Rodriguez. The last time I saw him he was higher up the bank behind some rocks—unwounded."

Dolby wondered then where Forte had been.

A radio message came in from Martin: "Leave your dead and pull back with your wounded."

Dolby handed his machine gun to Jaworski to carry. Jaworski had run out of medical supplies, anyway.

Spec. 4 Richard F. Lease, as large a man as Dolby, was the heaviest of the non-perambulant casualties. Peoples, on his own, had crawled to the foot of the hill some time earlier. There were no litters about.

Dolby got Lease on his back in a fireman's carry.

The other walking wounded had already cleared away.

Then with Mayberry, Forte, Walz and Fernandez, he went running down the hill.

By the time Dolby pulled up, somewhat short of wind, along the creek bank—the last man out—the three platoons in Captain Martin's reorganized line were advancing to the high ground with some celerity. This time Martin went with them. A tactical air strike called in just as dark fell had helped a lot. Now the rain was falling in sheets.

Lieutenant McCarran's Second Platoon was the first of the three to consolidate a position on the ridge crest. It was done by 2000: they were atop the knob on the right. They heard on radio that the platoons still lower down and advancing toward their left flank as they faced about were continuing to draw fire. Martin, who was with McCarran, possibly worried overmuch about this, considering that the line was not really being hurt.

He said to McCarran, "We'll sweep back toward them." Now there was so little visibility that they had to move shoulder to shoulder. Martin stumbled and almost fell going downtrail; he had tripped over enemy commo wire. While Sergeant Johnson stooped to cut it, four Congs, trying to get out of the fight, ran toward them. Martin and the others gunned them down.

They passed a line of bunkers, still occupied. They saw motion in the blackness as of heads popping out. So they grenaded through the doors and went on.

On radio Martin passed these words to the platoons lower down: "Fire only when you pick them out and are sure. Wait for the muzzle flash. Then fire low." McCarran's men were also told.

More VC tried to slip by on the platoon's left. They were shot. Another bunker, and Martin saw the nose of a machine gun jutting from the embrasure. The gunner was trying to get away through a side door, crawling on his belly. McCarran and Sergeant Lopez killed him.

Now all of the fixed positions were behind them, and the few enemy skirmishers still active were behind trees, firing uphill—in the wrong direction. Some were killed; others got away.

By 2200 the fight was over. Second and Third Platoons of Bravo Company had joined flanks on the low ground. Third Platoon of Charley Company set up a perimeter on the fortified hill across the creek within the bend. Third Platoon of Bravo went into a blocking position on the ground from which it had jumped off in midafternoon. Artillery fire continued to beat against the knobs and rear slope of the main ridge throughout the night. The dead and wounded were removed to the position across the creek.

What came of it, at last, is best given in the language of Bravo's after-action report: "The following morning Charley Company made it back up the hill. They counted 55 enemy bodies and picked up another machine gun. We had been unable to evacuate our dead and wounded because of a hard rain that fell all night causing a low ceiling. Evacuation was initiated at 0900 by C-47's using basket and winch. We estimate the enemy lost another 100 dead and wounded, not in the official count. We lost 8 KIA, 14 WIA."

By the hour the report was written, Captain Martin no longer had the company. He was badly hit while flying in a Huey two days later, the VC bullet shattering the leg bone. In the hospital ward at Qui Nhon, where he had to be operated on several times, he was cotted next to Sergeant Peoples, whose wound gave him, also, a ticket to the United States. Peoples talked mainly of Dolby. "... the bravest man I ever expect to see in my life, strong all the way."

Hennessey, once he looked into the case, was no less convinced than Peoples and decided that Dolby belonged in Medal of Honor company "all the way."

On 21 June, as summer opened, there was a great festival at Pleiku. It was called Heroes' Day. The idea had come to Gen. Vinh Loc, the ARVN commander of II Corps area. It was the right time to honor the two outstanding fighters in each division and brigade by pinning them with South Vietnam's highest decoration. So dignitaries collected from all around, as did the brass bands, entertainment troupes and platoons of school-age flag wavers; the weather turned out glorious.

The score of heroes, Dolby and Captain Carpenter among them, were formed on a platform facing the sun at 0930. They were to be the guests of honor at a banquet laid on that evening by Prime Minister Nguyen Cao Ky.

All the distinguished speakers, in particular the Vietnamese generals, lacked terminal facilities. The minute hand was moving toward the noon hour when at last the medals were pinned, the ceremonies ended and the formation began to dissolve. All of that time the heroes had been at attention, facing the sun.

Then the First Cavalry Division delegation moved forward to congratulate Dolby.

"Sorry about all that heat," one general said to him.

"I guess I can stand the heat once in my life," said Dolby, in his low-key, undramatic fashion, "when it's required by Army orders."

Men Facing Death

By the night of 21 May the Battle of Vinh Thanh Valley appeared to be slowing to a stop with the enemy fractionalized and everyone running for cover. Landing Zone Hereford, that well worked-over slope where the initial explosion had occurred, looked like the one safest place within the fire zone, such had been the constancy of armed traffic in and out of it.

That was about how Col. John J. Hennessey thought of it when he decided on a special mission for Charley Company, 1/12th, for the following morning. It was a courteous gesture, the main object being to return Charley Company to its parent battalion.

But for so doing, Hennessey planned to ask a small favor in return. The company, under Capt. Don F. Warren, a taciturn Georgian who had been with this same unit since winning his gold bars in 1961, was in perimeter on Hill 766, several ridges beyond Hereford. The airline distance was about 3000 meters. Hennessey directed Warren to sweep back over the high ground to Hereford after sunup. Unworried about that passage, he was most concerned that Charley Company should reconnoiter the lower slopes beyond the landing zone, which thus far no one had prowled. That task done, it could rejoin the battalion in the valley not far from the C.I.D.G. camp.

Hennessey had no reason to be suspicious; he was merely being cautious. The ground around Hereford had not been worked over carefully for several days. Capt. Jackie Cummings and Alpha Company were in perimeter on the landing zone at this same hour. They were not left wholly undisturbed. But the occasional sniper rounds and grenades that innocuously bit into their ground were attributed to enemy stragglers. Alpha Company was needed back at the An Khe base camp to man the defensive barrier and would be lifted from Hereford LZ as quickly as Charley Company appeared.

Word of what was afoot reached Maj. Charles Siler at An Khe shortly after Hennessey gave the order. The division's Public Information Officer was entertaining a visitor and weighing a problem all his own. Belatedly drawn by the news that Operation Crazy Horse was racking up a score, War Correspondent Sam Castan, a thirty-two-year-old Senior Editor of *Look* Magazine, had just arrived in camp, pursuing a theme worthy of the late Hemingway. Castan was the only correspondent drawn to the battle.

He said to Siler, "I wish to know the thoughts of men facing death."

Siler voiced an honest doubt that the quest was logical, men's fears and reflections not being all of one kind, and the soldier hardly knowing how he thinks about death until he feels he is dying. It is just not the kind of subject that makes for easy talk among combat men.

At that time General Norton had put the An Khe position on a semi-alert, and the whole camp was astir. Siler and his staff were in the bunkers around the press camp, realigning some of the sandbags.

"You don't have to worry about this ground tonight," said Castan. "I'm the luckiest reporter alive. Where I go, nothing happens."

Siler remembered the words, thinking them slightly ironic in view of what Castan sought.

"There's a big hill not far from here where a lot of men have died in the last few days," he said.

"Then I want to get up there first thing in the morning," said Castan, "and by the way, I intend to follow the subject all the way through—see the coffins in which you place the bodies."

"We put them in rubber bags," said Siler glumly, hoping to close the conversation. But Castan continued to fret about getting up to Hereford soon after dawn. Siler broke off work to arrange for Castan's certain departure.

These were the circumstances which resulted in Castan being delivered to Hereford by the same helicopter that carried ammunition, coffee and a hot breakfast to Cummings and Alpha Company. His first hours were unrewarding, that unit being too busy stacking supply and equipment for an early getaway to talk with Castan about death. Besides, the morning was disarmingly fair and quiet.

Warren and Charley Company meanwhile were beating their way along the ridge crest on the way back from Hill 766, having broken camp at 1000. A fairly wide trail runs the top of the scarp for the entire distance, which made the passage relatively rapid. It would have been faster had not Warren directed that the column reconnoiter the whole way. The point fired at every bend or covert where the enemy might wait in ambush. But it stirred up nothing and the column heard not an answering shot.

Alpha Company was lifted from LZ Hereford when Charley Company arrived at high noon. Castan stayed on. On the landing zone Warren talked briefly to Lieut. Col. Rutland P. Beard, Jr. the battalion commander, and his S-3, Maj. William Roll. It was arranged that Warren and the main body of the company would continue their stroll downslope, through the trees and across the river. The mortar platoon would remain on Hereford to cover its further advance with the fire from one 81 mm tube. The platoon, twenty-two strong, was led by Sgt. Robert L. Kirby, a twenty-nine-year-old Negro from Los Angeles. Slight of frame, solemn-faced, Kirby is rated one of the stoutest-hearted fighters in his brigade.

Few in numbers, his men seemed sufficiently armed. Each carried 300 or more rounds for his M-16 and from two to four hand grenades. The one heavy weapon was the 81 mm mortar for which Kirby had only eighteen rounds that, with the tube, was as much weight as the men could carry. Moreover, it had been agreed that as promptly as the descending company had passed beyond range the platoon would be lifted out by chopper. Alpha Company had left 100 or so mortar rounds behind; Kirby reckoned he would not need them.

Castan had decided to stay on Hereford, instead of moving with the company column.

"It will happen here, if anywhere," he said to Kirby.

"About that," said Kirby, "you're dead wrong."

And he honestly felt that way, though, as he looked about, what he saw of his position hardly warranted such assurance. It was all wrong from any reasoned tactical view.

Landing Zone Hereford was by then a burned-off, trampled and rubble-strewn glacis about double the size of a professional basketball court, running lengthwise down the edge of the ridge. Its scorched earth and grasses were less apparent than the foxholes distributed more or less evenly around the oval-shaped perimeter. Originally these had been enemy spiderholes and were subsequently enlarged by American occupancy. The trouble was that Kirby did not have enough men to round out this holding. So the position became a "U" pointed upslope. The uphill open end fronting toward the high ground was not covered by the weapons present, since the platoon was sighting its pieces downslope, the company having gone that way and the weapons platoon seeking mainly to cover the other platoons.

In neither direction was the prospect good if a fight was to be forthcoming, though there was beauty everywhere to soothe the eye. Upslope and bordering the very edge of the defended ground was a sea of elephant grass standing six to eight feet high. Downhill there was a sheer and rocky precipice extending thirty feet and giving way to an extension of the field of tall grasses, which also invested the flanks. Greenness was all about except where men looked to their weapons.

The company took off down the steep clutching to the

rocks and creepers for balance. No preparatory artillery fires or air strikes had been put on the slopes around Hereford, because of Warren's movement, the earlier presence of Alpha Company, and the all-around feeling that Crazy Horse Operation was slowing to a halt.

Kirby worried less about his platoon than about the movements and enterprise of Castan. The men had gone to ground. The correspondent was moving from position to position standing erect, taking photographs and asking numerous questions. Wanting to protect Castan, he did not know how to object to his freewheeling though he realized that his movements were describing the limitations of the force. In fact, these things little mattered.

Castan was enjoying himself hugely. He asked Kirby, "How do you feel about things?" Kirby answered, "If you think you're going to get a story out of this platoon, you're wrong. Nothing will happen here." Castan continued with his rounds of the perimeter, snapping pictures and asking the men, "How do you feel?" Kirby lost interest and Castan kept moving. The position of the one mortar was near the bottom of the sloped LZ just inside the bottom of the "U" where its crew had dug a little pit.

At approximately 1300 the platoon began supporting the descending company with the fire of the one 81 mm mortar—range 800 meters. It takes awhile to hack through jungle growth. Captain Warren got Kirby on the radio and told him to "bring it in closer," which Kirby tried to do.

One hour later Warren called Kirby again. This time the message was an uplift. Said Warren, "Choppers are coming in to take you out within thirty minutes." That was what Warren and Kirby both thought. But the choppers had put down at Landing Zone Savoy, Hennessey's command post hard by the C.I.D.G. camp in the valley, just to make certain that the orders given them still stood. From their delay, wholly unfaultable, came the denouement, rocking Gen. Jack Norton, rocking the High Command, rocking us all.

Kirby got off his seventeenth mortar round in support of the advancing company, that being the last one he fired. Then the thing happened. There was no advance warning.

Sgt. Louis Buckley and PFC Wade Taste were still collecting the company water cans and other matériel for the flight to the valley 2500 meters distant, moving carelessly in the open, even as was Correspondent Castan.

The other men, including Kirby, stayed put in their foxholes. That they did so was less a sign of their alertness than of their conforming to operational routine. Once lodged in the position, they had not moved to scout its surroundings. The long trek via the jungle trail had half bushed them. Over much of the distance they had had to move crouching because of the viny overhang. There was no shade where they sprawled, the sun beat directly down and the heat was not less than 100 degrees.

The word was passed round from hole to hole that they were returning to home base. Nothing much else, not even the eccentric movements and questions of Castan, interested them.

The hour must have been about 1330. From upslope, and from not more than fifty yards away, came the fire of a heavy machine gun. Its bullet stream was dead on the mortar, the first round ripping through the tube as if the weapon had been already zeroed in. Thereafter it beat directly on the mortar pit with never a pause. So came Kirby's first warning that he was engaged. He yelled out, "Fire!"

It was superfluous. Though he did not know it, being too close to the mortar, a split second before Kirby reacted, his own men had started to fight. On the left of the inverted "U" (it would have been the right flank had these men been facing uphill whence the fire was coming) Specs. 4 Paul J. Harrison and Charles Stuckey had seen three enemy skirmishers moving in through the elephant grass not five meters beyond their foxholes. Their M-16 fire signaled detection of the movement, to which the enemy machine gun instantly responded.

As swiftly as those three weapons spoke, from out the elephant grass on three sides of the perimeter rifle fire crackled, and Kirby sensed that his position was almost totally enveloped.

There was no time to reflect on that. He yelled to his radioman, Spec. 4 John F. Spranza, "Call the company, Get them back. We're being hit." As the message was relayed to Captain Warren, and as he remembered it, the words were: "Come back, we're being hit."

Though the main body, moving through jungle, was too far down the slope to get the sounds of the fight, Warren had his moment of agonized shock. He knew Kirby as a thoroughly brave soldier, too steady, too seasoned, to be stampeded by a little random fire. When he called for help, the thing had to be fully desperate. The confidence between the white captain from Georgia and the Negro sergeant from California was complete.

Wasting not an instant, Warren called back on radio to Lieut. Robert McClellan of First Platoon, bringing up the rear of the far-stretched column: "Get your ass back up that hill!" All hands reversed and started scrambling upward, men clutching at rocks, tearing their palms on the thorned vines, sliding, falling and panting in a desperate effort to race up the steep. All did not fully understand the reason why. There was no attempt to observe security, and had they been, without knowing, moving into ambush, the disaster that too soon followed could have been greater.

Far above them, on the slope of Hereford, men who could still move crouched low to escape the sheet of fire beating from all sides. Most of Kirby's men had died in the first ten minutes, though he did not yet know that. The return fire from his people grew steadily fainter.

Sgt. Isaac Johnson, a twenty-seven-year-old Negro, had been sitting with a plat board at the mortar pit when the fight began. He heard someone yell, "They're coming out of the woods!" In his agitation he tried to turn the mortar around to fire it uphill, not even noticing that it had been drilled through. The incoming fire was too great and his strength too little. So he slithered on his belly to the left flank and dropped into a foxhole. Upslope he could see forty to fifty men coming at a run out of the trees and into the elephant grass, where they were lost to sight. They were partly camouflaged and their shirts were of all colors.

Looking downhill, he saw as many more of the enemy, moving through the grass, some crawling, others hunched over, all firing as they moved in. It came to him as a sudden idea that he should fire too. He thought as he fired that he had dropped at least four enemy skirmishers with his M-16.

From the next foxhole, above him, PFCs Henry Benton and Joe L. Tamayo were alternately firing upslope and downhill, yelling as they pulled trigger. Johnson saw his last of them when he ran out of ammunition and crawled back to the mortar pit in search of a magazine. Inside the pit there were four men, heads down. The enemy machine gun and at least two automatic rifles were bearing directly on the hole and smashing its rim. Johnson could not be sure whether the men were ducking or dead.

Sgt. Paul Bucakloo, twenty-two years in the Army, was having his first go in combat. That opening fusillade cracked him wide open. He bolted straight across the perimeter, vanished into the elephant grass and was never heard from again.

Sergeant Johnson couldn't find his spare magazine. So he picked up an M-16 with fifteen rounds in it from the dead hand of Sgt. Edward Shepherd, who had no business being there that afternoon. Though he ranked Kirby and might have taken command, he was overdue to be lifted out by chopper for an appearance before a promotion board. So he passed up the honor and died inconspicuously from a bullet through his brain. Another long-time RA soldier under fire for the first time, he had stayed motionless, petrified by a personal terror as boundless as the horror exploding all about him.

His fifteen bullets gone, Johnson crawled toward the mortar pit, screaming, "Come on out! You'll all be killed." There was no response; it was minutes too late for that. The hole held four corpses, heads bashed in by bullet fire.

In the nearby hole with Kirby was another bloody welter. A rocket—the Russian-made P-40, a round so slow of motion that the eye easily follows the trajectory—came arcing in, dead center on the mark. Kirby saw it in flight and yelled, "Watch out!" So did his foxhole mates, Specs. 4 Austin L. Drummond and David S. Crocker, who cried warning in the same split second. Before any man could move, the rocket exploded just to the left of the hole. Crocker died instantly from a shard that crushed his skull in. Drummond took heavy fragments in the left arm and left leg; such gouts of blood spouted from him that Kirby, who had taken four pieces of steel in his head but remained conscious, knew that Drummond could not last long.

In physical torment, Drummond tried to rise. Kirby pulled at him. Drummond screamed, "Let me go. I'm hurting, hurting." Kirby pulled him down. Within a minute he died, under Kirby's body. Blood from Kirby's pate was streaming into his eyes, but the little sergeant could still see and think.

He yelled to his RTO, Spec. 4 Spranza, "Call Company. Say I'm being hit by mortars and rockets. We gotta have gunships and arty."

Spranza did his part. Captain Warren, struggling upward, remembered this piece of the message coming in: "We're hit by rockets and mortars." Later he could not recall that Spranza had also asked for gunfire and the air artillery. But anyhow, he relayed that message to the command capsule at LZ Savoy, and Spranza got the word back from him: "It's on the way."

Those were the final words. Right then communication between company and platoon ended. Both radios still worked; the mass of the ridge nose intervened. At that moment the front men in Warren's column were halfway back to Hereford. The breakoff doubled Warren's anxiety, though he was already doing everything possible. He had asked that the artillery be placed on the slopes alongside the perimeter, not on Hereford itself, for Kirby had passed on nothing about casualties, and Warren was still thinking of twenty-two live men holding the contested ground. The double-time climb had begun to slow from sheer exhaustion. Men stumbled, dropped in their tracks, were pulled to their feet by their mates, and reeled upward again. Warren realized now that if he continued the pressure, the company would reach the scene of the fight dead-beat. About that he no longer gave a damn.

Though the sounds of the struggle had not carried to LZ

Savoy in the distant valley bottom, that control point was athrob, partly because of Warren's call for help, still more because of the monitoring of conversations between eye-witnesses who were viewing the fight from platforms direct-ly overhead. What they saw and what they said in no way lessened the confusions.

Colonel Beard, the battalion commander, Major Roll, his S-3, and Capt. Robert Offer, artillery liaison, were at the brigade CP when the news came in. They took off in a Huey to view the fight from above.

Before they could reach the scene, out of sheer happen-stance, Maj. Otto Cantrell, battalion executive of the 1/12 Cavalry, was already hovering above it. He had been flying from An Khe in an H-13 and had arrived opposite the peak when he heard Warren's voice in his earphone saying that a platoon was being overrun on Hereford.

So he flew to station directly above it and began orbiting. Low enough to see people milling around and firing on the ground below him, Cantrell was yet too high to determine whether they were friend or enemy.

Lieut. William D. Fessenden, an artillery observer in another H-13 (one of the little bubble jobs), had flown the same way and was circling near Cantrell.

He asked Cantrell, "Sir, can I bring in fire?"

Cantrell replied, "No, I can't tell where our people are."

Cantrell then flew lower, and at about that time Beard and his party arrived. They could see forty or more men press-ing close to the perimeter.

"They must be VC," called Beard.

"Either that," replied Cantrell, "or GIs with uniforms soaking wet."

His words merely aggravated doubts all around. Cantrell's trouble was that he simply could not make himself believe one whole American platoon had been wiped out. Therein he was right.

Then he dropped to 100 feet for one swift pass. The phenomena of those few seconds doubled his perplexity. On the ridge crest above Hereford he saw a company of men in dark suits, marching to the fire. Shellfire was breaking into the landing zone. Cantrell had no way of knowing that these were enemy rocket rounds, not American rounds incoming from the bases of Savoy and Cobra.

The dark-suited men upslope he identified as enemy; he knew that camouflage rig, which from a distance made them to him "look like so many turtles." But where were the Americans, if not on Hereford? Just then he heard a friendly voice on his FM radio: "Please, please hurry. You must hurry." It was Spranza getting off his last message, but Cantrell had no way of knowing that, either.

Beard, viewing from the same height, was for the moment equally in the dark.

From the start of the fight, with good reason, Kirby had forgotten Castan, the correspondent. He remembered only when Castan slid into his position to ask, "When are we going to get the hell out of here?"

Kirby didn't answer. Then Castan said, "I've got to have a weapon," and Kirby silently handed him his own .357 Magnum. Quiet now, he briefly fitted into the hole beside Kirby. He spoke only once to say, "Sergeant Shepherd is dead."

All curiosity about the thoughts of men facing death was gone from Castan. He had been eagerly questioning Shepherd when the first shots were fired. That soldier's swift moral collapse and sudden death were his first shock contact with the realities which mocked his quest.

While Castan's opening words to Kirby rankled, they also rang a bell. Almost anywhere seemed better than the exposed ground to which the survivors clutched, now under a dust pall kicked up by the grazing fire.

The fight had been going somewhere between twenty and twenty-five minutes, and the fire was fast becoming wholly one-sided. Next Kirby's position the enemy skirmishers crawling through the elephant grass were not more than fifteen feet away; the fire build-up suggested they were bunching, probably for a rush. Kirby saw them fleetingly and vaguely, as through a haze, the flash of an arm, the bobbing of a head.

Kirby got off three hand grenades in that direction as

rapidly as he could throw. The explosions seemed to damp the close-up fire, but for not more than sixty seconds. In his moment of decision Kirby did not doubt that the ring had been closed and that other skirmishers waited on the lower slope amid the elephant grass, between him and the company, poised for the kill.

Still he yelled out, "Let's make it!" With that he rolled out of his hole and down the slope. Castan had jumped from the hole just ahead of him and was running upright and in the clear. PFC Bob Taste and Spec. 4 A.V. Spikes, from the foxhole above Kirby, went past Kirby, one rolling, the other sprinting. Then Spranza dashed by him.

As he rolled, Kirby thought he glimpsed Isaac Johnson off to his left firing two M-16s. He was wrong about that. Johnson had heard someone, not quite echoing Kirby, shout, "Move down the hill!" His own weapon was empty. He paused briefly to pick up another, only to find it in like condition. Kirby had seen him in that fleeting second when he clutched the two useless pieces before throwing both of them aside.

Johnson's face was already a bloody mask from three superficial grenade wounds. Such was his tension, he neither heard the blast of the grenade nor knew that he had been hurt. Now in panic because he was unarmed, he made a running dive at the rocky embankment giving off from Hereford's lower side. Then he rolled on and on downslope till his body could take no more beating. In that spinning descent he covered about 150 meters of rock-strewn trail.

When and where he stopped, a twisting, V-shaped cleft in the ridge-back gave off to the left. Along this slit there trickled a stream no wider than the palm of Johnson's hand. He crawled into the bed of it twenty yards or so, to where jungle growth stopped him. Then he gathered the bushes and vines down around him and lay with his face flat in the water. Not too far above him the ordeal of the other few survivors continued and grew worse. Of this Johnson felt and remembered nothing; thought paralyzed by the grip of exhaustion, he had closed his mind to the sounds.

Getting out separately, some running, others rolling, Kirby's men had stayed that way during the first few yards of flight through the short grass just off the LZ. Coming to the rocky steep, they began to converge toward center, whence the trail ran downhill. It is always so with men against fire; fear and herd instinct bring them together, which is the one worst thing that can happen since it shapes up a broad target.

Spranza was the first to get it as they approached the steep, Kirby still rolling, others crawling, Castan standing.

"I'm hit," Spranza yelled, and screamed like a panther. Three bullets, one in each leg, one in the head. But marvelously he still lived, and now he was erect and walking.

Castan yelled back, "Hell, everybody's hit!" That was news to the others. Castan had taken a bullet in one arm and several grenade frags in his back, saying nothing. In his last moments the correspondent had the courage of a lion. Here was a man, and they knew it.

Spikes yelled, "I'm hit!" It was a bullet through the right arm.

They had moved about twenty feet down the rock bank when Spranza yelled again: "Hold it up! They're in front of us."

Expecting it would come, Kirby froze right where he was.

Castan kept moving in long strides straight to the trail which led downhill through the elephant grass. He had made up his mind and Kirby did not bother to shout warning.

Standing clear on the trail was an enemy soldier, rifle aimed. Kirby heard a scream as Castan went down. Though Castan was not fifteen yards from him, he could not see the fall, as the body was enveloped by the sea of grass. But he heard the whack of the bullet and the thump of the body. The bullet had drilled Castan through his left temple.

Castan's personal effects were looted soon after he fell. The camera, films and purse were later recovered from the bodies of enemy dead in a fight that soon followed. Many next of kin get not even that grain of comfort. It is an agonizing matter for the commanders—having to explain why the dead soldier's most prized possessions and pictures cannot be returned.

Kirby could now hear enemy soldiers moving up the slope toward him—their chattering, the clang of metal from weapons being worked. He was down on his haunches, and so were Spranza, Spikes and Taste. None was firing; their only thought was to hide in the grass, which rose two feet higher than a standing man. They all knew Taste was slowly dying, two bullets in his neck, multiple mortar shards in his back. Though conscious, he made no complaint, only asking for water, of which there was none.

The skirmishers were moving up now and beating the grass on both sides of them. Kirby saw seven of them coming right toward him not ten feet away, and he knew he was discovered. He still held an M-79 grenade launcher. So did Spikes. They fired right together, and their blast killed five of the enemy; the other two crawled away, leaving blood trails.

Another skirmisher closed in from the left, spraying the ground between them with an automatic pistol. Kirby had his M-79 crooked in his arm; he had just taken another bullet through the right wrist and was feeling the wound. The skirmisher came on and looked through the grass straight at them. Spikes fired his M-79. The range was so short that the grenade didn't arm, though by sheer velocity it blew the man's head off. Had it armed, it would likely have killed both Spikes and Kirby.

A second VC closed in from the left, only to turn his back as he almost stumbled over them. Kirby killed him at range five feet.

Together two more groups closed in on them from right and left. Kirby took two hand grenades from Spranza, who by now was wholly down, and throwing in both directions with his wounded arm, he drove them off. He had no impression of how many he had killed or whether he had even scored a hit. He simply knew that they had faded back, easing the immediate pressure momentarily.

While this deadly hide-and-seek game went on downslope, Hereford LZ was being pounded by 105 and 155 mm howitzer fires from the valley bases at Savoy and Cobra LZs. Colonel Beard had called for it from his perch aloft, and still earlier, Warren had asked it. Whether it might have been brought in sooner, and done any good, is an open question. There was no right moment for its use until the Americans had cleared away, which movement could only be guessed at. Now that it had come, and the perimeter ground was being cratered, one of the effects was to drive more of the enemy to the grass field lower down where Kirby and his mates crouched.

The game was still on. From downslope a machine gun opened fire and scythed the grass beside them. Kirby went flat in the nick of time and the bullets zinged directly over his head. Spikes didn't quite make it. One burst caught him in the head. The sound was enough. Kirby, two feet from him, didn't have to look to know that he was dead. And he did not wish to look.

Kirby crawled downslope about ten feet, looking now for a weapon, thinking that the enemy might have dropped one. No luck. He was wholly out of ammunition and had no arm left but a flare pistol.

So he lay flat on his back, wondering what to do. Another skirmisher came up, parted the grass and looked directly down on him. Kirby rolled over on his side and in the same motion fired his pistol upward. The round smashed into the glaring face not three feet above him, getting it right between the eyes. The body was spun completely over by the blast, with the figure kicking.

Kirby did not wait to see more than that. He crawled back the way he had come to get to Spranza. The impulse was that if he had to die, he would rather not be alone.

Both men were silent now. There was nothing to say. Time had about run out. They thought they were the only survivors, though in this they were slightly wrong. Johnson was still face-down in his private cleft. Spec. 4 Charles Stuckey, whose swift reaction had started the fight, had moved obliquely to the others in getting away from the perimeter. Hidden in the grass alongside the knob, he had rare fortune, until in the final minutes he came under a grenade shower—the last of the survivors to get hit.

Directly toward Kirby and Spranza, another enemy group moved down the slope. Kirby didn't wait for them. Having nothing to fire, he crawled upward through the elephant grass, leaving Spranza and passing the skirmishers undetected.

They fairly stumbled across Spranza. He played dead. His head being gory from a bullet that had entered his left ear and emerged through his nose, it is less remarkable that the deception worked than that he stayed conscious and was still capable of thought. They rolled him over, searched his pockets, took his wallet, knife and cigarets and continued on. Having gone inert, Spranza stayed that way.

Kirby had had no sense of the barraging of Hereford, though the fire had been going all of ten minutes. Now as he crawled upward he at last heard the explosions and knew what they were. That determined him; he would crawl to the fire and try to hug it. Two thoughts were in his mind. "Charley will get as far away from this as possible." If he had to die, that way was still the preferable risk.

Halfway back to the perimeter, his ear told him that the shelling had suddenly ceased. Not knowing what that meant, he still crawled on. It was a tortured, most labored movement, as his last reserve of will and strength was draining away.

He got within six feet of the first foxhole before he looked up. What he saw almost numbed his senses and he felt that he would faint away. Sitting in the foxhole pointing an M-16 directly at his head was PFC Morgan of the First Platoon.

He crawled upward a few more feet and, still prone, looked around. Every hole on Hereford was occupied by an American. Captain Warren and company had returned to the hill.

Sgts. Owen L. Lewis and James W. Edwards came over to help Kirby to his feet. No words passed between them. They were not merely choked up, they were sobbing convulsively. And seeing them, Kirby knew tears for the first time that day.

Later Warren said, "If my men cried, it was because they were so damned mad." Kirby knew better than that; they were mourning the death of the platoon.

Kirby told them where to look for Spranza, not knowing that the company had found him on the way up, or that he had already been evacuated from Hereford by chopper. Stuckey appeared at about that moment, and he and Kirby were flown to An Khe aboard the same Huey. It was some time later that Johnson came in. When the hill went quiet, he started crawling upward. Coming to the tall grass, he saw his friend, Sgt. Wallace W. Hood, standing in the clear on the forward edge of Hereford, and that sight brought him to his feet. Days later he was still in a state of shock. Kirby, taken to hospital, of his own choice returned to company duty within ten days, still convalescent. Unlike Johnson, he was fully coherent, with his emotions under tight control, till he spoke of seeing the company in tears.

Warren and the company had made that frantic upward climb to Hereford in exactly thirty-five minutes. The descent over the same trail had taken them one hour longer. If a record march, it was to little avail. They saw dead Americans in all but six foxholes and thought at first that Spranza was the only survivor. All platoon weapons had been taken; every body had been stripped of personal effects.

Warren deployed two of his platoons for a 600-yard sweep to the eastward along both flanks of the ridge. The hunt proved almost barren of result. Though the blood trails were numerous and heavily marked, only five bodies were found, and they all too obviously had been felled by artillery. The fanatics must have hauled away a larger count of dead than was lost to the company.

So in the end they departed as they had come, more suddenly than mysteriously. How the trap had been sprung was easy enough to figure out in retrospect. This enemy force of about 200 was much too fresh to have followed along in Warren's wake as he came over the trail from Hill 766. The time interval was not long enough to have permitted ascent from the lower levels toward which Warren had kept moving. If there had been assembly and movement, still no sound had been detected; last, the enemy's main weapons were sighted dead on target. Thus the force must have been there all the time, some yards off the trail and along the ridge sides, as Warren's column had walked through.

Had Warren stayed in full strength on Hereford, there might have been no fight. He carried out his orders. Of that came the most melancholy episode in Operation Crazy Horse.

With Beauty All Around

The scene within that heavenly valley was not more extraordinary than the small company of strangers who entered it as silently as possible that evening, at one with the peace and quiet that came with sundown.

What they saw made the war seem remote and their mission incongruous. Given only a few minutes to enjoy the setting as they marched, they made the most of their opportunity. The picture thereafter would remain with them imperishably, for such is the nature of man under pressure. While excitement holds, the individual may rise high above his prior limits. Woodrow Wilson Sayre, writing of his fight against death on Mount Everest, put it this way: "Surprisingly the sense of beauty is still sharp. How deep that sense must be within us. Even a man waiting to die will notice the loveliness of trees and sunlight around him." I have found this to be true of much humbler men, combat hands who, unlike Sayre, did not normally possess an acute awareness of an unusual instance of order in art or in nature.

So they soaked up every new sight and sound. No approach march was ever more delightful. The path was smooth and soft, the air balmy, and at their backs was a refreshing breeze. Small puffs of fleecy cloud moved gently in the blue sky above. The nearest emerald hills that almost closed off the vale rolled smoothly and were of sufficient height to foreclose the view of the jungle-crowned heights beyond as well as muffle the booming from the nearby artillery base.

Thus almost shut off from care is a landscape of such exquisite beauty as to take the breath of the military wayfarer who for the first time views it from above. Forming the elliptical-shaped floor is a myriad of rice paddies in varying shades of green, all fitted together as if some artist had been thinking of the design as a whole and weaving a tapestry out of real estate. The water surfaces shimmer in the light instead of reflecting the scummy dull gray which bespeaks the stagnation of abandonment. All banks and dikes are either planted deep in flowers or lined with coconut palms, cultivated bamboo and shrubs. Where there are plots of firm earth, they are either checkered with tropical fruit trees or thickly clothed with greensward carefully tended. The one road and the intersecting paths run red as the tobacco clay of Virginia through this already ostentatious display of color. The farmhouses, nowhere tightly clustered, are symmetrically thatched under serpentined retaining bands, and the walls are of varying pastel shades. There was no blemish anywhere. In contrast to the shattered or temporary look of habitation elsewhere in the near countryside, all things within the vale looked lovely, wholesome and wholly impossible.

Few such garden spots of earth go nameless. This one is so. It is but a tucked-away extension of the much wider but harshly desolate Soui Ca Valley, which runs roughly parallel to Vinh Thanh Valley on the other side of the mountain mass. Whereas the Soui Ca River lower down is sluggish and no more inviting than the land it trenches, within the vale it runs clear and sweet over boulders through a rock bed, breaking enough white water to enchant any fly-caster. The final touch of unreality—within the vale there are five hamlets and all have the same name. So they are called Hoi Son One, Two, Three, Four and Five, as if they were little pigs bound for market. Only three of them appear on the military maps.

Hoi Son Five was their goal, the point of rendezvous, though it had not been honored by the cartographer. The hamlet had been fingered for one simple reason: drainage lines made it one of the most logical places for the illogical enemy to come if he was attempting to flee the battle area and get away to the east. The confluence of three small streams out of the ridges was next the hamlet. The jungle trails usually run parallel to drainage lines. The countryside to the north of the five Hoi Sons was not yet being beaten out.

Despite these reasonable deductions from a terrain study, not much was expected from the move by the operators. The enemy too frequently declined to react sensibly when he was getting away, and it was axiomatic that if any escape route was left unguarded, he would invariably find it. Evasion was his one great talent. The net cast around the mountains was not only very large but very loose, one wide sector going wholly unmanned for lack of troops. So there were large hopes and small expectations.

Bound for Hoi Son Five was the Red Platoon out of Delta Troop of the First Squadron of the 9th Cavalry. It was not a narrow conceit in Red Platoon that no unit of the Army was better qualified and equipped for the mission about to begin. Soldiers as a rule are not accustomed to thinking of themselves as key figures. With good reason, members of the First of the 9th are the exception. They think of themselves as something special, and what they think matters.

There is no other fighting organization like the First of the 9th under the American or any other flag. Its unique character, which nurtures a unit pride too genuine to permit boastfulness, is one more expression of the genius of Gen. Harry W. O. Kinnard, who formed and fielded the First Cavalry Division largely around this one air cavalry squadron. It is the dynamo. More than any other outfit, it serves to generate the division's extraordinary power to find the enemy, to reach out for him over unprecedented distance and to swiftly smash him.

Any American fighting element in Vietnam, including the infantry battalions of First Cavalry Division, may wing into battle aboard helicopters. The carriers are not their own organically and the crews much of the time are strangers to them. When the hour for their extraction comes, in all likelihood some other chopper company will lift them home.

Being the eyes and ears of the division—its reconnaissance part—the First of the 9th has its own Hueys, their pilots and crews. It is formed of three cavalry troops, thus already equipped to get moving at once, and one ground troop. In each air troop there is a scout platoon, a weapons platoon and an infantry platoon. They mount up in armored Huey Bravos with a mixed bag of rockets and machine guns. The scouts go forth and find the enemy; the infantry element then lands to exploit. The scouting is done from the air, usually just above the nap of earth. When anything is sighted that looks in any degree suspicious, the rifle platoon sets down to work it over.

So in the operation already going, the cavalry had reported seeing at Hoi Son Five a promising prospect and the Red Platoon had been given its task. It was led by Lieut. Thomas K. Holland of Oakland, Calif., one of its more youthful files, a bachelor with less than two years of Army service behind him. The mark of the warrior is all over Holland. He is the quiet type, without being either somber or boastful, and talks ever to the point. To a remarkable degree his men have this same reserve. Holland says it quite simply: "We know how to do our work." Red Platoon counts a high percentage of Negro soldiers; its pride in unit is not more noteworthy than the warm feeling and mutual regard its soldiers have for one another. That fabulous ingredient, and probably overpraised inheritance from yesterday—the cavalry spirit—is in them an all-pervading reality.

In late afternoon of 23 May, Red Platoon was lifted out of the base camp at An Khe. It counted twenty-nine men that, beyond the command group, divided into two squads, one with eleven men, the other with twelve. All were dropped 1800 meters short of Hoi Son Five, the predetermined ambush site, or that far to the south of it.

However, that was the third move of the late afternoon for

the Red Platoon and its lift. They had twice feinted just such a deployment along the edges of the big valley. Both times the choppers stayed down longer than was reckoned would be necessary on the pay run. For the choppers that was not the end of it. After the patrol was dropped the third time, they had to continue with two more fake passes into the dusk. So there was as much energy spent on deception as in the approach. The net gain from these extra precautions was probably nil, though about that there could be no way of knowing.

They went well loaded. Every man carried ten full magazines for his M-16, four fragmentation grenades, one claymore mine and one trip flare. Of food, there was enough in C rations to take care of six meals, since they figured they might be on their own for two days. Counting his rifle, bayonet and clothing, each soldier was carrying about fifty-five pounds. As is the custom with troops in Vietnam, they marched with belts unhooked, the buckles flapping loose, so that the weight might make the most natural adjustment to the body, reducing friction in this way. Where metal might hit against metal, producing sound, they were well taped and padded.

It took them not more than thirty minutes to walk from the landing zone to the ambush site. They had hoped to have about an hour of daylight after arrival, affording time to choose the best possible concealment, but had cut things a bit short, as dark comes early in that latitude. Still, their passage had been both swift and silent. Their footfalls being cushioned by the lush grass next the stream bed, they were quite sure they had not been detected.

About the population of Hoi Son Five, Holland had no need to worry. It and the other Hoi Sons were totally deserted, though each home looked as if it awaited the family's return from an evening stroll, so fresh did all things seem. Some of the windows were open, the doors unbolted. Missing were the skinny, homeless dogs that skulked around the average abandoned hamlet. There was something disquietingly eerie about all of this. Here was beauty all around, a garden for gracious living, a miniature Shangri

La, and they, the only people in position to view it this night, were compelled to rush their enjoyment of it.

In fact, too quickly the wonder of the landscape became a nuisance. When they drew onto the spot that had been designated by earlier reconnaissance for the rigging of the ambush, Holland immediately turned against it.

He said to S/Sgt. Herbert E. Jeffery, who was leading his scout squad, "This one won't do. We must find another location."

Jeffery simply nodded agreement. Jeffery is from Houston, Tex., with thirteen years in the Army.

Where they had stopped for one quick glance there was a U-shaped bend in the pathway several hundred feet short of Hoi Son Five. The path roughly paralleled the course of the Soui Ca and between them ran a ribbon of the neatly manicured paddies. The fault was that the bend itself was landscaped with shrubbery, mangos and palms which grew so thickly as to block out the other side of the bend and the hamlet beyond.

Holland and his men moved along looking for a place along the path where they could set up beside it in good concealment, with twenty to thirty feet of open space across their front and a clear sighting in both directions that would include the exit from Hoi Son Five. They needed at least that much room to their front to be safe from the back blast of the claymores, and they reckoned that if they were to have visitors, they would come from the direction of the houses.

Holland had only a few minutes in which to observe these things and complete his arrangements. They day was fast going now, the shadows were thickening, and the small clouds above them had turned red. Time for doting on the "casual tappings and twinklings of the countryside" had run out.

So they quickened their pace.

On the other side of the bend, and still a little short of Hoi Son Five, they found exactly what they sought—the perfect position made to their measure. Moreover, it was next door to an intersection where a trail, well marked, ran sharply uphill and into the tree line, so that it obviously served foot traffic between the bottom land and the jungle of trunks, roots and snarled bamboos. Here there was tall elephant grass beside the pathway. Beyond the grass were two small fields framed by closely clipped, low hedges. Here they would set their deadfall, extending somewhere between thirty and forty meters. The clearing to their front was more than adequate.

There was no need for talk about how to dispose themselves. Having rehearsed the exercise and discussed their plan numerous times, they went to their stations automatically, silently.

They divided in two lines. The eleven riflemen in the rear rank were to about-face and point weapons across the hedges, with one machine gun in the center. Here was the insurance against counter surprise.

The twelve men in the front line were to spring the ambush. Here, too, was a machine gun in the center, pointed leftward along the trail toward the village. The violence and fury of this trap lay, however, in the twenty claymore mines evenly distributed along it frontally. The closest claymore was about twenty meters from the trail. The blast of this mine approximately equals that of a 60 mm mortar round and its maximum effective range is about fifty meters. So as to concentration, the setup was superlative.

Holland and Jeffery walked up and down the front checking the positions. They adjusted the sighting of five of the claymores and added two more.

S/Sgt. Lester Everette, of Rocky Mount, N.C., the infantry squad leader, and S/Sgt. Russell C. Fordham, of Albany, Ga., the platoon boss man, checked the rear line. That, too, was according to plan, the better to save time.

By 1930 the position was fully cocked, every mine and trip flare having been checked. Nothing had been left to accident. The men in the rear line knew they were not to fire until the front rank engaged. Every member of the scout squad along the front had been briefed to this effect:

"Start nothing on your own. Either Holland or Fordham will spring the ambush." The lieutenant and the sergeant together shared the CP slightly to the rear of the extreme left flank, where contact was most likely. They had talked it over and agreed that whichever one saw the enemy first should explode the first claymore. The other would fire his own mine, then both would grenade the trail.

Since it might be a long, and even fruitless, wait, both lines went on 50 percent alert at once. The night was cool, the sky starlit, and the moon not yet risen. The cicadas strummed their fiddles.

There followed otherwise a prolonged silence louder than sound. Nothing stirred. The only sound to be heard was the rushing water of the Soui Ca. Very easily men get the feeling of being watched, in such a place under these conditions. But if there was any sign of tension in his camp, Holland missed it.

One hour later, at exactly 2030, they came, not as foxes but like a herd of elephants, their approach signaled by an overture of singsong conversation.

Holland saw them first. They were not more than thirty feet away and were walking directly into his position. He pointed and started to whisper to his second man. But Fordham was about twenty feet to his rear, resting next the RTO and the first-aid man. It would be his turn to relieve Holland on watch at midnight.

At first Holland counted only ten of the enemy, but in the darkness the figures blurred and he could not be certain. The hardest part was waiting until he reckoned that the lead man (Vietnamese almost invariably walk single file) came abreast of the extreme right of his position. That must have taken all of twenty seconds, with their chatter continuing all the way. So he knew in these moments that his position stayed undetected.

Then in the end he had to guess. For he lost track of the lead figure, as if he had ducked from sight into the grass. Then in a flash all the silhouettes were churning around and becoming bunched up as the chattering ceased. Looking to his left, Holland saw no more figures coming into the ambush.

Right then he blew both his and Jeffery's claymores

together. That was the first sound heard by Jeffery and Fordham. Everette had heard the intruders rattle the bamboo bridge as they came from Hoi Son Five perhaps half a minute before Holland sensed the movement. But following plan, he had waited for the front line to react. Now the whole camp had sprung to.

Even so, Holland got off his two hand grenades before anyone else fired anything. Then within a few seconds every claymore within the zone was exploded. With hand grenades they did less well, only four others following he pair Holland had thrown.

The men in the rear line stayed altogether quiet, neither firing nor yelling. To do either would have been a waste. Everette simply sat there, and not one of his soldiers called to him. Possibly this was the oddest touch of all; they remained there with their backs turned to the shooting just as if they were not part of the engagement.

Holland could dimly see a black mound just to his right along the path where none had been before. It changed form before his eyes as if part of the mass were writhing. Also he could hear muffled groans. For the moment he had no notion how many bodies were out there but realized some of the enemy were not quite dead. So he picked up an M-79 grenade launcher and fired several rounds against the black mass.

Missed by his eye, one enemy soldier hadn't quite entered the zone of destruction when Holland set off the claymores. He had been lagging twenty or so feet behind the others. PFC Theodore Simpson, who lay at the extreme position on the left, nailed the straggler with his M-16 as he turned to flee.

Save one, this was the only intensely personal round fired during the incident, which was no fight, no exchange of fire, but a mass execution carried out by men who were determined, painstakingly accurate, and intent on killing.

For a few minutes nothing more happened. All hands held their positions. Then the moon was up, bathing Hoi Son Five, the silver line of the Soui Ca and even the path of death in warm light. Except for what confronted them, it was a lovely evening, and concerning the former, they proceeded according to routine.

Holland ran back to Fordham's position and told the artillery observer, Lieut. Joseph Jordan, 2/17th Battalion, to bring in illumination from the 155 mm howitzers based on LZ Cobra in the big valley and keep the flares going directly above the path until the task was at last finished.

By their light he saw clearly enough that no more enemy were moving toward the position from any direction. Only then did he feel free to move any of the men out of their original positions. He had already popped the one parachute flare he was personally carrying just before the artillery rounds started coming in.

By its light he tentatively approached the pile of bodies just far enough to note that one figure still moved and groaned. Most of his face was gone and he was clearly beyond recovery. Holland administered the *coup de grâce* with his pistol.

Now Sgt. Rudolph Burns was sent forward with five soldiers—Spaulding, Carpenter, Hagen, Robinson and Polinsky—to count the bodies, police up all weapons and check the gear while searching the pockets and packs for papers.

Jeffery wasn't quite satisfied with this arrangement and tagged along to supervise the body count. It was hard to do. Most of these bodies had been brayed apart by the blast, and arms, legs and heads had been scattered over a wide space.

Faces were smashed beyond possibility of recognition.

But adding one thing and another, Jeffery counted fifteen enemy dead, most of them piled in the immediate foreground. It checked out. There were also fifteen weapons, many of them smashed beyond use.

Then came belatedly a cry for a medic. Until he heard it, Holland did not know that any of his soldiers had been hurt. Spec. 4 Larry Roberts had been hit by flying debris in the chin and arm, either the backlash of a claymore or a grenade that had exploded too close. PFC "Doc" Miller bandaged him. He wasn't badly hurt—just banged up enough to qualify for a Purple Heart.

Twenty minutes later Capt. William P. Gillette, the CC, told Holland on radio that he should march the Red Platoon back to the same landing zone to be lifted out by Hueys for return to the An Khe base. They returned silently as they had come. The only talking was between Holland and his main subordinates, the minimum necessary to maintain security and keep the column moving together. Lieutenant Jordan had called for a covering barrage which danced in front of them all the way back to the LZ.

At 2235 they were lifted out. By midnight they were securely asleep within the barrier of Camp Radcliff. This was the eighth ambush worked by Holland, Jeffery, Fordham and some of the older hands. They knew they were getting quite good at it.

There, quite rightly, this small affair should have ended. But the folk of the Hoi Son neighborhood did not return to their tidy vale while the main battle went on. The houses began to look a little sadder, the grass more neglected. The pile of putrefying flesh along the sloped trail not far from the bamboo bridge festered and fumed ever worse under the boiling sun. Obviously no more NVA soldiers had tried to slide away from the high ground via this same route or they would have buried their own.

So after four days Red Platoon was ordered by the division commander to fly back to Hoi Son Five to tidy up what they had wrought and put the dead decently below ground. Too many choppers were detouring that way so that passengers could take a look at the kill.

They went on dragging feet, feeling that a gross indignity had been heaped upon them. It was another glorious day, but they had no eye for it. By their own handiwork they were sickened.

Jeffery summed up their thoughts about it.

"If the reward for staging the perfect ambush is that you are busted to a gravedigger, why kill anybody?"

The Long Patrol

Landing zone corral was like a rainbow in the sky and probably the least plausible position ever to seat any artillery of the United States Army.

A hogback ridge, unconnected directly with any other outstanding terrain feature, the LZ, barren except for elephant grass quickly beaten down, was almost at dead center of the range being worked over by the troops under Hennessey.

Much higher ridges to the north, south and west directly overlooked it, and had the enemy possessed any field guns, it would have been untenable.

Why the NVA did not bring artillery along was a recurrent point for argument among troops, thanks to elephants. That the enemy used elephants as pack animals in his supply trains was commonly accepted as true, though no American had seen it done. The limiting factor, so it was said, is a congenital weakness in the elephant's back. The poor beast can carry only 350 pounds; "No, you're wrong about that, it will take up to five hundred pounds." So ran the argument. Then the May, 1966, issue of the *National Geographic* came in with a story about elephants: it said they could carry a one-half-ton load.

That made no difference. Read on LZ Corral, the article changed not one gunner's conviction that he was safe from counter-battery fire, because of disc trouble among elephants. The rumor was so delectable, and besides, the *National Geographic* was not official.

The guns of Charley Battery, 2/19th, under Capt. Thomas A. Ward, which had been lifted onto the sharp spine of the ridge by the Chinooks, were in delicate balance. Wheels and trails straddled this crest line. Shifted four or five meters in either direction, they would have careened down the steep slope. These bizarre touches made it a gunner's paradise, though when the supply Hueys and Chinooks arrived on either of the pads at the extreme ends of the quarter-mile-long position every half hour or so, pup tents were blown over, letters from home took wing for the jungle below, and soldiers rubbed brick-red dirt from their eyes.

The 8-inchers based on Vinh Thanh Valley, and the ARA—the air artillery—were the only fires from outside that could do LZ Corral any good. The 8-inchers could react to a call in three minutes. It took the ARA about two minutes to get off the ground and ten to fly there from the base camp. But they made it a practice to stick around.

Because the guns were there, daring attack from below, infantry had to be also. The hogback, sharp enough, was also, by an accident of nature, terraced at three levels. The guns bestrode the lower two. The upper was the CP of an infantry battalion, the First of the 8th. Lieut. Col. Levin B. Broughton had with him on the ridge only three of his platoons, or ninety riflemen, from Alpha Company. So the artillery had to provide part of the reaction power—twelve men and six machine guns covering the ground in the center. All patrolling and outguarding was done by the infantry.

The force and position were under Broughton's command, to do with as he wished—within limits. A very serious soldier whose dislike of sitting still is positively painful, what he wished mainly was to keep the guns secure.

But as that seemed not too difficult, with no one sweating about it, and the ridge stayed absolutely unmolested, Broughton thought of other ideas. There was a valley floor below, a beautiful far-spreading valley, green to the eye as an emerald. The enemy, not being too bright, might be loitering there. Rather than twiddle one's thumbs, it would be better to go forth and take a look.

There was a relaxed atmosphere about LZ Corral. At firing time gunners would stroll about saying to the casual visitors, "Be off, or cover your ears."

The patrol by the Reconnaissance Platoon of Delta Company came under S/Sgt. Rovert Grimes, Jr., a thirty-four-year-old Negro, born in Pensacola, Fla. That was unusual. 1st Sgt. Donald J. Johnson had always led on such missions, but he had been called before a promotion board.

Grimes, a small soldier, will never win a beauty prize. He is highly articulate, self-confident and wise about tactics, but for all that, not a bit inclined to throw his weight around. He is nicknamed the Headhunter.

Thirty-one of them took off at 0930 on 30 May, bound for the valley, 3500 meters away. For all that distance they would be dropping down. Otherwise they could not have made it, for they went laden like pack animals.

Every soldier carried 800 rounds for his M-16, most of them slung in crossed bandoliers around their shoulders, Mexican-guerrilla style. All carried six meals in C rations and four hand grenades. Then there were two M-60 machine guns with 800 pounds per weapon, nine claymore mines in each squad, three M-79 grenade launchers with 24 rounds for each, twelve smoke grenades and twelve trip flares.

These are nigh incredible loads for any patrol. With their canteens, aid packs, bayonets, pill bottles, etc., they must have weighed out with an average carry between sixty-five and seventy pounds.

Still they expected to be gone three days—thirty-one soldiers deep in enemy country. Every fourth soldier carried a bottle of hot sauce, which would be shared. That's something new added to the diet of the U.S. soldier and peculiar to the field force in Vietnam. Tabasco, or its equivalent, seems to counter the outward heat, while making more palatable the bland diet. They can't get enough of it.

They started as clean as the dust on LZ Corral permitted. They wore no pigment on their faces. That touch, which is shown in old pictures of paratroopers about to launch for Normandy, they regard as kiddy stuff. It could be so, but one thing about them was not less ingenuous. Some wore insect repellant, some did not. Young Americans are so conditioned to deodorants that many of these soldiers stick with cologne and after-shave lotion and dare the anopheles mosquito to have at it. Doctors and generals may lecture, but they cannot do much about it.

Within two minutes they were lost to sight by the people atop the hogback. A deep ravine feeds off to the north from the western edge of LZ Corral. Its course is hidden by jungle growth almost to the brow of the ridge. This was the natural line of descent to the valley, for there was bound to be a stream bed, and no other way was even relatively open.

It was a column in single file. S/Sgt. Terry W. Lawson was in charge of the five-man point, which moved fifteen meters in advance of the main body and would try to stay that way.

Spec. 4 Keymo Hyvonen was the first scout, PFC Frank A. Bishop the second scout. This last soldier deserves a closer look, though there is really no explaining him. He is the average all-American boy, age nineteen, no bird-watcher or child of nature, but normally urban-reared in Arlington, State of Washington. If he had any special gift or sixth sense for tracking his fellow man, he did not know of it. He thought of himself as a rifleman, engaged in a routine. When he was named second scout, that meant nothing special save that he was supposed to stay extra alert. He had never scouted before; his case is like that of the Georgia boy who, at Fort Knox in 1942, was found to be the speediest and most accurate cryptologist in the Army, though he had been nonplussed that his superiors wished him to try. Most men have talents in themselves beyond their imagining. The simple fact is that on this prolonged patrol Bishop made all the sightings that counted, though he was never the front man. If conceivably his big score was an accident of numbers, greater modesty than his still is not to be found. Everything he did was put into this chronicle by his comrades.

Though the weather was fair and the sky cloudless, they lost all track of the sun as they entered upon the stream bed, so close was the bush matted above their heads. From that point on, in the words of S/Sgt. Cole L. Blease, "the operation ceased to be a dry-run exercise."

The jungle itself had changed subtly in the height and overstructure of the trees and the way that the vines from both sides coiled and interlocked a few feet overhead, making the air oppressive. There was a different smell than on the relatively high and occasionally wind-swept rim of LZ Corral. It was like musk, with a cloying sweetness, possibly rising from rotting vegetation.

The tumbling stream that they had to walk, in water around their knees, was not refreshing. The runoff was too silt-laden, whipped to chocolate brown by the recent monsoon rains. The boulders around which the water swirled were their main problem. Some were high as a man and closed so tight together that there was no way around any. So their advance was concertina-fashion. The rear files would close up on the scouts while they were giving one another a leg-up. Then the scouts would scramble on, and the column following would again become stretched too far. It was more like an obstacle race than a military movement.

This bothered Grimes only when, on two occasions, the scouts approached trail openings along the edge of the stream. At such points he would have set an ambush, had this been his task. Coming to them, he was wary and tried harder to keep his men together, fearing he would be jumped by the enemy. Nothing happened.

At 1100 they emerged into the clear of the valley, sweated through from the waist up, water-soaked from the waist down.

There they might have taken a breather, had they not immediately sighted the first sign of enemy presence. Next where the stream spilled onto a flat bed and became placid was a small hut; in the doorway lay a pair of black pajamas.

They walked on and came to three more huts. All had

been knocked about by artillery fire from LZ Corral. One had been occupied within the last hour or so. There were ashes on the floor—warm ashes.

While Lawson and the five-man point secured the area by outposting it in a circle thirty meters from the huts, the rest under S/Sgt. Luis G. Sepulveda made the ten-minute search. They found nothing further of significance but dried blood and one dud U.S. illuminating round.

The point moved on another 100 meters and came to a trail six feet wide, expertly corduroyed with six-inch logs. This was something new in their experience, and they walked that path for seven or eight minutes. It took them to a cluster of eight larger buildings just off the trail, one of them a mess hall. They knew then that the valley was a Viet Cong training center. Some of the houses had been blasted by the artillery; shell-smashed trees lay all about.

Just about then they began to feel that special sweat—a cold sweat—that tells the jungle fighter he is leech-infested. "Here it comes again," said PFC Randall Campbell. They all knew what he was talking about; they were sharing it with him. The leeches were in their boots and inside the waists of their fatigues. They had dropped from the trees, not from the water, on their way down. It was now too late to bother about removing them. The cold sweat was body reaction to the drainage of blood. The leeches would drink their fill, turn into a ball and drop off.

Grimes closed discussion of the subject with a wisecrack: "Maybe it's time for us to knock off for lunch also."

A call on the radio from Battalion derailed that train of thought. The mission was being changed. The original purpose had been to rig an ambush in the valley that night. Now they were to work 1200 meters farther north, run up the first ridge finger on the valley's far side, and do it at once. The reason—someone had sent in a report that a VC platoon was marching across their front.

They walked the corduroy road all the way up the first finger. But they found no Victor Charleys. Everybody was dog-tired. Grimes said, "Break it off for lunch." Security guards were thrown out forty meters up trail and down, to cover them while they ate.

Bishop was with Hyvonen on the upside. As they stopped on the designated spot, both saw movement twenty meters off to their right. It was an enemy soldier, wearing a jungle (camouflage) suit and carrying a rucksack. He turned to bolt as Bishop and Hyvonen fired—one round apiece. He fell flat on his back, wriggled out of his pack, and was up and running again before Hyvonen reached the place where he had fallen. There was no blood. Both bullets had hit him in the rucksack; it was packed hard with rice, in the center of which was an aluminum cup. The rice had acted as a buffer; both bullets were inside the cup.

Grimes and Lawson had heard the shots just as they sat to eat. They rallied two squads, and for the next thirty minutes these men beat through the bushes. Though the trail was too cold, the search was not wholly in vain. Returning, PFCs Robert N. Carriger and Donald F. Barrett, some distance ahead of the others, heard a noise off to the right. So they went that way, Sepulveda following them.

Thirty yards off trail was a twelve-by-twelve building with tin walls, rosewood pillars and a mahogany door. The sheeting was printed with the labels of two of America's nationally better-known beers.

"Man, what a hootch!" said Barrett.

Carriger opened the door. To the level of his chin, the building was loaded with bulk, unhulled rice. "There must be four tons of it," said Barrett.

Blease left his squad there on guard and went to tell Grimes about the find.

"How do you destroy four tons of rice?" Grimes asked.

They were both puzzled by the problem.

They tried to burn it with a white phosphorus grenade; the grain simply smothered the bomb.

Grimes called Broughton for advice. He wanted to know if the rice could be gotten out. "Is there a PZ [pickup zone] nearby?"

Then Grimes had a sudden thought. "We are still trying

to stage a surprise. If we mess around with this stuff any more, there won't be any surprise."

On that note the conversation broke off.

Bishop and Hyvonen came along to see the rice.

Bishop pointed and yelled, "There's one!"

An enemy soldier had popped up fifteen feet from the building and was dashing away.

Barrett, who had been looking at exactly the same spot, fired and missed. The man was lost to sight in a split second. Barrett dashed after him. Twenty feet on Barrett stumbled over his pack and helmet. In the pack were three sets of clothing—blue, black and khaki—100 rifle rounds and a hand mirror.

Very suddenly PFC Raymond N. Carley developed a raging fever. Grimes knew it was malaria. Grimes helped him down to the creek and had him lie flat in the water. That cooled him a little but for only a few minutes at a time. So Grimes knew he had to call a Huey in and ship Carley out. Along with him went some documents taken from the VC's pack. It was plain enough now that, with the landing of the chopper, the enemy knew of their presence in the valley.

There was no point any longer in playing make-believe. So Grimes called in the artillery. He thought it important to get the fires registered before nightfall. The time was about 1700, the temperature was around 105°. Only two smoke and one HE round were fired by the battery from the ridge above—which was enough. The shells fell 150 meters ahead of them in the valley.

Returning to the flat ground, they pushed along and came to a field circled with spider holes. The holes showed no sign of recent occupation. At exactly 1800 Grimes held up the platoon, at a fork where two creeks met; it was within 500 meters of the ambush site that he had chosen in the first place. By then the platoon had been going ten hours and had covered about 7,000 meters.

There they had chow—cold meat, corned beef hash and cold soup out of cans, along with crackers and the hot sauce. (Salmon and baked beans have returned to favor in Vietnam, having been banned from Army menus ever since

World War I.) There was enough room in their snug corner, though it was pretty well covered with miniature greening paddies with narrow earth banks, that they could set up a fair-size perimeter. The main trail ran directly north; the main stream ran directly east and west.

Grimes, Lawson and Blease went over the map together. It showed a hamlet not more than 300 meters from where they were sitting.

Grimes said to Lawson, "Take your four-man point and probe toward it." Carley had been with the point earlier.

The light was still fairly full when they started out.

They walked along a dike. Lawson saw a foxhole on his side of the bank and knew sudden caution.

He looked left at Bishop; the private had frozen still and was acting for all the world "like a well-bred setter."

To his front Bishop saw "an expansive system of rice paddies, three water buffaloes, ducks swimming in one of the paddies, and off to the flank, a 'Victor Charley' in a tiger [camouflage] suit, walking along the creek bank toward the village. The Victor Charley carried a rifle slung."

Lawson looked at the same scene and saw only the buffaloes. He thought that that was the sight giving Bishop pause.

Bishop, a few yards ahead of Lawson, had already turned and was coming back.

Bishop said, "Go for cover."

They dropped back fifty yards into a patch of elephant grass by which they could work, concealed, toward the village on another line.

First stopping off and caching their noisy equipment, they crawled forward, came to a paddy dike, and wiggled on their bellies along its nigh side for about fifty meters. The dike was high enough, being three feet or so above the paddy. Now there were just the two of them. Hyvonen and PFC Ted Hale had been left behind to give them a covering fire if they had to get out in a hurry. Hale had the radio. These may have been the minutes that told. Lawson had not known Bishop. He was getting the feeling that the youngster had something special, worth careful attention. Why he felt so he could not say exactly; but he knew he was fascinated by Bishop's placidity combined with his ability to see all parts of a picture at one time and impart it to others. He had never run into anyone like him before.

They turned a corner of the dike and lay silent a few moments among the reeds of the bank before they looked. Just beyond them the creek ran white rapids through jagged rocks, noisy enough to drown out whatever sounds they made. (And it seemed to both of them that they had been anything but stealthy.) A good stone's throw on from the far bank of the creek were four huts, solidly built, undamaged. Smoke was rising from at least three fires; there was a loud banging, as of someone pounding on a pan.

For twenty minutes they watched. In that time they saw eight men come from the buildings. All wore khaki uniforms— NVA soldiers; always they moved in pairs, side by side. The last two came directly toward them. Lawson started to pull away, fearing discovery.

Bishop held his wrist and whispered, "It's just a changing of the guard."

His keen eye had seen a man standing with sloped rifle waist-deep in a large hole, next a tree, well off to the right. He had guessed the rest. They saw the old sentry go off, his relief jump into the hole. The other man went on to a second post.

Lawson knew it was time to give a full report to Grimes. So he crawled back to Hale, Hyvonen and the radio. Bishop stayed on, watching.

"There's at least a squad there—maybe a platoon," he said to Grimes.

Grimes wanted to know how many weapons.

Lawson said, "We saw six, none automatic."

Then he added, "I recommend we attack; I'm in the ideal spot to support you with automatic fire."

Grimes called the battalion, asking that Broughton alert the artillery to be ready with a concentration. Lawson had crawled up to rejoin Bishop but had sent Hyvonen and Hale back to rejoin the platoon.

Grimes assembled the platoon, told them what Lawson

had found and what he proposed to do—hit 'em with everything.

He led them forward, at first walking, then crawling. First he had formed them in line, Third Squad on right, Second on left, his headquarters group a connecting link in the center. Five men were dropped off with the heavy weapons to stay fifty meters behind the general line and serve as a rear guard.

Their approach lay across the flat surfaces of a chain of small paddies, not under water, but still muddy enough that it was sticky going in the ooze. The movement became distressingly tedious and labored. The light of day was fast fading, and that was what worried Grimes more than all else.

A plan formed in his mind as he sloshed along. With his left flank he would set up a base of fire, centered with two machine guns. They would sight to fire straight in the doors. The right flank, still crawling, would circle around and get within grenade range. The left would fire with all weapons for two minutes; the right would close with a bound and finish the thing with grenades.

If that did not smash the resistance, he would fall back and call for artillery.

He got up to Lawson and Bishop and lay there watching. Then for the first time that day Grimes knew doubt.

What made him hesitate was that he could not see the outline of the buildings through the gloaming. The whole foreground had come under the shadow of the ridges to the west. Several thoughts were racing through Grimes's mind. The huts might have a rear entrance. There could be caves in the rocky hill a few feet to the rear of them. Seemingly a pushover, it might be a trap. The enemy must know by now that his party was in the valley.

He whispered to Lawson, "It's too late; we gotta call it off."

Lawson whispered back, "Man, you were never more mistaken in your life. Let's go get them now."

Bishop, too, murmured a protest.

Grimes started crawling back to his radio. The other two

followed him, Lawson still trying to win his point as they moved along. The argument wasn't easy on anyone's nerves.

They were not arch rivals, these two, but wary and mutually respectful competitors. Lawson, the white man, was not challenging Grimes, the Negro. Convinced that he was tactically wrong, he was trying to avert a blunder by the platoon. Grimes, on the other hand, had no desire to ride Lawson down with rank; Lawson might be right: the book said nothing about any such problem.

So it was time to appeal to a higher court. Grimes got Broughton on radio, described his situation, and said what he proposed to do. Broughton replied, "I think you're quite right, Sergeant; do as you think best." Broughton didn't really feel that way. Some sentiment for the emotional stresses upon Grimes and Lawson, or maybe the code of the gentleman, guided him. Deep down, he believed that Grimes was wholly wrong, and in that, having only a cursory knowledge of the facts, Broughton was not more mistaken than Lawson, who was judging from close up. The Negro sergeant was right as rain. Doing anything other than withdraw would have been begging for trouble.

The battalion commander had more specific instructions. The platoon should return to the corduroy trail where it looped north over the high ground and there establish an ambush. If nothing came along the trail during the next seven hours (the time was about 1900), they should break off the ambush about 0200, return and attack the position in the valley. The enemy might be caught sleeping.

Grimes got the word out to his squad leaders slowly. While he was still proceeding, an NVA soldier came from one of the huts and stopped within fifteen feet of their line. They froze, while he stood there. Then he took off in the direction of the corduroy trail.

Five minutes were lost.

Then Grimes said to Lawson, "Go after that man."

Lawson picked Bishop and Hyvonen to go with him. They took a short cut, trying for an interception, but somehow missed it. The three of them returned to the spot where the platoon earlier had gone into perimeter. There they paused briefly for a cigaret, standing and watching the trail. Bishop tapped Lawson on the shoulder and whispered, "I see two VC." He pointed in opposite directions along the corduroy. There were vague shapes out there, perhaps thirty meters on either side of them. They had stopped, as if listening. Lawson ran one way, Bishop the other. Again they missed. They did not fire because in the dark it would have been futile, and besides, they wanted a prisoner.

Lawson said, "I think it's time for us to go after them."

These three took the corduroy to the high ground again, splashing through the knee-deep creek on the way. The hour was about 2100. They would set up their own ambush, rigging it with Lawson and Bishop on one side, Hyvonen on the other. If anyone came singly, Lawson would shoot; if there were two, Bishop would also fire. Hyvonen would join only if it was a bigger bag.

This scheme they worked out as they walked north, Bishop leading, Hyvonen in the rear.

Lawson looked back for Hyvonen but could not see him. (Hyvonen had stopped next to the bush to urinate.)

So Lawson looked ahead to see if somehow Hyvonen had caught up with Bishop.

There stood Bishop again, M-16 pointed at a dark shape that had just turned from the corduroy onto a side trail ten feet ahead.

Lawson cried, "Don't shoot! Don't shoot!" thinking it might be Hyvonen.

So Bishop withheld fire.

This thing was getting pretty sticky. It came to Lawson that a three-man ambush had its complications. It might be wiser to return to the main body.

Grimes had taken his time about pulling back the platoon to set an ambush. The men seemed worn down and listless. To ask them to climb the hill again was too much; he withdrew them only the 250-meter distance between the creek bank where they had faced toward the huts and the lower end of the corduroy trail.

One place seemed as good as another. There he was, trying to organize his ambush, when the trio returned, about

2145. Lawson's assistant squad leader, Sgt. Kenneth Smith, sat sprawled with his feet in the trail. So did half a dozen of the others. Lawson said, "Smith, how in hell can you rig an ambush with your big feet out in the trail? All of you get those feet in."

Grimes turned to Lawson, saying, "You and the scouts go back along the trail about two hundred meters and stay there as an OP."

But Hyvonen was hungry, having missed his noon meal because of the flurry over the rice cache. So he took a C ration from his pack and for a few minutes sat there munching. The other two tarried with him—a brief break that may have saved their lives.

Grimes passed along the word to the others that if only two or three enemy came into the ambush they would "try to wrestle them down, or at the worst, use knives."

Bishop said suddenly to Lawson, "I think I hear somebody closing in on us."

Sergeant Sepulveda and his squad were on the extreme left, the direction in which Lawson and the two scouts should have gone. He was trying to get his men down and they were giving him a hard time.

First he heard a singsong chatter.

The moon was just rising.

By its light he saw four or five shapes coming his way some thirty meters off. The figures wore black pajamas and conical hats.

They were ambling along single file, as is the local custom, but they all seemed to be jabbering at one time, another quaint native habit, exceptionally helpful in the circumstances.

Sepulveda passed along the word to Grimes, "VC coming into the ambush," then moved to the extreme end of his line.

He looked again and counted six this time—the same conical hats and black suits.

Grimes and Sepulveda let them come on—nine men all told, five in the first group, four in the second.

It took about thirty seconds before both groups were well within the block, with every M-16 trained on them.

Still prone, Grimes yelled, "Kill them! Kill them! Kill them all!"

The fifth man, directly in front of Sepulveda, had whirled and screamed an instant before. He must have seen the glint on a rifle barrel not more than five feet away.

Of the twenty-three weapons in that line, all fired, and none stopped until the clip was empty. All the shapes along the path seemed to topple at one time. Within thirty seconds of the first shot Grimes cried, "Cease fire!"

It was a gory mess. The nine bodies lying on the corduroy had been pretty well pulped.

Lawson thought he saw a tenth man spin and get away. No one else did. Still Lawson must have been right about it.

A grenade came sailing in, to explode among Sepulveda's people. Spec. 4 Cunningham was wounded badly in the stomach. Sergeant Hoskinson and Privates First Class Cunningham and Roberts were also hit by fragments.

So there was work at last for Spec. 4 William Winchester, the aid man, who till then had done nothing but fight.

Grimes uprooted his ambush right after putting in a call for the medevac Huey to come on from An Khe. The casualties were lifted out forty minutes later. By then the platoon had backed away 300 meters or so to a better 'ole—a well-banked paddy where it could go into a tight perimeter with satisfactory fields of fire.

This done, Grimes called on the artillery to shell the huts. The first rounds were 300 meters off target. Then the guns got right on it and quickly the thatches were blazing with a glare that illumined the valley. Next morning the position was ashes which no one chose to rake over.

They stayed in the valley two more days, more as a gesture of defiance than anything else. Pestered by leeches all the while, they fought off nothing else. The hope that more of the enemy might be drawn out by their small numbers proved vain; the enemy knew too well about those guns lining the ridge above.

On the third night they were lifted back to LZ Corral by Hueys. Though they had set forth on the adventure with a generous distribution of flamboyance, no one suggested that it would be more soldierly to walk.

The Place Called Monkey

Hollywood could not have done it better. In the scenario of Operation Crazy Horse, here rechristened the Battle of Vinh Thanh Valley, the hero returns to stage center in the final act, not having held the spotlight since he introduced the play.

Large as life in the prelude, but still an outsider whose quick wit and bold action pointed First Cavalry Division to a profitable battleground, Special Forces Sergeant Freeman had been sitting at the C.I.D.G. camp ever since, watching the winged chariots fly by.

To the Division Command at An Khe he remained anonymous. His name was nowhere in the records. With the pressure full on, no one had found time to seek out Freeman and learn exactly how things got started. All armies are a little careless that way.

Now the operation had entered a new phase, or at least so everybody thought. The scattered and routed enemy forces appeared to be fleeing the battle zone. Instead of punching in air, therefore, the high mobility and fire power of the division had better be employed around the outer circle, blocking the exits from the mountains and closing the bag.

So there were weighty staff conferences. Gen. Jack Norton talked things over with Gen. Jack Wright. The Acting Corps

Commander, Gen. H. W. O. Kinnard, flew into camp from Nha Trang again to consult. Wright flew off to Qui Nhon to ask the ROK Division Commander and the ARVN Division Commander to provide battalions so that the circle of force could be made complete. Both agreed to cooperate.

These things happened as May turned toward June. As an upshot of the many conversations, four C.I.D.G. companies were to deploy to the center of the massif beyond LZ Hereford where all the hot action had taken place.

These Montagnards are extremely good at scouting and patrolling and not much more than that was expected of them, now that the heat was off, and certainly no heavy and sustained fighting was anticipated.

To the companies committed this was both good news and bad. They were overjoyed that they would be working with regular forces for the first time. They were chagrined that the call came only after the battle had petered out, for these men love to fight; one thing they ask in return, that if killed in action their bodies he returned to home soil for burial.

General Norton pledged them that they would have the full support of the cavalry division. Its fires and heavy weapons would be on call. Its men would come if re-enforcement were needed. They would be treated exactly like his own troops. With this promise they were content.

Some of them were less happy, however, when after being lifted from the Vinh Thanh redoubt at 0830 on 26 May, they were set down on Landing Zone Monkey and saw it for the first time.

This was the Son Hai Company, 110 strong, under Commander Dimh Ghim, the same unit, the same leader, that brought home the bacon from the long patrol that opened the battle.

Sergeant Freeman was the first American, the first man, to step from the lead Huey onto the ugly surface of LZ Monkey.

He turned to his friend, Sergeant Adams, and said, "I don't like the look of this place."

For David C. Freeman, of Baltimore, Md., twenty-two years of age, RA 1380034, that was quite a long speech.

Strikingly blond, and handsome enough, he impresses most of all by his manner. Some early training must have given him a high regard for silence and self-control as tactical weapons. The voice is ever low-toned, the face immobile except when he smiles, and rarely is a word wasted.

By training Freeman is a medic. In his first service to the cavalry division he functioned like an intelligence specialist. Now as he viewed the frowning face of Monkey, he was thinking like a tactician with little prospect that he would have to act like one. He ranked fourth among the American advisers who would be present, and the two Montagnard officers were nominally his superiors.

Monkey was a horizonless hollow, hemmed in by jungle-clad heights that pressed in too close. Worse still, its rumpled surface was strewn with monstrous boulders, rock slabs, blown stumps and fallen trees. It was a clearing only in the sense that here the litter of basaltic debris lay so thick as to forbid growth by the surrounding forest. There was just enough flat, fairly clear space to serve as pad for the landing of two choppers at a time, if both took extreme care.

The cramping effect on operations of this strait jacket was quickly made evident. The third Huey to arrive over Monkey crashed from fifty feet up when its tail rotor caught in the limb of a tree. In the fall the pilot broke his hip and the co-pilot smashed his jaw. So any movement outward from Monkey had to be delayed for ninety minutes.

Freeman doctored the two men. The two door gunners, who had escaped injury, stripped the chopper of everything that could be salvaged, and the Montagnards piled these parts in the center of the LZ. Then the helicopter had to be blown up by Sergeant Adams and Sgt. Turner Lawhorn, Jr., age thirty-four, home, Brainbridge, Ga. The latter had brought along a squad from Alpha Company of the 8th Engineer Battalion, supposedly to clear Monkey of stumps and rocks, which was a proper labor for Hercules. Last, with the wreckage cleared and more choppers coming in, the casualties had to be flown out.

During the prolonged delay, which killed half the morning, the Montagnards had outguarded the position. But not a shot had been fired or suspicious sound heard, which circumstance allayed the earlier worries about the unsuitability of Monkey. They had made enough noise to jar the ridge tops, and an enemy not given to attacking in the full heat of day had failed to respond.

At 1000 they started up the mountain and were glad of it. They were in patrol formation, a point of one squad, followed at forty yards by the main body, all moving single file. It would have been so even had the jungle trail been wide enough to permit two men to walk abreast. After the clangor in the valley all was now strangely silent, as from the intense sunlight of the LZ they moved into the semi-gloom cast by the canopy.

The march was NNW. Fifty minutes later they were atop the first ridge, 300 meters higher than where they started. There the whole company went into defensive perimeter, where Freeman and Adams were able to get in radio contact with their own base camp for the first time.

Under the Montagnard assistant commander, Dinh Tach, the I & R Platoon moved out to scout along the ridge crest for another 600 yards. Within fifteen minutes they were back, and Dinh Tach had a story to tell.

"Not more than three hundred meters out," he said, "I see one VC carrying six canteens."

"For just once," Adams wryly remarked to Freeman, "they did what they were told. Instead of shooting, they looked."

Immediately Adams and Freeman and the two Montagnard chiefs fell to bickering over what to do about it. The six canteens bespoke the presence of an enemy group, and the trail atop the ridge was wider than before and looked well beaten down.

Dimh Ghim was all for throwing the whole company forward.

Adams, who had been with Dinh Tach on the point, was dead against it. Tempers flared. Adams said, "No, absolutely not."

He put his counter proposal this way: "Give me twenty of your men and Freeman and I will recon with them. If we find anything big enough for a company, then we'll decide what to do about it.''

Dimh Ghim was willing to compromise, provided he could go along too. So they agreed on the unorthodox arrangement—three leaders forward with a patrol, one rearward with the main body.

It was time to get off the trail and move through the bamboo forest that enfolded it. They split in three parties, Adams' group advancing along the trail edge, Freeman's being on the slope to right of it and Dimh Ghim's taking the left flank.

Just ten minutes and fifty yards further along, still far short of the spot where the guerrilla with six canteens had been sighted, Adams' group came under intense automatic fire at close range.

A first bullet hit Adams in the rucksack and spun him around. He reached back with his right arm to see what damage had been done. A second bullet hit the arm, shattering it, severing the ulna nerve, and knocking him flat. The bone thrust out.

Curtained off by the bamboo thicket, Freeman had not seen his friend fall. That first fire had hit no one else, and the movement perforce continued, for the Montagnards charged right on.

They were going against a strong position—a tier of three bunkers extending for thirty yards in depth, going upgrade on both sides of the trail. They maneuvered as the Americans had trained them to do, half of them firing while the other half bounded ten yards or so, there to resume fire while the other half came forward.

Done according to the book, the reduction of these works took one-half hour. By the end three of the Montagnards were dead and eight had been wounded in action. What grieved Freeman most was that out of a small Vietnamese detachment accompanying the Montagnards, he had lost by death his most prized soldier. But there was one compensation. Of the fifteen VC bodies counted, his M-16 had downed four. The loot was seven AK47 rifles and one 7.62 light machine gun.

Even as they were getting away and Freeman, after patching the Montagnard wounded, was doing what he could to help Adams, he realized they had not finished the job. For more than 100 yards, as they back-trailed, rifle fire, an impressive volume, followed them out. Most of the company had moved up to support the patrol from the flanks at some time during the thirty-minute fight, though fewer than fifteen men had borne the brunt of it.

They returned to the old perimeter atop the ridge. Adams was mobile but in such pain that Freeman had taken over. He still doubted that he had left behind any formidable concentration of strength. But to be on the safe side he asked the TOC (Tactical Operations Center) at LZ Savoy to lay on a tactical air strike according to the coordinates he read from the map. He preferred that damper because the Montagnards always got rattled by friendly artillery and would break and run if it got anywhere close. Most of the bombs came in on the right spot, but one 500-pounder blew within fifty yards of them, shaking their earth much, but shaking the mountain men more. Freeman could hear much yakking and teeth chattering. Still, no more fire came from whence they had been, and he judged that the resisters had been wiped out.

It was now high noon. Freeman called Savoy, asking that choppers be sent to evacuate his casualties. Then on radio he asked Lawhorn to bring up his squad from the hollow. When they arrived, the engineers set about blasting a hasty LZ amid the bamboo atop the mountain. It took them about one hour to clear enough space for a Chinook to settle. Above all, Freeman did not want to return to Monkey.

At last the Chinook came over, but vainly. It could not find the LZ. As these ridges are folded, with so many forest-clad knobs, switches and cutbacks, such small spots can be easily missed.

With that failure the company was directed from Savoy to return to Monkey. Freeman and Adams both stoutly protested, Freeman saying, "Anywhere but Monkey; that's no place for a fight." It was no go. So they packed up and moved downhill.

At the landing zone in the hollow a security force had been trying to bring off a little military order out of a scene of topographical chaos. There was one platoon of Montagnards; then there was Sgt. Cecil Broome, the senior among the Special Forces people present. It was not a happy combination. Broome, though an older head, was new to the country, awkward with the mountain men, and unacquainted with their folkways. Little had been done to straighten out this inefficient, tangled warren.

It was still noontide when the company resettled among the boulders to take a break for a lunch of rice and cold canned chicken, flavored with hot sauce. Shortly afterward Hueys came in to evacuate the wounded and dead. Incoming, one of the choppers had two passengers who intended to stay.

The first was Sgt. Alan M. Arrowsmith of Headquarters Company, First Brigade, Cavalry Division. A twenty-five-year-old citizen of Fort Charlotte, Fla., but calling himself a "service brat," Arrowsmith had come to the mark only because he burned with curiosity about how Special Forces soldiers performed. He had his camera along and his notebook and was ready to make himself useful in any other way.

Second was Lieutenant Walker of Special Forces who, since he ranked all others present, quite naturally took charge, if only for a brief span.

Thereafter for a piece things went, if not smoothly, at least more so than before. At about 1400, on Walker's order, Broome took one platoon of the mountain men and posted them 150 meters up the trail they had walked that morning, where they rigged an ambush for the further protection of the force on LZ Monkey. That done, he rejoined Freeman on the LZ where the latter had just shown Dimh Ghim how to place the security guard.

The slippage started when at 1630 another Huey arrived with an ammunition resupply that was not really needed. Though this is a complaint virtually without precedent among fighting forces afield, it was the peg from which large confusions became suspended. The natural condition of Monkey and the burning desire of the force to get away from that fell spot and stay mobile in order to live longer so made it. Too much ammunition tied it to the unwanted base; either so, or it had to be used up, even if wastefully.

One hundred additional rounds had come in for the only 60 mm mortar present. There had been unloaded 200 additional cartridges for every Montagnard rifleman—not a great abundance, but still seeming an overburden to small men confronted by large hills.

At least the mortar supply seemed easy of liquidation. The logical thing was to shoot it off against the enemy position NNW which had been braced that morning. That's what they started to do, and straight off they ran into trouble.

Of the first twenty rounds, twelve misfired, which is to say that they wouldn't eject from the tube, though test showed that the mortar itself was in working order. Now shaking a sensitive mortar round out of a tube is a very delicate, devilish and time-consuming business and hardly a task for amateurs. But somehow, though slowly, they made it and decided to fire no more.

The still larger problem then arose—how to dispose of the useless and dangerous ammunition. If left behind, it might be carted off by the Viet Cong and used for booby traps and mines.

Lawhorn and his engineers dug a very large hole just off the LZ. The most overworked men present, they then filled it with the bad ammunition and prepared the pit with a blasting charge for demolition.

That's when the mountain men bucked. If the mortar shells were to be blown, so must their overload of rifle ammunition. They began to toss their magazines into the pit.

Lawhorn held off the blast while the argument rose to high pitch. Dimh Ghim supported what his men were doing. Walker stormed at him, "We'll get no resupply till Saturday; if you refuse to take that ammo, I want no squawking if your men get killed."

Dimh Ghim answered, "That's O.K. I say blow it."

Suddenly Dinh Tach entered the row to break with his

chief and support Walker. Such a large man physically that he stands more than a head above his people, who are scarce smaller than Americans, he spoke no words. He began grabbing men by the neck, walking them to the pit and forcing them to pick up the magazines. He was effective while he lasted, which wasn't long.

A volley of automatic fire cracked somewhere above and echoed through the hollow, returning them to reality. The sound was unmistakable but was so diffused by the jungle growth that no one could tell its direction.

Broome went at a dead run up the jungle trail where he had posted the ambush. The others still figured the shooting might come from a few stray Viet Cong or possibly their own men. In three minutes Broome was back, shouting, "The ambush is attacked from three sides; they must fight their way back."

Lawhorn still squatted, demolition lever in hand.

Walker yelled, "Don't blow that ammunition!"

With that, fire in large volume swept across Monkey from three sides of the perimeter. All had happened in a matter of seconds.

There followed a total silence of two minutes. Montagnards and Americans, who had flattened and begun working weapons though they saw no targets, broke off when they heard nothing coming in.

Then came a heavy fusillade of rifle and automatic fire from the ambush side. Tracers bounced like fireflies amid the boulders, and machine-gun bursts cut swaths in the elephant grass just beyond. Then bullets came in from all sides and the force knew for the first time it was surrounded.

Arrowsmith had squeezed into a small hole next a large boulder, wholly astonished that he had come to a fight.

Came another cessation lasting four minutes. The defenders had thrown out a heavy counter fire all around the circle, and confidence rose that the repulse was complete.

A few Montagnards rose and walked about.

Walker called the TOC at LZ Savoy, asking that a strike by the rocketeers of the air artillery be put on the bush all around Monkey.

Then a few random bullets came in.

Arrowsmith stood to look about for a possible target. Broome said to him, "Sarge, you crawl right back in your hole."

Arrowsmith said, "Yes, sir," and jumped for it.

Yet Broome still stood there, moving uncertainly as if about to change his position. Walker also was in the open. Arrowsmith thought this so odd that he pointed his camera and snapped both men in the two seconds while they stayed hearty and whole.

There came from the bush just one bullet. It got Broome in the back just under the left shoulder blade. He clutched at his heart, screamed, "Mother—," tottered for a second or two, then pitched forward and rolled over.

Starting to crawl to him, Arrowsmith pulled out his aid pack.

Walker yelled, "You get back in your hole!" Arrowsmith did.

Walker's mouth was still open from the yelling. The second bullet hit him in the right cheek and came out of the lower jaw. Otherwise the shot might have killed him.

Freeman, the medic, had also yelled to Arrowsmith to get back. Having started moving to Broome, Freeman at once deviated to Walker. One glance told him Broome was dead. He saw wide eyes staring up but could detect not the slightest motion beyond.

Both bullets had whined directly past Freeman's ear. So he knew they came from one marksman who was still out there. Still he knelt in the open, bandaging Walker and giving him an injection of morphine, which took him ten minutes. Slugs continued to kick up rocks around him, but he was wearing a lot of horseshoes.

The lieutenant was in bad shape, not that he was likely to die, but with the shattered jaw and flow of blood he could no longer talk. The result of trying to communicate was an unintelligible mumble.

So Freeman knew now that he had to take over command, though there were two lieutenants present, including the artillery forward observer, Lieut. Wade W. Hathaway, and even Sergeant Lawhorn ranked him.

While he was bandaging Walker, Arrowsmith grabbed the radio and called 3-8 Savoy to ask for help. Before he could get through, Freeman had finished and taken over from him. First, however, together they carried Walker and the radio over to the right of the perimeter where several logs provided them with a dubious revetment. The fire around the circle continued to build up steadily. Freeman described what had happened to the people at the Savoy TOC. He said, "I must have re-enforcements. I estimate this as a two-company attack."

At that point Arrowsmith, by his own account, took three precautions. He checked his rifle ammunition, straightened the cotter pins on his four hand grenades and said his prayers. Feeling positive that otherwise he would not survive the night, though the prospect did not too greatly alarm him, he could not put at discount the possibility of Divine intervention.

Freeman was not troubled in the same way. Another sort of worry pressed on him, though for the moment he was keeping it in the back of his mind. As for the chances of life or death, the few Americans with him had responded so wholeheartedly that he felt more confidence than his situation warranted.

Hathaway, who hails from Charleston, S.C., was about twenty-five meters to Arrowsmith's right.

Freeman called, "Where's the FO?"

Arrowsmith pointed.

"You get him!"

When Hathaway crawled over, Freeman said, "You bring in that air artillery."

Hathaway did. The rocket Hueys swooped down on the hollow just about dusk and plastered the walls all around it. But the most prolonged stage of the close-in fire fight had lasted all that time—just about thirty minutes.

Well before the respite came, it was self-evident that the tumult of the small fight had reverberated in the First Cavalry Division command. Jack Norton and Hennessey kept their word. Before the latest inning of the fire fight had closed off, the promised re-enforcements began to arrive and the view from above which convinced them that Monkey stayed combustible, did not deter them.

The men on perimeter saw the Hueys circling and they intensified their defensive fires. All of Bravo Company, 1/8th Cavalry, was scheduled to come in. The first ship came in and dropped its men—five riflemen under a sergeant who scampered to position under fire—then was away and aloft in a trice with its door machine guns blazing.

The second ship was three feet off the ground and going away, having dropped its riflemen passengers during a hover, when it was shot down. There was a tremendous puff audible, well audible, above the small-arms exchange which resounded like the rhythmic drone of a highly vocal bee swarm.

That was how it looked and sounded from ground level. The fact was the Huey had been stricken while making a steep descent 100 feet in air by a burst which riddled its power structure, coming in on the left side and rupturing the hydraulics system. The pilot, CWO Francisco G. Moreno, twenty-seven, of Dos Cabezas, Ariz., who had been ''shot up'' three times in earlier fights but never shot down before, said gently over the intercom to his people, ''The panel says we are losing power, so I will set down.''

Not wishing to make things sound too final, he alone sweated out for the rest of the descent the certainty that he was about to lose directional control. Luck certainly smiled on this high heart, for it was only five feet above ground that she went out. The bump was gentle, the landing missing by a hair one of the largest boulders. The five riflemen aboard had jumped clear before the Huey settled.

Arrowsmith saw Moreno pulling frantically at all switches during the last stage of the drop so there would be no fire. Next morning Moreno could recall nothing of that; he had responded automatically. What he did remember vividly was the impeccable conduct of his crew. The two gunners, S/Sgt. Herbert R. McDuffy, Hattiesburg, Miss., and Spec. 4 Angel L. Cumba, Hato Rey, Puerto Rico, kept their M-60s blazing till the last moment, then jumped out with their weapons and ran to ground positions. But that was only after McDuffy had whipped around and opened Moreno's panel and Cumba had stood by to cover him with fire as he popped out.

Moreno got over to Freeman, who was bandaging some of his Montagnard wounded. The warrant officer did not understand at first that he was talking to the soldier in charge. The mountain men were calling Freeman "Doc."

Freeman had turned to rebandage Walker when Moreno asked, "What's your situation?"

To his surprise it was Freeman who answered, "Just look about you."

"How much force have you got?"

"Mainly what is left of a C.I.D.G. company."

His calm fascinated Moreno; "he was acting as if he did the same thing every day of his life."

Then Freeman said, "You and your crew are stuck here for the night. Be sure to make yourselves comfortable."

His medical work done, he led them to the positions where they could do the most good for this oddly assorted garrison. Moreno had come armed only with a .38 revolver and was now presented with an M-16 which made him feel a little better.

For ten minutes following Moreno's crash, the fire from outside beat against the boulders on Monkey—some mortar, one machine gun, several automatic pistols and numerous rifles. Then suddenly again the crunch and crackle and the whining of the ricochets ceased. Freeman took this opening to check the Montagnard positions on the north and west flanks of the LZ. Counting the men he had just worked upon, the C.I.D.G. company now had another 3 KIA and 11 WIA. Most of the wounded had been hit by grenade fragments.

Taking stock of how the Americans were distributed and armed, Freeman took away one of Sergeant McDuffy's M-60 machine guns and gave it to the infantry squad led by Sgt. Kenneth L. Wells, of Kansas City, Kan. It was while he was checking the numbers that the ARA strike came in beautifully, the rocket salvos pounding at the jungle on all four sides of the LZ, the closest rounds falling not more than 200 feet away. As the strike lifted, from the base at LZ Cobra the battery of 155s put fifty rounds on the slope NNW.

There were now twenty-two armed Americans under Freeman's charge, along with the wounded Walker; and Freeman was junior in age and grade to almost half of them. They were with him all the way, irrespective of that, for as had happened to Arrowsmith, he had won them swiftly with his poise and self-confidence. But now that the heat was off momentarily, what weighed heaviest with this Special Forces soldier was not the problem of directing the defense as a whole but that he was responsible for the lives of more than a score of his countrymen, most of them still strangers to him.

No SF soldier had a higher esteem for the mountain men. Days earlier he had said to me, "This is the happiest bunch of people I have ever known. They stay well-groomed, keep themselves clean. Well-disciplined, they keep their rifles the same way. I enjoy serving with them."

The one dark thought he had harbored now came forward again. It fretted him sorely, obscuring all other considerations. When the two bullets that killed Sergeant Broome and felled Lieutenant Walker had zinged past his ear, the sound had followed too quickly the two cracks of the rifle. The firer had to be only a few feet away. Probably a VC sniper had worked right in among the boulders of the sector defended by the mountain men. But then there was an uglier alternative possibility, and about that he dared not take chances.

This reflection he would keep to himself. He would still have to call the Americans together and give them a logical explanation of why he was regrouping the defenders. The sun had dropped below the westernmost ridge, the hollow was already darkening, and the thing must be done at once.

Arrowsmith helped him round up the others and is the best witness as to what he said to them.

It went something like this: "The VC may come on in

great numbers. Our position could get worse. I think that for now one thing helping us is that they overrate our strength and the chance we may be re-enforced tonight, which can't happen.

"This thing could go wrong. If it does, the VC might offer to let the C.I.D.G.'s go free if they will kill or surrender the Americans. I have confidence in these men, but I want nothing like that to happen because it would make confusion."

So he outlined his plan. The Americans would group together in a closed circle, forming a perimeter within a perimeter, but holding to one side of the LZ. Next that side a deep creek bed ran directly past the flank. Should any crisis impose threatening the integrity of the force as a whole, the Americans would shoot their way to the creek bed and make for the high ground.

Then he added, "In any case, if we seem about to be overrun, I would choose to pull out with the whole force and fight from the woods higher up. We are holding the worst possible ground."

There was no argument. The Americans drew together as the dark became full and a large quiet filled the hollow.

With that came another assault, lasting twenty minutes. The fire was high and seemed to be ranging from greater distance. There were no casualties. The night wore on, bringing only a few halfhearted probes by small groups of snipers.

Freeman sent out the word: "No more defensive firing unless you see live targets."

He was worrying about ammo supply and the possibility of full-scale attack after dawn.

Hathaway had already set it that as soon as possible after first light the ARA and the 155's at Cobra would work over the slopes on all sides of them, bringing their fires in just as close as possible.

Freeman and Arrowsmith took turns at the radio. No one slept. The moon rose but cast only a thin shaft of light to within the hollow. Smokey the Bear and Puff the Magic

Dragon stayed on call all night and periodically circled above Monkey to drop their flares and illuminate the scene.

Moreno, from his position in between a fallen tree and a rock outcropping on the downslope next the creek bed, saw Freeman move only twice during the night. Both times it was to put fresh dressings on Walker. He and his crew members said nothing to one another; they had nothing to discuss. Long before they had agreed that they would never be taken alive by the enemy, which is how many American fighters in Vietnam feel on that subject. As Moreno said, "It gives one a bit of comfort to come to such a decision early and stick with it."

Long before their sweated jungle suits had dried, a heavy dew descended, the air chilled markedly and they shivered. The tree leeches working on them only intensified that misery.

Almost before they were aware the night had ended, so deep was the shadow from the eastward ridge, the ARA was over them. The strikes were precise beyond fault, the nearest rockets rocking the timber less than 100 yards from where they lay. With that, Freeman for the first time felt a great relief, saying to himself, "They will not come now."

Then the sun came over the hill, bathing the hollow and washing them. Dull, bone-ache wakefulness gave way to the feeling of being freshened. They arose and stretched and no fire came against them. At first it was hardly believable. A few hands began breaking out rations: they had not eaten since the previous noon.

Patrols were sent out for short distances on all four sides, this maneuver being done without abruptness. There was no sign of a live enemy. The bodies of thirty-seven Vietnamese regulars were counted scattered around the immediate foreground. How many others had been dragged off was beyond telling, though there were well-spattered blood trails in many directions.

The first medevac Huey arrived at 0700. Shortly there was another Huey coming into the only pad, to make adjustments on Moreno's downed chopper so that the Flying

Crane could lift it out some hours later, to be patched for further use.

Arrowsmith rode out on the Huey that had come to do the prep job. So did Moreno, McDuffy and other members of that crew. The surcease from pressure had made them suddenly vocal. They confessed to each other that they had not expected to last the night.

Freeman stayed on in the despised hollow for a few hours longer. He felt a little more content with how things had worked out at Monkey. There was no protest from the mountain men when he told them the adventure was over.

The Big Picture

Somewhere along in a chronicle such as this it is necessary to "take a breath and then reprise in a different key."

Otherwise there cannot be understanding of how the main battle is being played. The essential drama of war lies in what is thought and done by men in the close-joined fire fight where their lives are at stake from minute to minute.

The deliberations and decisions of generals, the aims and reasonings of the planners, the hopes and fears, expectations and disappointments at all higher levels, play their part and indeed receive disproportionate attention from the romanticists who write of war.

But as the hucksters say, it's what's up front that counts. Only there can the issue be joined and decided. Nothing willed by any genius in high command as to the action of fighting forces has any real importance until the rank and file directly under the gun do it and thereby validate his judgment while sustaining his reputation for wisdom and boldness.

No great land battle is ever a tidy affair, precisely managed and giving those of its participants who directly face fire a feeling for the thing as a whole. Flanks are never really "hurled forward"; large troop bodies do not arise, at the wave of a baton, and charge on as one man. Only novelists dream such things, thereby perpetuating the myth. Composing the large battle are any number of small fights, little connected, and sometimes at cross-purposes one with the other. Each is local and limited in the feelings of the men who engage. Company fights company, platoon goes against platoon. How the regiment or brigade fared as a whole is something that has to be computed later.

In this particular, the Battle of Vinh Thanh was not different from Omaha Beachhead, Kwajalein or Pork Chop Hill. The distinction is that the separate actions were spread over more time and greater space because of the irregular character of the enemy. True, it was not called a battle by our press or government when it was fought. For political reasons, more obscure than sensible, the large-scale operations in South Vietnam are always termed "campaigns" even when large numbers of the enemy are encountered and decisively beaten as was done when the cavalry division first hit the North Vietnam formations around Plei Mei and in the Ia Drang Valley. This mistaken terminology is a defeat for both history and for military English. To go to the root of the word, campaign means only a sweep through country. There are many campaigns in Vietnam which prove futile.

This one did not. It brought on a battle which, once its proportions and possibilities were understood by the forces of the attack, became highly productive only because it was systematically run. Linking the seemingly disparate and unrelated actions was a broad design, subject to day-to-day change, not only because of enemy reaction, but because of the limited availability of hitting forces. Remaining constant were the two general purposes: to purge the mountain country beyond LZ Hereford of Communist forces and to make it so costly to them that they would be loath ever again to attempt using it as a sanctuary.

In relation to these objectives, the roles of the commanders responsible for the pivotal decisions were greatly unlike.

Gen. Jack Norton was coping with the division's problems as a whole, which task the unexpected opening of Crazy Horse had turned into a Roman ride. One of his brigades was in the Ia Drang Valley joined with other forces in a sweep toward the Cambodian border. The greater part of another brigade had to remain fully occupied manning the eighteen-kilometer-long barrier protecting the An Khe base camp. That left too few troops to keep safe watch over the division's piece of vital Highway No. 19, running from the sea to Pleiku. Bridges had to be guarded. Patrolling both ways from the road and outward from the barrier was done daily. Every morning mine-sweeping operations had to be run from the Deo Mang Pass westward to the Mang Yang Pass, before the military convoys could start moving.

Gen. Jack Wright's portion was that of serving as deputy for the division commander by overseeing this one battle and assisting the chief to conserve forces, while making sure that the man running the fight had enough.

Col. Jack Hennessey's part was to keep the battle energized by feeding more troops into the area, pushing forward with them, and pressing upward when he felt that he was running short.

Though the Three Jacks were not always eye-to-eye, as is true of any deck, it was still a good hand.

In the maneuvering that had already taken place the First of the Fifth (1/5th), from out of LZ Monkey, had swept north toward the Crow's Foot, its people moving along the trails of the ridge and through the valleys to LZ Mortimer on high ground overlooking that area.

At the same time the First of the Eighth (1/8th) pushed from LZ Horse northeast along the trails toward the Soui Ca Valley. This maneuver had hardly begun when Captain Martin's company made its onfall. At Division HQ the feeling was that Martin had dealt the hardest blow of all, though so rating it is pure speculation.

Through these moves outward the central mountain area had become, in effect, a vacuum. The command felt, however, that major elements of the enemy were still somewhere within it. Yet there was no way of knowing but to search. By then the failure to take even one prisoner had hit hard. What little was known of the enemy, fleeing or still present, could only be guessed from scanning captured documents. The catch included current memoranda or orders published by five battalions of two different regiments, the 93rd, 95th and 97th of the Second Viet Cong and the 8th and 9th of the Twenty-Second, Army of North Vietnam.

At this stage, what to do next had become the big question for the operations managers, the division in the hour having nothing more to send forth to stir the fire. Its own battalions were now deployed on the outer rim of the mountain area, plugging what were reckoned to be the main exits therefrom. That was when the four C.I.D.G. companies were dropped into the central zone. Only one of them was familiar with the highland interior. They were supposed to establish a unit patrol base with each company and then, using squad-size groups, work the streams and trails within 100 meters of their perimeters and rig ambushes by night. They were not supposed to launch on a big brawl. But as happened to the Montagnard company around Sergeant Freeman, the planners proposed, and the fortunes of war disposed.

With this commitment, 1/8th was lifted to a new position to the south of the battle zone, 2/8th was shifted to a new position at the north end of the Soui Ca Valley, 1/5th was sent to seal off exits from the Crow's Foot and 1/12th was disposed as a screen along the Vinh Thanh Valley.

There were no troops with which to cover the northern arc. The plan was to saturate it with tear gas, spread in the form of crystals dropped from a Huey. The plan didn't work; rains came and washed out the crystals which otherwise might have persisted for a week or so. That stratagem was then supplemented by the first B-52 strike against the northern arc on the evening of 25 May, which made much thunder and may have smitten a few Philistines, though no one knows.

To Jack Norton it had become self-apparent that the division was overextended, in view of the demands on its resources from elsewhere, and had to pull in its horns a little. That was when Jack Wright besought the ROK Tiger Division and the 22nd ARVNs both to send up a battalion from the coastal plain. They moved in on 28 May; the body count of enemy was by then 392.

Not a prisoner had been taken. The ROKs took position where 1/8th had held forth, 1/8th filled in where 1/5th had been, 1/5th was moved to a ridge line directly north of Hereford, the ARVN battalion moved into position at the south end of the Soui Ca Valley, and the division put out an instruction to forces: "Try to shoot them in the legs only." It didn't go to the ARVNs; they were running their own show. Furthermore, the instruction did no good. That night one VC was shot in the hip by one of 1/8th's outposts. Four men lifted this great prize to choggey it downtrail. He bled to death before the chopper could come get him.

So there, for the most part, they stood and waited, or patrolled, and in either case served. The highland interior was no longer being prowled and pounded. The wishful hope was that the enemy, deprived of his stores, driven by hunger, would emerge, poking through the holes in large numbers, looking for rice.

At 1253 on 29 May it happened. The first *chieu hoi*, *rallier* or POW of the battle came into Division's eager embrace. He didn't fall in; he walked in via the 405th Scout Company of the 22nd ARVNs, which was doing a little snooping to the east of the old French fort. The act of surrender, or quitting, goes by various names in Vietnam, and the psywarriors, like the troops, use them pretty much interchangeably. *Chieu hoi* literally translates as "open arms." But as applied to this specific problem, *chieu hoi* is synonymous with "returnee." Even as the French word *rallier,* which means "rejoiner," it is so much more refined and acceptable than deserter, quitter or POW. It conjures up a picture of the prodigal coming home, the lost sheep back in the fold.

This *rallier* was about to bust his gut or the last two buttons left on his shirt, so anxious was he to talk. He said he had walked in from a two-platoon position about one kilometer from the cap of Hereford. All members of his force were feeling mighty low and in a mood to surrender, so great a beating had they taken from shot, shell and malaria. So he said. He was willing to finger the ground where they sat and help in any way to persuade them to come on over to the L & M (Legal & Magnanimous) side.

Jack Wright flew to LZ Savoy at once to make sure that a real treasure was in hand. There was no doubt of it; the *chieu hoi* was as cooperative as Flubber or Flipper. Even before Wright talked to him at 1430, he had already agreed to board a Huey at 1600, guide the pilot in, and then from his platform in the sky appeal to his brethren through a bull horn to lay down their arms and be sensible.

Said Wright to Hennessey, "It looks now as if all we have to do is make certain that none of the artillery blows those two platoons apart before we gather them in." And that was what he thought.

Wright then flew back to the Division HQ at An Khe to make certain that everything was laid on for the exploitation. He told the Division Psywar Officer, "There is one other point—the two platoons must be given an ultimatum; if they do not surrender at 1600, we will go after them with artillery, air and all we've got at 1700."

The ax was to be applied in two whacks. The guns would fire at 1700. Then there would be a lull and a second appeal. If the enemy remained contrary, the air would put on the big whammy at 1800.

To take no chances on a slip-up, Wright personally dealt with the division fire direction center and made the stand-by arrangements.

Right then the hard facts of life began to pile up on him. Psywar, and the technological appurtenances therefor, were administered from Nha Trang by Corps, one hour's flying time distant.

Said the Psywar Officer: "The only ship Corps has which is equipped for broadcasting is a U-10 which takes only one pilot and one passenger."

So if Wright or the Psywar Officer were to go along, that would exclude the *chieu hoi* and the interpreter.

Armed with all of this refreshing information, Wright took the Psywar Officer and flew back to LZ Savoy to talk this problem over with the *chieu hoi* and to tell Hennessey that the show might have to go on later than first scheduled.

En route the Psywar Officer gave him another piece of news: "By the way, the U-10 was told to put down at Phu Cat airfield to receive its instructions."

Wright swallowed hard while calculating that the extra stop would cost at least another thirty minutes.

He then asked, "How long would it take us to rig a helicopter of our own so that it could do the work?"

The PO said, "Oh, maybe by tomorrow morning."

Wright suggested it might be a pious idea to proceed with it at once, but for use some other time.

They landed at LZ Savoy to learn that some helpful fellow had flown the *chieu hoi* back to the open arms of the 405th Scout Company, redelivering the prisoner to the rightful possessor, or something of the sort. Wright had to fly on to the next valley to replevin the little rascal.

Then he barreled straight for Phu Cat. But no U-10 was sitting there; idling nearby, however, was a Huey rigged with a manned PA system that wouldn't work.

Instead of puffing from outrage, Wright was filled with a sense of wonder that things could go so far, far wrong. He remembered a saying of his friend, H. W. O. Kinnard: "When you are a general, you no longer direct traffic." Now he was less sure of its worth; somebody had to, or it didn't get done.

The *chieu hoi* squatted there on the runway, a picture of self-composure. The U-10 came in and plopped beside them.

The pilot popped his head out and said, "General, what do you think? We have been broadcasting to those two platoons in the boonies for the past hour."

That left Wright speechless. He thought to himself: Isn't it remarkable? The only reason we arranged the broadcast was so the *chieu hoi* could speak. The broadcast goes on; the *chieu hoi* isn't there. It's like the two drunks who stagger onto the railway platform as the train pulls away. One has a ticket; the other has come along to see him off.

They both dash for it. One throws himself aboard. The other misses. But the wrong drunk has caught the train.

It was 1800. Time had run out. Wright called the Division TOC to say, "Cancel the artillery; cancel the air strike; we won't need them tonight." Then he said to the psywarrior piloting the U-10, "You might as well return to the hills and continue broadcasting; after all, there's nothing to lose."

The *chieu hoi* and the interpreter were flown by helicopter back to the ARVN CP, along with a word of counsel: "You might as well teach this *rallier* how to use a PA system; it could come in handy one of these days."

Then Wright asked for one of the infantry platoons in bivouac near LZ Savoy to wing on over and rendezvous on the ground with the *chieu hoi* and his mouthpiece. Together they would try it the old-fashioned way. The platoon arrived about 1830, and the *chieu hoi* led them via the trail to the place where he had left his unit in midday. There wasn't a sign of anyone about. They saw no reason to doubt that an enemy force had been there; but the iron had not been struck while it was hot.

On seeing only emptiness, the *chieu hoi* lay down in the middle of the trail and bawled like a hurt child. Whether the weeping was because he had not succeeded in plucking a few brands from the burning, or that he feared he would be killed for not delivering the goods, no one was able to figure out.

Back at Camp Radcliff, Jack Wright, pensive as usual, was feeling somewhat better than that, though not because a light had dawned and he understood the lesson.

He was sipping a martini, a very good martini.

To the Last Valley

The Republic of Korea Battalion had been beating the bushes on the toes of the Crow's Foot countryside, as well as patrolling into the flat land between the ridges for three days, and had found so little to do that its people felt faintly disgusted.

Called too late, they had been launched on a wild-goose chase. So they believed.

These were strong companies, 180–185 men in each, forty-one men to a platoon. Each squad had nine men, like the U.S. infantry structure of the 1950–53 war, unlike our design for 1966. The Koreans were also armed with the U.S. weapons of that earlier war, while regretting that there were not enough Armalites to go around.

The battalion under Lieut. Col. Kim Yong Jin, as June opened, had its rifle companies bivouacked in a roughly triangular relationship to one another, on three separate landing zones, located several klicks (kilometers) apart. The base of this inverted pyramid was LZ Colt, where was placed the battalion CP, with 5th Company guarding the perimeter.

LZ Colt was no picnic ground from any point of view. Periodically it was being shelled by an 81 mm mortar, the position of which, somewhere amid the hills, remained a mystery. The daytime temperature of this hard-baked flat averaged 110° F. The Korean enlisted men on base, including those who worked in the 105 mm howitzer pits, did duty wearing nothing but sandals, shorts and dog tags and managed a grin, though no visitor could understand how or why. The flow of whirlybird traffic into their thornbush-bordered base, sized and shaped like a gridiron, kept the pup tents flattened and the turbulent atmosphere charged with dust. Except where the rotors raised their dirt storms, there was dead calm all around.

At evening the battalion received new orders; they came from the First Cavalry Division, the Koreans being under its operational control. The ROKs, heretofore beating around the Crow's Foot, were to take a larger bite toward the northwest. The shift was predicated more on hunch than on solid information.

Colonel Kim decided to loose the 7th Company, with an LZ at the northwest apex of the battalion triangle, and let it go on, if it could, until it reached someone else's boundary (TAOR) line. The 6th Company, making like a whirling dervish and using eight choppers in shuttle, would go to the center of the battalion's tactical zone. Some of it, following the first lift, would be carried on to the southern slope of Hill 754, where there was a negotiable flat, within a draw, large enough to receive one chopper—in a pinch. Two other platoons would face the other way, so that the company's deployment would be an expanding circle. Elements would search to the east, north and west.

The plan sounds crazy; many things do in Vietnam; it is a crazy war. The irony is that it was out of this pinwheel, not out of the deep and orderly thrust of 7th Company into enemy country, that the last hurrah developed.

First Platoon and the HQ detachment searched to the west after morning came. Its soldiers very quickly came across some large enemy rice caches. There were also documents, grenades and rucksacks in the huts. While the search went on, five Viet Cong, returning to this small base, were killed by ROKs guarding the trail. All of these things, in the end, proved somewhat irrelevant.

Two other platoons, moving in the opposite direction, saw a line of people walking a road in the distance. Though they were too far away for it to be certain, they seemed to be carrying arms. The platoons took out after them.

That morning I started out in the Huey with Jack Wright. The aim was to visit the active LZs and reconnoiter some of the forward positions. By 0815 we were at the old French fort where Sergeant Freeman and the Montagnard companies based. Next door to it was the pod that Colonel Hennessey was using as his TOC. The corn patch just outside the door was LZ Savoy.

Hennessey told us it had just come over the radio that the ROK battalion had made contact with the enemy in another wide valley fifteen klicks to the east. Wright said, "Let's get over there and watch it from above." Having persuaded the Koreans to come along, he felt responsible.

Halfway to our destination there came another message: "Contact has been broken; somehow the enemy slipped away." We flew on to the coordinates that had been given us. It was no valley but a great flat plain, almost denuded of trees or any healthy-seeming vegetation. The whole flat was repulsive and almost desolate. There were a few streaks, pea green in color, running through it like striped ribbons— the partitioned rice paddies. A house or hut stood forth every hundred yards or so, though there were no villages. A few palms around the houses, a few cattle and buffalo in the fields. But most of the land was parched gray and white, looking not unlike Bonneville Flat, as if nothing worth while could grow there.

Streaming across the flat, from 1500 feet above, we saw several columns of people headed southeast. At that distance they could as well have been mites. We dropped down to 700 feet and still could not tell much about them. Some carried bicycles. Others rode them. It was all according to whether the wheels could be downed on a solid bank or had to be hefted across a mud flat. None seemed in a great hurry. They ambled. Yet none lagged behind.

They wore their wide mushroom hats to shield their shoulders. That was the trouble. From above they were as ageless and sexless as marching ants. They were dressed like the VC; it could possibly be the lost company mixing in with many women and children.

Worried, Wright called the An Khe base, asking that a rifle platoon be sent out by chopper to land and see what was going on. For an hour or more we held just above them, waiting for the platoon to come on. When we got word that the force was on its way, having already supplied the coordinates of the area we had been watching, Wright pulled off so that we could witness a B-52 strike along a valley eleven kilometers to the northwest. It was a beaut— as a spectacle. We watched it for the full thirty-five minutes, flying on a parallel line three klicks off. Only one bomb missed the target line. The smoke clouds rose out of that valley evenly spaced and standing above the so-green hills like as many great ostrich plumes unfolding in white and gray. So far as could be learned afterward, the only other effect worth mentioning was the denting of good earth.

As the strike ended, we got word on radio that the U.S. platoon's choppers were over the area we had scouted earlier but no one could see what Wright and I had been talking about. So we buzzed back. This time there was no fooling around. We came in low and continued to fly at fifty feet above the columns (there were now four of them) for the next twenty-five minutes. If they fired, they would be at least unfriendly. If they did not, the negative proved nothing. It was altogether unlikely that, exposed as they were in the open, the hardest bucko among them would risk firing at our Huey with three other ships circling overhead.

As we gained elevation and the other ships descended, Wright told the platoon, "Do not fire! Do not fire!" We saw them, with their interpreter in the forefront, flag down the two columns on the extreme right. The leader called back, "Negative! They are old men, women and children. They say they are getting away because the ROKs are in the area. They said they were told to leave because a big fight is coming."

There was no checking of the other two columns. We had flown on to an LZ where 1/5th was based several miles to the southeast because we were running out of gas; and somehow the search platoon missed the movement on the left flank. Whether that mattered, later there was no way of knowing. We moved on at noon. Later, in the midday, in this same vicinity, the ROK sweepers got on the hot scent again and were able to hold the trail.

The two platoons of the 6th Company that had traveled east through the early morning, then lost the quarry, reversed direction some time before noon and struck out northwest. The flat plain seemed to hold no promise. After a one-hour march they were approaching the first line of small hills and ridge fingers. Then, once more in the distance, moving in the same direction that they were bound, they saw what appeared to be the same column of moving figures they had tried to track during the morning. While they gazed, the file of figures vanished into a cut in the hills. Quickening their pace, the platoons marched for that spot.

No real tactician, with a proper eye for ground, on viewing that pinched landscape, would have imagined it a place which a military force was holding, much less that it had fortified it, unless it hugged no better hope than to hide away.

Here two ridges, not more than 250 feet higher than the nearby terrain, ran closely parallel for approximately 900 meters, both tailing off at either end, rather than connecting with any larger hill mass. The crests ran evenly for the greater part of this distance, not more than 300 meters apart. There was no vale or flat floor between them, not one spot large enough to turn about a squad. The inner walls sloped down sharply in a lazy "V."

This slot could be blocked off readily at both ends, and not many hands or weapons would be required to do it. With one exception the inside slopes were even enough that they might be saturated with napalm, shellfire, or tear gas. At approximately midpoint of the northern ridge the base curved inward to form a rock-walled draw. The southern ridge had no such feature. It was timber-covered uninterruptedly for the whole distance except for a large slashing cleared by some Montagnard which was strewn with fallen trees and

boulders. This blemish on the slope was not directly opposite the rock-walled draw but about 100 meters farther on,
taken from the point where the platoon of ROK soldiers first
looked upon the scene.

Lieut. Chung Mun Ki, who directed the search, was
taking no chances—yet. He decided to drop off Third
Platoon at one end of the slot, where it would hold for a
while. With Second Platoon he proceeded to his recon,
moving along the crest of the southern ridge. If he flushed
out any enemy, it would be time enough for Third Platoon to
enter the slot via the narrow trail at bottom of the V.

The view from the top was unsatisfactory; too many
treetops in the way. None in his party saw the rock-walled
draw on the other side. Progress was very slow. Third
Platoon got impatient and, taking the path, went past him
and was just about to exit from the far end of the defile.

That was when Chung saw the enemy. At 1400 he
messaged the battalion base: "Made my first sighting."
Below Chung, standing clear in the path 150 meters away,
were seven men wearing NVA khaki. Third Platoon had
already moved too far to do anything about it.

Though the range was long for snap shooting, Chung
opened fire. One light machine gun and ten rifles poured it
out. (The ROKs are armed with the U.S. M-1, carbine and
Browning.) Chung was certain he saw seven bodies fall. It
was time to descend the hill and claim the weapons.

He took twenty men with him and they were at least
fifteen minutes laboring down the slope, such was the
thickness of the undergrowth. His men on the crest did not
see him reappear. They thought it a reasonable assumption,
even as had he, that the foray engaged no real danger, since
Third Platoon had walked unmolested over the same ground.

Breaking the quiet, a sharp volley of small-arms fire from
below—all of it enemy—told them they were wrong. Chung
and party had walked straight into an ambush, bullets
coming at them from all directions.

Thereupon all communication with Chung ended. His
men on the crest line waited uncertainly; the one radio had
gone with him. More than one hour later a badly wounded

soldier, who had gone along with Chung to carry ammo for the light machine gun, came crawling to the crest.

By some miracle he had saved the radio but couldn't remember how. He said to them, "I saw the lieutenant shot down. I don't know if he was killed. I saw his RTO killed, I saw others fall." The rest of his experience had fogged out.

They sent the news along to Capt. Lee Tae Il, the company commander, who was at LZ Echo. This was a new chopper landing, set in a grassy bowl almost encircled by high ground, within close reach of the fight now opening. The surroundings were so lovely as to be disarming. The slopes above were not jungle-grown. Only that morning it had been decided to stage supply for the ROKs out of Echo. So a Chinook crew was given the task of setting a bulldozer there so that the pad could be leveled. I flew along with Gen. Jack Wright in a Huey to watch the operation. The Chinook had already called for help from another Huey; it couldn't locate the spot. The Huey lowered to fifty feet above Echo to mark it with green smoke. Our Huey dropped to thirty feet lower than that and circled around the smoke for two minutes simply to have a closer look. When we lifted, another Huey was dropping toward Echo, piloted by W. O. Owen, fresh from helicopter school at Fort Rucker and making his first combat run. When he was 200 feet above LZ Echo, a VC bullet hit Owen in the right leg, wounding him gravely. His co-pilot barreled for the ROK's main base. Owen had already been evacuated to hospital when we put down. Wright commented, "It's better to have a charmed life, if you can get it."

Now Captain Lee was on LZ Echo, weighing his problem and being given a hard time by snipers. Seven had been killed in the tall grass around the pad during a quick mop-up that followed his landing. Lee, a much-decorated Korean, handsome, with cinnamon-colored eyes, is rated by his mates "a little too aggressive." He first thought he would order Third Platoon to march back through the slot, firing. Then he realized that an ambush that had smashed the greater part of one platoon might do the same with another. A reasonable thought.

He recommended that the 7th Company, under Capt. Park Jong Sung, be turned about to assault this prickly groove from the western side. At the same time the Reconnaissance Company would be lifted about three kilometers and set down where it could easiest deploy to block the exits. These notions made sense to Colonel Kim, the battalion commander, and were converted into orders.

Then Lee had an afterthought. He still had one platoon on hand. A few of his people held a precarious toehold somewhere above the ambush site. It was his duty to get up to them promptly and re-enforce. So he entered upon the defile, instead of coming over the high ground as Chung had done, and at once the boom was lowered against him, at the same spot where Chung had been bushwhacked.

Lee was not trying to get in the first punch, nor was he seeking glory. His motives are quite clear and are almost beyond fault. He knew that he had a lost squad or so on the high ground along the southern ridge and had reason to believe that a number of his wounded, and probably a few of his dead, were among the trees at the base of the ridge. With one platoon, proceeding in single file in the manner of a patrol, he should be able to steal into the area, rescue his wounded, and while avoiding engagement, link up with the other survivors on the ridge crest. The reasoning was all right as far as it went: the trouble was that he could not imagine what the ground was like and he did not understand the enemy.

The 7th Company was still two kilometers to the west, marching over the ridges. Lee's message was: "We are being attacked from all sides. We think there are two VC companies around us." The call was monitored by the 7th Company, marching east, and by Chung's survivors waiting on the crest above. Somehow the battalion missed it. This happened at 1700 on 2 June. From a ridge top in the distance, using field glasses, Captain Park of 7th Company could see "VC milling around at the bottom of the defile" but could make out no friends. He thought he was barely within machine-gun range, so he tried it. The distance was too great, though a few bullets tumbled spent among Chung's survivors atop the southern ridge.

7th Company closed on the position of 6th Company at 1800. The sun was still one hour above the horizon in distant Vinh Thanh Valley. But where Lee's platoon fought on, the dark was closing fast. The company had taken more hard loss—three dead, three critically wounded and fifteen more lightly wounded.

More depressing, the mystery of Lieutenant Chung and the other nineteen missing had not been solved. Not one body had been found. There was no sign of the fight in their foreground and they were too well occupied to look farther.

The dark and 7th Company arriving together, the enemy quickly slipped away. Whether they had gone for good, no one knew at first. The ROKs went into perimeter on the only open ground within sight—the cleared patch littered with fallen trees and granite slabs on the south slope where the mountain man had toiled.

The moon came up full and flooded the scene. Captain Lee took a patrol of volunteers to prowl along the notch for signs of the missing men. They found none. But the patrol did see one thing clearly—a group of men moving toward them. They wore cone-shaped hats. Before they could raise weapons, the enemy patrol had vanished into the rocky draw at the center of the northern ridge.

Lee knew in that instant, and for the first time, that this was the enemy citadel that he had missed on his first passage through. And he guessed, rightly as it turned out, that their presence at this hour meant they had no intention of quitting the battleground.

There were gunships aloft and not too far away, bent on some mission for the cavalry division. Lee asked for a strike against the draw on the opposite slope. The ships came on and put their rockets on target. They were wasting their fire. Though Lee had yet to learn it, the position was proof against air bombardment, and field artillery could get at it no better. A projecting ledge above it gave it almost perfect protection. And there were other reasons.

That evening Gen. Jack Wright had talked over the

situation with Major General Lee, the commander of ROK Tiger Division. This was at the battalion CP on LZ Colt.

Wright said, "We are as much concerned about twenty missing Koreans as if we had lost that many of our men." He wanted to know what the cavalry division could do to help, and the two men agreed on certain measures.

Some of the ARA Hueys would be kept on station above the fight ground. The Second of the Eighth (2/8th), that much overworked battalion, would be moved into a blocking position on the west right next the exit from the two ridges. At first light the two ROK companies would be resupplied with ammo and food by Hueys that would come low over the slashing, kick the bundles out and zoom away. The Koreans by that time would have missed five meals.

Under the moon, outside the perimeter, Lee and his patrol counted the enemy dead they had killed that afternoon. There were nineteen. The score was not yet even.

The Reconnaissance Company marched through the night so that the eastern exit from the vale would be blocked when morning came. Captain Park sent one of his platoons to the top of the ridge opposite the slashing to serve as a blocking force should the enemy try to break away to the northeast. That still left too many air holes; both ridges were so densely timbered and rock-crusted that the closing of all escape routes was manifestly impossible.

On 3 June the action developed like a reel in slow motion, except for the buzzing traffic overhead. There were numerous reasons why.

Morning ground fog cloaked the enemy notch in the center of the north ridge, and though rifle and automatic fire came against the ROKs in the slashing, they could not see where to return it. That is the nasty thing about fog in war; its reputation for impartiality is rarely deserved.

So the Hueys were slow in getting in with their loads of food and ammunition. The first chopper was hit hard and driven off. The others delivered. There were only three of them, and all came and got out in a hurry; the bundles were loosed from not more than thirty feet above the steep-sloped slashing; yet not a few of them missed it wholly. Two of these choppers were ripped by machine-gun bullets during this quick pass but continued in flight with their crews unhurt.

Capt. Johng Sung, operations officer of the battalion, was on one of the Hueys. He caught a fleeting glimpse of the main enemy position as the pilot banked sharply to get away from the fire slot. Within the clifflike structure of the draw, which was roughly semicircular, with a radius of about a hundred meters, were twelve or fifteen odd-looking spots deep with shadow which he took to be the mouths of caves.

Had the Huey been able to hover so that Johng could look at the position carefully from the same level, he would have seen much more to worry him. The positions were about one-third of the way up the ridge. They were not natural caves but deep recesses dug or blasted out of the evenly stratified limerock. Then they had been made into sangars; the mouth of each hole had a waist-high protective wall of loose rock. The rest of the rubble from these excavations had been strewn evenly over the surface of the 45-degree embankment below. A charging man could not climb that steep against fire; his feet would find no firmness and he would fall on his face. All of this had been skillfully done. The works had been there long.

Clever is the word for it. Artillery could not get at these holes because of the angle. They could not be knocked out by recoilless weapons from the opposite ridge. Half a dozen machine guns had that slope covered, and besides, the density of forest and undergrowth forbade use of such weapons. Napalm might work but probably would not.

Johng told Park on radio what he had observed in one swift pass. That bit of information was filed for the time being. The ROKs were interested, first, in getting their own back, whether the quick or the dead. After that they would deal with the enemy. Their higher commanders had so ordered it, and the leaders on the spot would have given it that priority, anyway. So would any of Jack Norton's commanders, had it been their problem, their people.

Park and most of his men stayed primed in the slashing, ready to defend the ground if counterattacked. They were not in foxholes; their cover was the fallen trees and boulders. Lee and the men with him went on with their search, formed as patrols, armed and munitioned to stand and fight, even if jumped by superior forces. In that event Park's command would probably quit the perimeter and join them, depending on the circumstance.

They found the bodies of Lieutenant Chung and seven of his men at 1500 that day. They were strewn through the timber right by the ambush site. Lee on his prowl the night before had simply overlooked them. Scattered through the brush along their front were sixteen enemy bodies. So Chung's survivors, who had listened to the ambuscade from atop the ridge, had been wrong about one thing: there had been friendly fire and it had done good work.

Soon after that find I flew with Jack Wright in a Huey to make a reconnaissance of this grim vale at close range. He felt he had to see it, the better to know what might be done. Twice we sped back and forth through the gut, four trips altogether, not quite as high as the crest line, or about 150 feet above the central trail. It is a tingling experience— maybe like a roller coaster, though I have never ridden one. No fire came against us, at least none that we felt. But we could hear faintly above the noise of the rotors the steady bark of fire below. Snipers had thickened around Captain Lee and his search party. Of this we saw almost nothing; in the four trips I observed only nine human figures, and from above it was impossible to tell what suits they wore or what they were doing. Under the strong sunlight, however, we four times got a good look at the enemy's walled nests in the cliffside.

Wright thought something could be done. He called General Lee and recommended the use of tear gas. Lee agreed. The chopper arrived on station, bringing the gas dispenser, and was just ready to make the run. At that moment the message came through: "Don't use the gas; contact is too close."

There is good reason for doubt that it would have worked, and in any case, the countermand was sound. Lee and his patrol were continuing their search, and their exact location was unknown.

General Norton sent two flame throwers to them; there was no way to employ the weapons; the hazard was too great.

The patrol found a few more of its dead. Then, marvelously, one live survivor of Ki's patrol stepped from the woods, unhurt.

His story was this: Along with Chung's wounded RTO, he had crawled away from the ambush. They had worked their way upslope on the other ridge and entered a cave for refuge, not knowing there were four able-bodied VC in there, who were also trying to escape the fight. Mutual hostages, the runaway VCs and the refugee ROKs had spent the two days ignoring one another. When Lee's patrol began crowding in close and shooting up the woods, the enemy soldiers broke and literally went over the hill. Kim then did what came naturally. The RTO had lost much blood and was so enfeebled that he could not go with him. Guided by Kim, Lee and his party climbed to the cave and saved the RTO to sing another day, which was the penultimate good deed of the afternoon.

At Park's position some of his men, having reconnoitered the enemy position in the rocked-walled notch, by working to it through the trees along the ridge flank, thought they had a bright idea.

So a patrol was formed shortly before sunset, going normally armed, but with a very special weapon in addition. A Korean sergeant had the inspiration. This was the standard claymore mine, with something extra added—a piece of ordinary commo wire attached as a lanyard, so that the mine could be dangled and still exploded. In fact, the arrangement took two wires.

The patrol moved through the trees along the crest line of the northern ridge just before the dark gathered, then descended to the projecting ledge above the caves. Once that passage was made, the ledge itself changed function; it was now protecting the ROKs against the fire of the people in the caves. The claymore was lowered just to even with the top of the central cave and there exploded: the enemy within had not detected arrival of the patrol. The ledge and the height protected the patrol from any back blast. The slaughter within must have been grim and great. Having fired the one mine, the ROKs returned to their perimeter. They now had their method.

That night I wrote my wife, Cate: "One thing about life over here, it is not routine. This may not be the best war ever fought by the United States. There is none such. But it is the most interesting, and has more changes of pace than any other. These soldiers seem more self-helpful, more generous and less windy than any I have ever known. There are no smart alecks among them. They are workmen."

It could have been written, as well, of our friends, the soldiers from Korea.

During the night, from the ridge opposite, they kept enough bullet fire going against the holes in the cliffside that many in the enemy force were contained, though doubtless still more risked the flail and, either through sliding down the embankment or slipping flankward through the trees, got away.

Next day the ROKs renewed the attack, using the device of the evening before, with one additional refinement. Smoke grenades were first lowered on lassos of commo wire so that they could be looped into the caves to blind the inmates. Right on the heels of that the claymores were lowered and exploded. Captain Lee had brought both of these ideas forward by saying to the men, "Let's be cautious. We have already lost too many soldiers. Think of something that will get them without costing us anything."

It had to be slow work because it was delicate; one mine mishandled might have wiped them out. It was also thorough; not one ROK soldier was hit during the day, though under cover of the smoke lowered from above, some of Park's grenadiers crawled up the rock-strewn bank to within easy throwing range. By 1800 on 4 June, as the valley again fell under shadow, they were content that the task was finished.

They pulled back and waited a little while to see if any fire came forth. There was only silence.

Sixty-five enemy bodies were pulled out of the caves. There were also four heavy machine guns, two 57 recoilless, twenty-seven automatic rifles and a large store of Russian-made carbines, hand grenades and rifle ammunition. These numbers, added to what had gone before, made the count of enemy dead within the vale 103. That made the exchange rate a little less than one to five. As General Lee said to Captain Lee, "It isn't good enough."

While they took stock, five enemy soldiers came out of the woods with hands in air, to surrender meek as kittens. Save for one item of possible use to history, the capture came too late to be of any value. The curtain was dropping on the finale, and the battle called Crazy Horse was all but over. Not one POW had been taken during the fighting; everything had been done the hard way. The generals were unhappy about that. The ranks didn't care one way or the other, or even think about it.

The five prisoners said they were from "the 9th Battalion of the 27th PAVN Regiment" and that two full-strength companies had been positioned within the vale when the ROKs entered it.

That surprised the Koreans not a little. They had thought they were taking a pushing around mainly from local VC. So they winged back to home base feeling a bit more cocky.

Old operations in the Vietnam war, like old soldiers at the time and everywhere, never die; they just fray away. There is always another plan somewhere on the burner. Invariably the plan has a jump-off date.

When the mill seems to be running low on grist, and what remains for the grinding is reckoned to be no longer worth the cost of the power expenditure, commanders and troops turn to something promising a surer return.

The break-off date for Operation Crazy Horse—which in more reasonable times than these will be called the Battle of Vinh Thanh—had already been set for 5 June. Had another enemy battalion sprung from the brow of any of the nearby hills fully armed, it would have been kept going for a while longer.

But that was not to be. The mountains beyond LZ Hereford had been well flailed out. The slopes soon smoked with the only signs of a resumption of normal activity—the burnings that followed the clearing of some new patch by a Montagnard for the growing of his corn, beans and tomatoes.

The cavalry division, still having a few lives to give to its country, had already gone to Operation Nathan Hale.

BOOK II

The Trail to Toumorong

From the Checkerboard

During the first five days in May, Lieut. Col. Hank Emerson's battalion (2/502nd of First Brigade 101st Airborne Division) carried on a sweep roughly thirty miles to the north of Bn Gia Map in the vicinity of Bu Prang.

A Regional Force Company of Vietnamese garrisoned Bu Prang. The rumor was circulating that the outpost, nine kilometers east of the Cambodian border, had been marked for overrunning by a North Vietnam battalion. There had been a small thrust against Bu Prang in mid-April which the defenders had beaten back with little loss to either side.

It was at a time when the command in Saigon was acutely concerned about the rate of North Vietnam's buildup along the western frontier. The southwest monsoon was coming on. Force levels were too low to permit screening the whole border. Saigon was wholly convinced that the flow of enemy traffic out of Cambodia into the Central Highlands was a major threat. With more heat than light, Phnom Penh, the capital of Cambodia, denied it was so. For reasons better known to itself than were clear to the army afield, Washington also ridiculed the idea.

Emerson and his men would at least have a fair chance to look for some of the alleged infiltration routes out of Cambodia. General Westmoreland had made an exception;

when on missions of this kind, corps boundaries did not have to be considered inviolate.

That was what Emerson remembered when, after a futile beating of the bushes around Bu Prang for most of one week, where he had expected to find something hot, the bag remained empty. Bn Gia Map was in III Corps territory. On the other hand, Bn Gia Map, abandoned in the 1965 summer in the face of an attack, had been a Special Forces camp and for that reason was fitted with an air strip that could receive C-130s. Theater intelligence had come up with nothing suggesting that Bn Gia Map might be on an invasion route or could be worth working over. Emerson went that way only because it was something to do and seemed like a good idea at the time. That's par for the course in Vietnam: most of the better finds are uncovered in no other manner.

On the morning of 5 May, very early, Emerson reconnoitered the area around Bn Gia Map in an L-19, a two-man operation chopper. So much ground fire came against him in flying both ways from the air strip that he didn't bother to put down. He thought this very encouraging. One other thing, however, did worry him; he knew that the Special Forces group had left a store of mines behind on abandoning the camp; it was possible the mines were waiting along the air strip.

Emerson called his force the "502nd Light Infantry Brigade," and it wasn't altogether a joke. Attached to the battalion were Third Platoon, Alpha Company, 326th Engineers, a seventeen-man element of Vietnamese from the Regional Force Company at Bu Prang, and a crew of thirty Montagnard porters who were being given a trial run. Then there was a squad of the National Police, who served as interpreters, and the Third Company, 4th Battalion, 9th Regiment, ARVN, with its U.S. advisers. The battalion had its own scouting force, called the Recondo Platoon, and in addition a group of thirty Montagnard trackers, called the Apache Platoon by their Special Forces trainers, six of whom were with them. The name fits; they do look like Apaches.

No preliminary air strike was put on Bn Gia Map. Emerson thought it wiser to sneak in. The Recondo Platoon and the Engineers were landed from Hueys at 1000 on 6 May in a melon patch belonging to a Montagnard, three kilometers to the southwest of the air strip.

The battalion had been scheduled to set down in midafternoon. But the Recondo force went like the wind and by noon had some of the air strip, the surface of which was staked with tall sharpened bamboo intended to foul the rotor blades but hardly suited to the object. Also there were strewn about numerous rocks the size of a curling stone that were painted to look like mines. All of it superficial, the litter was quickly cleared away, and Emerson rammed the battalion into the south end of the strip during the lunch hour, which passed without grace or meal. The atmosphere did not allow for either. Snipers were busy north of the strip. Spec. 4 Will Scott of the Recondos was downed by a bullet. One figure in black pajamas came out of the elephant grass, reeling with malaria, and collapsed amid the Recondos. He said, when he revived for a bit, that he was from the 608th Viet Cong Battalion and that the battalion had cleared away, leaving him because of his illness. Then he went into a coma. On his person was a document showing the location of a large arms cache not far from the st

A few of the local Montagnards had been rounded up. They spoke of "many, many VC." (They cannot deal in numbers.) They said "recently." (They do not count days.)

Emerson at once launched his companies on a "checkerboarding" maneuver to sweep an area about ten kilometers square. Bravo Company was to go east, Alpha Company to the north, and the Recondo and Apache Platoons to the south, while Charley Company and the Regional Force stayed around to guard the air strip. There were contacts almost immediately. Bravo Company drove off a few VC who were guarding the arms cache; it was found to hold more than 4,000 rounds for various heavy weapons. Right afterward the VC surged back, and there was a brief fire fight, without loss or gain, no bodies being found.

That was all for one day. Emerson was by now convinced

that his net was not being cast in vain, and it was time to make more certain that the central position was properly organized. The companies would proceed with their checker-boarding and would be on their own through the night.

In checkerboarding, a company splits into groups of half-platoon size, called "Recondos." The task of the group is to work over a section of land, roughly five kilometers square, searching for enemy forces. If nothing is found, they proceed diagonally to another such square, alternate squares being left untouched. The use of helicopters for resupply would likely expose the pattern of such a deploy-ment, for the groups work the jungle continuously five days at a time. So for secrecy they do the whole thing afoot and must enter upon it carrying five days' fighting supply and rations. Water they do not carry; they depend upon jungle streams. To handle such a load, the men have to swing over to an Asiatic diet. They take along rice, and a powdered B-ration soup for flavor, and eat only two meals a day, taking these past the main danger point in the morning and just before dark in the evening. Reserve food and ammo are cached centrally as soon as there is found a central place where it can be kept under guard; the Recondos work the ground carrying not more than fifteen-pound loads, in addi-tion to the rifle. They stick close to the streams and paralleling paths, for that is where they find the VC and NVA. Vietnam has proved quite well that U.S. soldiers can hold up under the strain of such operations. The main physical trials, apart from malaria and bullets, are leeches and jungle rot. In a day's travel through the bush a man picks up between twelve and twenty leeches. Insect repellant will knock them off, once he stops for it. Jungle rot, which usually starts with a thorn prick becoming infected, he can do nothing about, unless he moves to a drier atmosphere. The Recondos set up ambushes at night. So doing, they rarely dig in. They set up at a bend in the trail, with some natural protection and concealment that may be augmented with camouflage—vines, branches and fronds.

Sgt. Billy Watson of Bravo Company and Murphysville, Ill., led one such ambush party through the night of May

6–7. There were seven men in the squad. The ambush was set up at a trail intersection, with three men facing north, two to the south, one covering the flank and Watson in the center, next to his RTO.

At each position the men would alternate sleeping, with the extra from the three-man guard relieving the flanker. Watson would check on the others occasionally. Talk was kept minimum and then in whispers. It had been pre-set that if anyone walked into the blind, Watson would fire the first round.

At 0600 he called his commander, Lieut. Louis Sill, of Washington, D.C., and his platoon leader, Sgt. Camillo Gonzales, of Sacramento, Calif., and said, "Negative. No contact." It was the sort of report that made wearier the weary.

Gonzales said, "Hang on a little longer."

At 0645 four men came downtrail into the position. Watson saw them when they were forty meters away. They were stopped and he was afraid of losing them, though in the dim light the distance was long. So he took aim and fired the M-16. Spec. 4 Charles Brown and PFC Thomas Duncan got off at least half a clip.

The targets disappeared. There was a momentous pause. Then half the squad went scrambling uptrail while the other half stayed guarding. They found two bodies within the tree line fifty meters higher up the path. Between the bodies, kneeling and trembling all over, was a third figure, clutching a French-made machine gun.

Watson at once called Sill on radio, saying, "This guy acts like he's in shock."

Sill answered, "Treat him gently. Give him water and something to eat. Try to get him quieted." Then because Sill and his party were 1500 meters more distant from the air strip, he told Watson to take the prisoner back to Emerson.

Under interrogation at the air strip, and after he had been given a malaria pill and several hours' sleep, the POW began to talk. He said he was an ammunition bearer for a heavy-weapons company. He couldn't read a map. But as he pointed with his finger at a distant ridge, it became fairly clear that he had left the company at about center of the area that Bravo Company was working over. The information was put on radio to Sill.

He said, "One man escaped the trap; that company will be long gone."

Emerson asked the POW, "Will you help us?"

The POW said, "Yes."

Then the question: "Will you lead us to the place?"

At that point he again began shaking so violently that they let him sleep for a few more hours.

The favorite timepiece with the U.S. soldiers in Vietnam is a cheap Japanese watch, the dial of which shows the date and day of the week. Emerson did not need to be told that he was extending as wide as possible on the twelfth anniversary of the surrender of the French at Dienbienphu. General Pearson at Brigade HQ and General Kinnard at Corps in Nha Trang also thought of it as they monitored the movement. Kinnard had been so many times cautioned by the four-star admiral from Oahu during his rounds: "Remember, we don't want any Dienbienphus, not one, not even a little one."

To the north, Alpha Company was having a less satisfying go than Bravo. The Recondos were moving up steep mountain trails, amid ever-thickening jungle, with no inhabitants and meager trails. Also Capt. Henrik Lunde was irritated: Bravo Company was getting all of the action. He called Emerson and said, "I'm not the boy for this kind of country. We're too tied up here to do a good job. Why don't you turn us around?"

Emerson couldn't resist baiting him. Lunde is a Norwegian with a German father and a very low boiling point. Emerson said, "Why don't you call Four-Six? That CC [Sill] will tell you how to make a Recondo work."

At that crack Lunde really bridled. He said, "I want to get on another axis or I'm not with you."

Emerson laughed, then replied, "All right, if you must have it, get on a line going south." That would bring Lunde back on a parallel to the air strip.

Lunde turned at once, even as, without their knowing, the whole operation pivoted on this hard-kidding conversation.

Just after sunset Gonzales, who had brought his whole platoon back to the air strip, hit the trail again, the platoon and the prisoner going with him. The farther they marched, the more the POW dragged his feet, and by midnight he would not move at all. They had then gone five kilometers of rugged, boulder-strewn trail. The men were tired. So Gonzales rested the platoon. By 0500 they were going again. Four hours and 2,000 meters later the POW again tried to hold back. They picked him up bodily. Just ahead was a small village. It proved to be a VC base camp, with a mess area, lean-to huts, and a small hospital strewn with bloody bandages, all showing signs of recent use and hasty flight.

Sill and the rest of the company had fallen in with Gonzales. The base camp was torched.

Sill called Emerson and said, "They have gone south, I think. I'd like to go after them."

Emerson replied, "If that's how you want it, get going."

Sill deployed the company on three axes, and these several columns were off again at 1100.

Beginning exactly at 0730 that morning, Alpha Company had become engaged in one shoot after another. Groups of three to five Charleys moved into their ambushes, all armed with the AK47, the NVA weapon. The ambush parties that had pulled stakes and started moving had the same fortune. There were six contacts, one after the other, and most of the killings were done by a point on the move. At that, the marksmanship was nothing to write home about. By noon the company had racked up seven bodies and was in possession of five AK47s, one Soviet sniperscope, eight packs, twenty-four antitank rounds and one Chinese-made bolt action rifle. The rest of the day was a blank, for both Alpha and Bravo, and not one nocturnal visitor disturbed the sleep of anyone on the ambushes through that night.

For Alpha, the morning of 9 May began with another small fire fight, which drew no blood. They moved out through a forest of nothing but bamboo, the stalks of which were so close together that they had difficulty slipping through. Of a sudden Lunde broke into the widest, hardest-beaten trail he had yet seen in Vietnam.

He called Emerson, saying, "I think I'm on an invasion route."

Emerson asked, "Are you going to turn the checkerboard?"

From Lunde: "I've already turned it—ninety degrees—headed straight west."

On the new line, the company at once began bumping more small groups, killed a dozen of the enemy, captured a few weapons.

Sill, despite the blank of the day before, still believed he was on a hot trail and would find another base camp when he got to the Song Be River. That happened not long before noon.

Gonzales, who had killed more VC (18) than anyone else in Alpha Company, always insisted on being point man. He was in front now, and the group with him was 500 meters in front of the main body. So more idly than otherwise, they sat in ambush and waited for the company to close, as they neared the Song Be. Two VC walked into the ambush within a minute thereafter. At twenty-five meters the front man saw the Americans. He sat down in the trail and began laughing like a fool.

Spec. 4 Alfredo Gonzales walked out to nail him as a POW.

PFC Freddy Williamson yelled, "Look out! He's reaching for a grenade!"

Williamson fired with his Colt .45—and missed.

Sergeant Gonzales killed him with his M-16 and then killed the second man, forty yards farther on, across the Song Be.

A typical incident, illuminating why the taking of prisoners is so difficult in Vietnam, it ended well only because the right soldier was in the swing seat. An odd bird, this one. Gonzales has twice extended his stay in Vietnam. Asked why, he says, "I like hot climates, and I feel sorry for the people of Vietnam." He looks as if he means it.

By 1200 on 9 May, Sill was about eight kilometers to the

southeast of the air strip and Lunde was four kilometers to the southwest. In between them, turning up nothing, were the two scout platoons. Sill was told to swing his formation southwestward toward the Recondo flank. Emerson wanted to get his people closer together as Lunde walked toward the Cambodian border along the spacious trail. These lines of movement were extended through the afternoon without sensation. This peculiar enemy seems to love a vespertinal rest, and though one may not always depend on that, it does condition the American attitude. Men slog on, no less dutiful, but not quite so wary.

"When you are checkerboarding, how do you close the trap?" In midmorning of 10 May, Emerson asked himself the question in dead earnest. He had not faced it before. His grid pattern had never been intended as a battle deployment; its purpose was to find, rather than fix; and, spread out as were his forces, he now sensed that he might have to form fast for a fight, or opportunity would slip through his fingers. Some resources were at hand. Alpha Troop of the 17th Cavalry, now at the air strip, afforded him some reserve. Capt. Ronald Brown, who had been the battalion S 3, was shifted to take charge of the two scout platoons in the center checkerboard and strengthen it with one platoon of Charley Company.

Lunde, on the right, was colliding with enemy soldiers at a great rate—singles, twosomes, more singles, and last five men bunched tight together. These were not patrols, sent to scout Emerson's movement. All were hauled down while going the other way. All had NVA weapons.

The break came when the five-man squad was overrun. Its wounded leader was grabbed before he could wriggle away. A National Police interpreter went to work on him and he sang like a canary.

What he spilled was passed swiftly from Lunde to Emerson and went like this: "Ahead of us, on this same trail, forty minutes' march distance, are four companies in fortified, strongly protected positions. Between them and the Cambodian border are six more companies of the same regiment, the 141st NVA."

So far as the prisoner knew, the positioned NVA battalion did not know Emerson's forces were approaching.

All Emerson could do for the moment was alert Capt. George A. Hamilton, leading the cavalry troop, to prepare for movement.

Captain Brown and his people were entoiled in a bamboo forest. It was not true jungle. Amid the bamboo there were teaks and mahoganys that rose to more than a hundred feet. The growth was festooned with thorn vines and flowering creepers. But the bamboo was the problem. Where it grew straight, it topped off half as high as the big trees. Little of it was that way. It lay mostly in twisted and intertwined tangles, fairly close to the ground, and these clusters were in such profusion that Brown's people were forced frequently to cut back and detour, more than doubling the straight-line distance.

By 1020 Emerson knew it was time to blow the whistle. Going against earthworks defended by a battalion, he would either redeploy to put a force on the enemy rear or put his operation in grave jeopardy.

He called Lunde and said, "Get your people off the trail about fifty meters. Stay well dispersed and hold there. You may send a Recondo element forward to feel things out, but tell them to be careful as hell."

To Sill he gave these instructions: "We must stop bushbeating and concentrate. Gather your company and move north and west as fast as you can travel, prepared to re-enforce."

This went to Brown: "Move northwest and get on Alpha's left flank."

Hamilton's cavalry troop, re-enforced by another platoon of Charley Company, was ordered to march by trail and get on the rear of Alpha Company—seven kilometers distant. Emerson added one precautionary bit of advice: "Go as light as you dare or you'll never make it in time." So they shucked off most of their ammunition, spare canteens and whatever else could be discarded.

Even so, to Lieut. Fowler Goodowens, Hamilton's second, that seemed the hardest march he ever made in his

ife. That "capacious trail" proved to be only seven meters
wide and in places narrowed down so that the wheeled
machine gun they dragged along ripped bark from the trees
on either side. So dense was the canopy above the trail that
they marched all the way in semi-darkness and did not once
see the sky. Fallen trees blocked their way from point to
point, too high to clamber over; the gun had to be manhandled
through the surrounding bush. They passed enemy corpses.
The stench thickened. Maggots and flies were already at
work. Still they could not rush on to fresh air. There was
none, and the column moved on haltingly, at half the pace
men had anticipated.

Emerson called Brown: "Bravo is coming across country.
I don't know where. The critical thing is to get you up as
fast as possible."

Brown was doing his best, though his forces were still
spread out in a checkerboard, there being no way to concentrate them. The platoon of Charley Company was off a full
kilometer to the west and falling behind. The bush in front
of these thirty-one men steadily thickened. Now all hands in
Brown's three platoons had their machetes out and were
hacking their way through; it was faster that way, yet still,
agonizingly slow. In four and one-half hours, slashing the
bamboo all the way, they gained only 3000 meters.

Brown figured he must be almost abreast of Lunde and
was probably somewhere to the west of him. So he called
Lunde, who said, "No, I don't think so. Continue cutting
your way north. You'll know it when you break through into
a big trail. Then turn left toward me."

Lunde had already sent forth his patrol to feel out the
enemy front. It was led by Sgt. José S. Laguama, a
Guamanian, commonly rated as the stoutest-hearted squad
leader in the battalion. The patrol slithered westward
along the trail for another 700 meters. There Laguama
halted. He could hear sounds of digging, the shouting
of men, and the clanging of metal from somewhere
ahead.

These things he reported to Lunde on radio, who passed it
to Emerson.

Emerson said, "Tell him to hold it right there. Don't move one foot. We have pushed our luck far enough."

Laguama did as told.

At exactly 1430, still cutting their way, Brown's point men broke onto a trail and called back to him. The discovery doubled his confusion: the trail did not run east and west. So he sent out two five-man patrols to reconnoiter along it.

Five minutes passed. Then he heard shooting on his left—first a few rifle rounds, then many of them . . . a lull, and a storm of automatic fire. So it seemed to him.

Platoon Sgt. Lawrence Koontz said to him, "I'm going forward, sir. I have to see what it's all about." Brown nodded and Koontz was off running. The rest of the platoon had pulled off the trail and folded within the bush, the men standing, with weapons ready.

Two minutes passed. Then the fire on the left crescendoed. Brown guessed the buildup signaled Koontz's entry into the fray. The man loved to fight and was carrying 480 rounds for his M-16 that day.

Brown grabbed Sgt. Roy Roedel and said, "Let's go for the action."

Roedel replied, "Let's go!"

They ran.

Two hundred meters along, Brown saw two men of the leftward-turning patrol pulled off the trail, flattened amid the bamboo.

He asked, "What's happening?"

One man replied, "We don't know, sir; we were just told to stay off the trail."

Three hundred meters farther along, at the point of fire, Brown found Koontz and Sgt. Henry Schiavoni of Philadelphia, Pa., lying five feet off the trail. Schiavoni was on his back, his chest was bare, and he was bleeding from many wounds.

It had come about this way.

Finding the trail still led in the wrong direction, Schiavoni had dropped part of the patrol, along with most of his equipment, then taking two men, had continued on to scout more of it.

He saw one enemy soldier, ducking behind a bush, range seventy-five meters, and fired. He thought he hit the man: there was no return fire. After waiting a few seconds, he walked on, searched, but couldn't find the body—only a pair of sandals.

As he looked up, a figure moved in the bush, not twenty feet away. Before he could raise his M-16, a bullet exploded into the magazine of his weapon and knocked him flat, while from the jolt of the exploding rounds the M-16 was hurled twenty feet forward.

His first thought was: I must get my weapon back. He did not know how badly he was wounded; he had never been wounded before. So he crawled on to the weapon, to find it wrecked and useless.

Just as he threw it away, he saw another enemy soldier prone, twenty feet away. His uniform blended so perfectly with the bush that only a slight motion betrayed his presence.

He called to Sgt. Willie J. Peppers, who had come to the unit as a replacement only that morning and was in a fight for the first time: "Come on up and cover me, Peppers, so that I can crawl out of here. I'm hit." It annoyed him that he could not remember Peppers' first name.

As Peppers came up, Schiavoni was fumbling with his first-aid packet and didn't notice that Peppers advanced standing, instead of crawling. He knew it only when Peppers leaned over him.

Schiavoni yelled, "Get down! Get down!"

It was already too late. A burst got Peppers in the chest. He spun and fell flat on his back beside Schiavoni. His eyes were wide open and staring, so Schiavoni did not understand the meaning of the fall.

He asked, "You all right? You all right?" then picked up Peppers' M-16 and started firing.

Slowly it dawned on him that Peppers must have been wounded.

He called to his second man, PFC Jerry Ramsey, "Go get a medic. Peppers must be hurt—maybe bad."

Ramsey, twenty meters behind Schiavoni, took time to fire another clip, then ran back along the trail, crying, "Medic!" In the excitement of their forward rush Brown and Roedel missed Ramsey altogether. But Ramsey did find the medic, Spec. 4 George Kirkley, to hustle him forward.

Schiavoni was hugging earth. He was weaponless and alone, and every time he had called, the bush all around him had blazed with fire. It seemed to him that thirty minutes went by, though it was less than ten.

Then he heard Koontz call out for him. Koontz had picked up Sgt. Roy Romans as he came forward. There was a lull in the firing. Schiavoni called to them, "Be careful; they're all around me."

They got to him, crawling on their bellies.

Koontz asked, "Can you crawl out?"

Schiavoni was already started, heading for the rear. He still did not understand that Peppers was dead and had been killed instantly. Koontz and Romans lay there, firing as fast as they could pour the stuff out. By the time Kirkley, meeting Schiavoni on the trail, stopped to bandage him, Koontz was out of action, stopped by a bullet through his thigh.

That's when Brown and Roedel came up. They were greeted by a wave of fire all along their front and from both flanks. Brown took one look at Peppers and knew that he was dead. Brown felt it was time to back away from this thing, if they could, and let Emerson know all about it. Luck was with them. Koontz could crawl, despite the wound. They got away on their bellies.

Hearing the report, Emerson concluded that one enemy company had been intercepted in the act of probing for Brown's rear. And if it was a full company, Brown's strength was so little that Emerson's whole plan was in jeopardy.

Just then came a report from Lunde. Sergeant Laguama's squad, maneuvering in front of Alpha, had "killed two Charleys who had walked into the ambush." Laguama had the enemy weapons.

Lunde said, "Let me charge them! I've got them on my hip. Don't let them get away. Turn me loose!"

Emerson had his "soul-searing moment." He was tempted to let Lunde go on. But what Brown had said cooled him. He could not afford two widely separated actions, though he was reasonably certain that a major force was not being turned against Brown. Besides, the cavalry troop was not yet up to Lunde.

He said to Lunde, "Keep a covering fire to your front for a time but try to back away with most of the company until you can link with Brown." He was sure Brown and Lunde must be somewhere close together.

By this time Emerson was in his Huey above the general scene of action, wishing his eyes could penetrate the canopy and reveal the whereabouts of his several flanks. He had already called for an air strike by the F4C's and been told they were on their way.

He told Brown, "Put out some violet smoke."

Brown said, "I have only green smoke."

From Emerson: "Hell, I can't see that; I'm damn near color-blind."

The green smoke and the green hell were just too much of one color.

But it was an afternoon in which trouble over signals rose almost as high and thickened as promptly as the smoke itself. The cavalry troop was still plodding along through the gloom. Some gunships that Emerson had ordered into action came over, feeling blind for the enemy front forward of Brown. Their rockets—two of them—and their M-60 machine-gun fire broke amid this column which at that moment needed anything but a strafe. The cavalrymen went flat. Bamboo splinters, sharp as javelins, flew in all directions. Six of Hamilton's prone men were slashed, by the wood, not the steel.

Hamilton and his platoon leaders all threw out smoke—on his order. It was green smoke and diffused among the canopies.

"Throw red smoke!" yelled Hamilton.

They did. It wouldn't rise high enough.

Somebody thought of the white phosphorus grenade and heaved one. It made a beautiful plume that in two minutes was standing straight, well above the top canopy. By then the armed Hueys had flown too far beyond to be interested.

By the interruption the cavalry column lost ten minutes. The Hueys had gone on to shower rockets, first 100 meters in front of Brown's position, then closer, so that they broke at thirty meters. The concussion blew some of Brown's people violently back against the nearest bamboo.

The cavalrymen continued on and were shortly on the left of the force that had been attacking Brown. There was no need for them to fire: the enemy had pulled back, probably warned by an outpost of the column's arrival.

The back-pedaling enemy had gone through the woods, not via the trail, which a short distance to the west joined the main trail that Lunde had taken. Lunde and company, retrograding altogether 2000 yards, missed them wholly. By 1800 he was between Hamilton's ground and Brown's. So the forces became joined and it was full dark in the jungle—too late to do anything about it.

Emerson was thinking only of what to do with his forces so that he would have the best possible chance next day.

Lunde was either doing some hard kidding or was sore as a boil. To Emerson, who was back on the ground, he said on radio, "You have cost me my last chance."

Emerson said, "Let's wait and see."

Sill's hard-pushed Bravo Company came up about then; the men were pretty much beat, having marched nine kilometers through the jungle. A bit late, Emerson decided he did not need Bravo as a central reserve. He said to Sill, "Start checkerboarding to the southwest; they might make that same kind of move again, or they might try to get away." So Bravo resumed the march.

Then Emerson gave them all via radio his plan for the next day.

Alpha Company was to fan out, with its center moving west along the trail. The cavalry troop was to go one kilometer straight north through the bush, then turn west so as to get on the enemy rear. Brown would support Lunde during the movement. These things were to start as soon as possible after first light.

The word was passed around: "No lights, no smoking." They sent out their ambush patrols, all of which were to pass a restless and catchless night. Lunde, along with the others, was too weary to fret about what had been; he had tried to make his point while it still might put pressure on Emerson. Now he was ready to accept any rest that might come his way. The jungle dark, a great equalizer, did not withhold all comfort. Worn men could sleep a little, despite the insect pests, knowing the enemy could see no better in the blackness and had no special immunity to the fears, aches and irritants troubling them. The jungle, as somebody said, was the great neutral.

At the time of giving his orders, the Gun Fighter hadn't the foggiest notion whether the enemy battalion within the fortification forward would hold in place while he went through his elaborate, time-consuming maneuver the next day. As had happened more times than not, it might be another strenuous windup for a large letdown. He knew that the enemy knew that he was there; he knew, also, that this enemy was disposed to stand and fight only when convinced that all things were in his favor.

So the Gun Fighter merely hoped and prayed. To have the last word in the argument with Lunde would be good, very, very good.

All the Way

Captain Hamilton and his troop started their flankward march at 0700—if march is the right word for it.

All the way it was trail-blazing with machetes, through as resistant a stretch of the bamboo forest as had baffled Brown and his men the day before.

Hamilton hadn't quite believed Brown's recital of the difficulty. So from the trail he started out with his men in line, thinking that they could wiggle through the bush. They got scattered in the first five minutes; the movement stalled; worse still, the noise of all the machetes hacking hard rang through the forest. So he brought them back to file column, then kept rotating platoons to the front, so as to equalize the strain of the toil among all of his men.

After three hours of cutting and slashing his command lay due north of Lunde's column one kilometer. That it had maintained direction in the trackless bush was due to Emerson's work overhead in a Huey. Every fifteen minutes a white phosphorus grenade would be tossed out by someone on Hamilton's point. Emerson would see the plume, then readjust the movement by azimuth.

By 1000 the cavalrymen were set to attack westward parallel with Alpha Company. Lunde and his people moved on the hour. By 1040 Lunde's forward element was looking at the enemy position. Forward of it twenty meters and pointing along the trail from an independent position were two enemy machine guns. One was so well camouflaged with bushes and trees that the Americans didn't see it.

Lieut. William Otto, eying the other gun, called Lunde on radio to say, "There's a machine gun in front of me; I'll have it for you in a few minutes."

Lunde said, "You play it cool; no gun is that important."

Otto stayed unconvinced. He turned to Lieut. Robert Vaughn to remark, "There are only four companies waiting for us. That ought to take five minutes. Then we'll get to the six companies behind them."

Vaughn remained skeptical. Beyond the guns he could see the tops of a long line of log bunkers, rock-revetted, aligned at the topographical crest of a steep hill, the length of a city block. Both flanks of the position ran down to creek beds. The banks along the front and both ends had been stripped back, leaving almost vertical walls. That bunker line would not even be fazed by small-arms fire. To Vaughn's mind, to assault the hill frontally would be suicidal.

Otto said to his RTO, Spec. 5 Clyde D. Tipton, "Get the word to First and Second Squads to come up here; we'll have a go at them."

The men came forward and formed roughly in line, flattened for firing. They had chosen their general position not too carefully. While they deployed, the enemy weapons stayed silent.

On Otto's order the First Squad, from left of the trail, opened fire. Immediately the enemy machine gun pointing directly down the center of the trail returned it, as did several machine guns from the bunker line.

Tipton said to Otto, "Sir, you better be careful; that fire is awful heavy."

Otto seemed not to hear. He still stood upright. He kept yelling, "Move forward! Move forward!"—this to Sgt. Robert Drake's Second Squad, that on the right side of the trail was echeloned about ten meters to the rear. He called to Drake, "Bring those men up here!"

From directly in front of him, not ten feet away, the

camouflaged gun opened fire. Tipton's first warning of its presence was when he saw the flame pulse from the barrel: he went absolutely flat, his M-16 on the ground. The first burst riddled Otto's chest, and as his body doubled and fell in a heap, the bullet stream kept boring into it.

Tipton called the platoon sergeant, Raymond Soto, and said, "I'm sorry, but the lieutenant is dead."

Soto waited for the bullet stream to lift to some other target, then wormed his way to Otto's body and confirmed the fact of his death. Nothing more could be done about that. Prone, he looked about him. The forward men were much too exposed. Such was the thickness of the bamboo growth about him that to attempt grenading the two guns would most likely result in his own death.

Still covered by Otto's corpse, he yelled to the others, "Get back! Behind the rocks. Or trees. Defilade. But get back!" Some of them, including Tipton, had already taken that precaution.

They were given no time to think over the problem of getting at the two guns. It was 1125 when Lunde passed to Emerson the news of Otto's death. Emerson told him, "Have them keep the heat [the fire] going, but they are not to press; I want to keep casualties down." They were allowed no choice in this matter; nor did Lunde bother to relay the message. He was being hit by a counterattack—estimated at company size—all along his left side. All that the column strung out along the trail knew about it was that plenty of fire—rifle and automatic—was coming out of the bamboo.

Lunde called to Brown, who was farther back along the trail, "They're trying to outflank me. Can you help?"

Brown answered, "I'll go myself."

He took one platoon, cartwheeled with it, enveloped the right flank of the enemy line, and came on firing, once his men had drawn a few rounds from the other side and were certain of the direction. The enemy attack faltered. Brown sensed a withdrawal but did not follow it up. There was too much risk of colliding with Lunde's people up forward. One half hour later came another call from Lunde: "Now they are doing the same thing on my right flank." Brown took the Charley Company platoon, repeated his maneuver in reverse, and again drove the counterattack off without losing a man.

Throughout this time Charley Battery, 2/320th Field, based next the air strip at Bn Gia Map, six kilometers away, had been shelling the northern end of the enemy hill, and several air strikes had been put on the south end. These fires were so laid on as to keep the enemy force heads-down in the bunkers and to block escape routes down the western slope, to the limit possible. Between 1000 and 1300 the 320th battery put 1600 rounds on this one broad target, or roughly ten rounds per minute.

Lunde was working more of his firers up to where they could bear on the bunker line, though so doing was largely a waste of bullets. Over to the north, somewhere, the cavalry troop was still hacking its way westward, and Emerson was becoming increasingly anxious.

He got aloft in his Huey to check firsthand where his pinning force (Lunde's) and his enveloping force (Hamilton's) were positioned with respect to one another. Flying first toward the sounds of the fire fight, he said on radio to Hamilton's RTO, "Use white smoke as you have been doing," then gave this order to Lunde's people: "You put out green smoke."

Now he was almost over Lunde's forward element. Directly ahead of him rose two plumes of smoke within 100 meters of one another—one white, the other green.

His heart rose to his brisket. Aloud he said, "My God, they're about to collide!"

The cavalrymen had complied with the order perfectly. Their signal was standing so far away above the jungle roof that Emerson did not see it. Alpha Company, beset by other problems, had misunderstood. Soto had thrown the white smoke grenade, Vaughn the green.

Emerson told both forces, "Hold everything; don't make a move." At that moment Hamilton and the troop were 1000 meters directly to the north. Lunde replied, "We'd better make a move; I'm running out of ammunition."

Twenty minutes were lost before Emerson, without yet knowing what had happened, got a fix on Hamilton's location. Now, because of Lunde's comment, he was sweating for another reason. He told Hamilton, "Abandon all caution and get on the enemy rear as soon as possible."

More time passed. At 1330 Emerson went aloft once more, flew almost to the enemy hill (the Huey was at 200 feet altitude, just above the treetops) and told Hamilton to use white phosphorus again. This time the plume was on beyond the bunker line and to the right of it. The troop's advance had stayed undetected. The F4Cs, F100s and AIEs (they made altogether eleven stories during the fight) were striking in between the cavalry column and the fortification. It was uncomfortably close. One bomb frag smashed the radio of Lieutenant Goodowens' RTO. One napalm container exploded behind the column, starting a fire that spread swiftly southwest.

Emerson, in his two passes back and forth, could see nothing of the cavalrymen below. The jungle hid them. Yet the plume told him all he needed to know. He said to Hamilton, "You must hook directly south, right now."

They had come to a trail. As they turned south into it, the Second Platoon bestrode the path, with Fourth and Third Platoons a hundred meters on either side of Second, working through the bush. The attached Charley Company platoon stayed as reserve 100 meters to the rear.

Goodowens, in the center, dallied with the main body while sending one squad on to reconnoiter. It moved only twenty meters, the leader returning to say, "I got the information as soon as I moved away from the noise of the column. The enemy position is six hundred yards directly southeast of us. I can hear shooting, yelling and digging."

Goodowens ran forward to have a listen. Then four NVA soldiers, stringing commo wire, with their weapons slung, stepped onto the trail between Goodowens and the squad, who were only twenty meters apart. The surprise was mutual and total. Except that the squad killed two Charleys and wounded the others, who were killed by Goodowens before they could get away.

Knowing this fire would give away the movement, Goodowens called to his men, "We've got to move in and go fast." That was at 1350. They ran on and swiftly deployed in line behind the enemy hill some 200 meters to the rear. Their foreground was littered with the dead and dying and with enemy wounded—and some of the able-bodied—trying to break out and head west. As the platoon closed, the fugitives dropped behind rocks and trees. They were ineffective. Some had arms missing; others dragged along on shattered legs. Human limbs were strewn among the shattered timber. The entire scene was shockingly, revoltingly bloody; such was Goodowens' most awesome impression. Even the broken bamboo seemed to reek of the smell of death.

Knowing nothing of what was happening on the other jaw of the pincers, Lieutenant Vaughn and the men about him who confronted the enemy hill felt the magic, yes, delicious, moment when the cavalrymen faced toward their field of human misery. Suddenly all of the fire that had been turned against them ceased, and the pressure they had known for three hours lifted. It was like a holiday.

Emerson was hearing from Hamilton about the deployment. He shifted the artillery fire to both ends of the hill so there would be no escape in these directions.

PFC Louis Aguila (the one real eagle among the flock of Screaming Eagles) was age nineteen, a Puerto Rican raised in New Jersey. It was his first fire fight, and in his own words, he was feeling "mighty scared." Aguila is a ballplayer, second baseman and catcher.

Minutes before the cavalrymen arrived, his sergeant, Elmo Tacuban, a Hawaiian, had become disgusted because Alpha Company, as he saw it, wasn't contributing anything to the fight.

Tacuban said to his squad, "Let's get in line and let's keep crawling up." So they went. There was so much yelling among the Americans that Aguila, the scared boy, again, according to his own words, "became confused," crawled on too fast beyond the others. He saw "a spray of bullets coming out from under the roots of a tree." This was the artfully camouflaged machine-gun position that had dealt lieutenant Otto's death in the morning. Aguila crawled five meters more and threw a grenade. It struck the tree and glanced off, hitting a rock and bouncing back on him to explode within a few feet of his flattened body. One bit of metal cut his cheek.

Tacuban, right behind him, had yelled, "Hit the ground!" but Aguila was already down by then. He crawled on five more meters. His second grenade was a bull's-eye, straight through the hole in the tree. It destroyed the gun and killed two men of the crew. He was sitting fifteen meters away this time, confident that he was on the mark. Thus was born a new hero.

Four more enemy soldiers jumped out from behind the tree. Sgt. Sidney Oliver, who had just come up, yelled, "Those are mine!" Aguila heard some shots. Oliver worked over to him, rubbing his hands and saying, "Well, I got 'em." The two men crawled on to the machine-gun position in the roots of the tree.

It was then that the fire against them died, owing to the cavalry troop having closed on the enemy rear.

This sense of relief and release was felt wherever Alpha Company men were deployed, farther to the rear, on the flanks, or in the far fringes of the deployment.

Sgt. Willie Harris, Birmingham, Ala., had had his bad moment before it happened. When the artillery had begun spraying the hill, he noted that the enemy fire slackened somewhat, as if its people were crowding toward the cover of the bunkers. But enough bullets buzzed about him that it was difficult to prod his rifle squad forward. Still his men did come along, and that gratified him. They got to ground where they had the enemy hill in sight. To his fore, the point man, Spec. 4 Wayne Trayler, Heflin, Ala., saw a machine gun (not one of the pair that had stopped Otto). It was spraying the Third Platoon front. Trayler called to Harris, saying, "Somebody ought to get that gun." Trayler started forward. A bullet hit him in the side. He was still alive when Harris got up to him, crawling. Trayler was bleeding badly from the nose and mouth.

Trayler kept saying, "Don't stay here, you shouldn't be here; you can't help me." Harris sat there in the open, holding Trayler in his arms, saying, "Take it easy, take it easy," until he felt the body slump and he knew that Trayler was dead. Some instinct had told him that there was no hope for Trayler, but he didn't want him to feel "like a motherless child."

Harris picked up Trayler's M-16 (the battalion had never lost a body or a weapon) and started for the cover of the nearest tree. The enemy machine gunner must have seen him move, since he didn't quite make it. A bullet took off the end of his nose. It felt to Harris "like a right-hand punch from Cassius Clay." He blacked out. Minutes later he recovered consciousness and crawled rearward, carrying two rifles—his own and Trayler's. That was what he had been told to do and he would do it.

PFC Larry Neal was at the extreme left of Lunde's forward deployment. He could see the enemy's main position. He was more concerned with a bamboo thicket twenty meters directly ahead of where he lay. He could hear voices raised within it, the patch being about twenty meters square. The voices sounded as if "someone were telling kids in a school what to do." So he kept firing, convinced that his bullets were not cutting to where they counted. In three hours he fired 270 rounds and told himself disconsolately that he had wasted a lot of ammunition.

PFC Clarence Cubby, on the extreme right flank, fired very little. He is another Negro. The main hill of the enemy was 200 meters away and he "didn't believe in wasting rifle ammunition, for it might be needed later." Cubby was already convinced that the fight was won. Cubby had a good sensing of things.

Pvt. William D. Hines had gone through the whole fight looking in the wrong direction. One of Otto's men, he had been put on special duty guarding the rear of Lunde's CP,

125 yards east of the trail's end. So he sat on his hunkies beneath a big tree, facing back the way they had come and feeling foolish about it. On hearing that morning that Otto was dead, he had said, "I don't believe it." Now he crawled forward to see for himself; he was certain the report had been a mistake and that Otto would be the first to welcome him.

When the fire died along Lunde's front, Emerson still, though he knew of it, did not order him on. Lunde was told: "Stay where you are." The cavalry troop in rear of the hill had all the advantage of surprise and position; one determined enemy survivor with one automatic weapon, on the other hand, might deal a doleful anticlimax to Lunde's men from out of the ruins if they moved into the clear space forward of the bunkers. Emerson had made up his mind that, with the fight already won, the thing had to be finished without risking further loss to any of his forces.

Such battle honor as attends any mop-up on a stricken field therefore fell to Hamilton and his men. They closed on the smashed bunker line after they had ended such resistance as the few derelicts facing them were able to put up. It was an expert disposal of a frenzied, unrelenting opposition. Not one of Hamilton's soldiers was even scratched; and not one NVA soldier indicated by any sign a desire to surrender. Fighting to the last man, they were killed that way.

One hundred and six enemy bodies were counted in the open. How many other bodies were entombed under the shattered walls and roofs of the hilltop bunker line is beyond saying or estimate. The victors had no wish to delve and dig for the sake of such meaningless statistics. Emerson, Lunde and the others were well aware that the war in Vietnam is so little understood by their countrymen that the relative death rate of the two sides is given wholly disproportionate emphasis and inflates the permissible puffery of the outfit that has done extremely well. For once they might be able to convince the home folk that they had gotten the best of it by a measure of twenty to one; and why bother about that? For much the same reason their capture of enemy arms and ammunition is beneath the dignity of this report, though the hard figures are at hand.

Emerson's companies checkerboarded westward for the next several days toward the Cambodian border, searching for the six companies of the NVA 141st Regiment that the wounded POW had said would be there. These they did not find, though from the enemy hill they did track after a rash of blood trails, most of which ran northwest. The country through which they traveled now was much lower and more open. The heat was not more, yet their energy was markedly less. They were in their thirteenth day of continuous movement afield. They had been that long without a hot meal or a night of unbroken sleep. Their twills, mud-caked and ragged, were foully damp; many wore jungle boots that had been laid open by the thorned vines and pungi sticks. That the big excitement lay behind them did not make the almost fruitless aftermath any easier to take. A few Viet Cong walked into their ambushes night after night and were killed for being careless. Still nothing that they found justified the expenditure in energy or the hardship. Emerson would have called it off had not the possibility of overtaking the rest of 141st Regiment beyond the next river tantalized him like a mirage.

On 13 May at 0100 the B-52s from Guam put on a strike ahead of their line of march, at Emerson's request. It was a precaution taken because they were approaching the Cambodian border; whether the bombs accomplished anything worth doing, no one later knew.

Next day at 1840 they got to the frontier. With them was an NVA soldier, who had been captured that noon. Much of his lower jaw was shot away; a piece of artillery shell had done that to him as he fought on the hill that they had taken. They doctored him. To their amazement, he could still talk and, moreover, was anxious to tell them what the defenders had been through.

He said that of the original battalion of 450 men about fifty remained alive and reasonably whole-bodied. They had quit the fight before the artillery and rocket ships had sealed in the other men. He was sure that by now these survivors had found sanctuary in Cambodia.

Prisoners of war, much of the time, are self-serving liars, prone to say what they think the captor wishes to hear. This one, with the beat-up jaw, ran on true to form. So they paid him not too much heed.

Later in the evening one of their ambushes caught three more runaways from the same battalion. Under interrogation they said much the same thing as the first POW.

By then they were almost ready to believe.

The Fishing Expedition

On 10 May, as Colonel Emerson buckled to his task around Bn Gia Map, another expedition, built out of scratch forces, was loosed on a sweep toward the Cambodian border.

Though there was less fighting by Task Force Walker in Operation Paul Revere than by the First Cavalry Division or the First Brigade of the 101st Division in those weeks of early summer, in the TF's prolonged maneuvering lay the key to General Westmoreland's strategy. Unless its role and purpose are understood, the big picture of operations in the Central Highlands as the 1966 southwest monsoon began remains incomplete.

In the 1965 summer monsoon the main NVA threat had come from that quarter; Pleiku and Kontum had been saved, though the fight to stave off disaster had been a cliff hanger all the way.

Westmoreland now had enough U.S. Army combat strength at hand to be fully confident that nothing of that sort would happen again. But it was still insufficient to piece out a deployment-in-strength to maintain continuous screening of the Laos-Cambodian border.

The next best thing—the essential in his over-all planning— was a relatively light, mobile screen that by frequent shifting of its hitting forces would keep the enemy off balance.

Intelligence continued to report the presence of a great part of six to seven NVA regiments stacked up across the border in Cambodia, though Prince Sihanouk continued bitterly to protest that the enemy had no sanctuary in his domain. Provided these forces could be held in check, or their movement east reduced to a trickle, the NVA and VC units east of the Kontum-Pleiku line would be dealt a rough summer.

In his estimate of the enemy Westmoreland neither underrated his elements of strength nor overlooked his main point of weakness. His appreciation of how the North Vietnamese Army operated went something like this after one year of being at grips with the problem:

1. At the tactical level this opponent is a capable planner who organizes offensive operations in four successive steps.

2. The plan itself will always accent deception or the staging of an entrapment.

3. His intelligence stems primarily from comprehensive reconnaissance of the chosen battleground and forces adjacent to it.

4. He will usually prepare the battlefield, moving up and caching ammunition and other supply; while that goes on, the hitting forces rehearse the attack, using sand tables, mockups and similar ground in the training exercise.

5. If while that preparation goes on, as a result of counter intelligence, his over-all maneuver can be divined, parried and blocked, he will have to start all over again.

6. Because of his set-piece approach to operations, he is hurt far more by spoiling attacks than is an average, conventional opponent in war.

By this line of reasoning Westmoreland had arrived at a concept of how to fight the war that was the direct opposite of the proposal that U.S. forces should adopt an essentially defensive posture within coastal enclaves. The deployment of a relatively small task force to engage in continuous sparring along the Cambodian border logically derived from the concept.

Operation Paul Revere was under an uncommonly able commander, Brig. Gen. Glenn Walker, born in Rapides

Parish, La., a 1939 graduate of Mississippi College. Alone among the commanders who appear in this chronicle, Walker could be described as a traditional infantry type. He is tall, spare, quiet of speech and seemingly proof against any kind of jar from the outside. No man ever wasted fewer words or expressed himself with greater clarity and conciseness.

Walker and his troops took unto themselves the safeguarding of a zone eighty kilometers wide by half that in depth to the west of Pleiku. The zone ran southwest to the Chu Pong Mountains and northwest as far as the outpost of Duc Co, and the eastern border was on a line with Plei Me. They were to keep watch especially on the Ia Drang River Valley, an invasion route that had figured prominently in the first full-length campaign of the First Cavalry Division in November, 1965.

To begin, the force was composed of three infantry battalions from the 25th Division (Walker's own organization), one company of medium armor, one armored cavalry troop, one air cavalry troop, one battalion of 105 mm artillery, one battery of 175s, one battery of 155s and one battery of 8-inchers. Here was far more gun power than was given any other operation in the Central Highlands.

Where to base was the first question. Plei Me, otherwise suitable, was knocked out by Walker because the roads round about are fifth-rate and its air strip is inadequate. Duc Co, though served by a satisfactory air field, was rejected because of its location in the extreme northwest, eleven kilometers from the Cambodian border.

Walker picked an abandoned base twenty-five kilometers west of Pleiku which the Americans had named Oasis. The First Cavalry Division had put in an air strip there in late 1965; it had fallen into disrepair, the neighboring Montagnards having stripped the membrane from its surface for use in weatherproofing their huts. But to Walker's eye it looked good. Oasis was on high ground, well sloped for quick drainage. Water was plentiful. Roads were serviceable. There was more than enough room on the high ground to afford storage for all requirements, and Walker planned to keep at least 600 tons of ammunition ever on hand.

His first step was to secure the area to the eastward. One infantry battalion was lifted to a point ten kilometers to the northwest of Plei Me, another to the southwest of it the same distance. They beat out the bush as they swept straight westward to a line even with Oasis, thus clearing Walker's rear of Viet Cong. As they continued on, a central column moved directly west from Oasis, within it being one troop of armored cavalry, one platoon of medium tanks and one company of infantry. The riflemen went cross-country in the armored personnel carrier M-113, which was ideally suited to the terrain that had to be crossed. The three columns, advancing west on parallel lines, would continue to move abreast. The central column, having much more mobility than the others, would be able to assist either flank, in case of need. The troop of air cavalry was sent to work over the twenty kilometers of Cambodian border that lay to the south of their operating zone and beyond their reach.

The operating method was conventional—at least it was not more unconventional than the U.S. Army way of going elsewhere in the Central Highlands. However, the tactical pattern to which Walker adhered and his reasoning in support of it were markedly at variance with the operations of the cavalry division and Pearson's brigade. It is the difference between the several approaches that makes Operation Nathan Hale of interest chiefly to tacticians.

In screening, Walker believes in saturating every area with patrols. The patrols stay out all night, every night, working from a battalion base, which always keeps to itself one rifle company, one artillery battery and the battalion headquarters, with part of the time a reconnaissance platoon.

Ahead of the battalion base there are set up two rifle company bases; one would be armed with 4.2 mortars, within reach of the second base. Both perimeters would be within range of the 105 mm battery, which stricture would still enable the guns to fire over a twenty-kilometer circle.

Thus maximum attention is given to so situating both battalion and company positions that they can be supported by the heaviest weapons while mutually supporting one another. There is certainly nothing unusual about such an aim. Nothing could be better, provided that the terrain is accommodating. Where Walker's tactical pattern was in marked contrast to the others was that his smallest deployments were more daring while his larger ones were more conservative.

His surveillance parties, operating in detachment from main bodies, were fire-team size—five men. Through the use of such small packets one of his rifle battalions could coordinate screening across a twenty-kilometer front. That stretched the battalion's radio reach to the limit, without exceeding it.

His theory of larger deployments is best put in his own words.

"I figure one U.S. rifle company, when backed up by the artillery we have, can stand off a VC or NVA battalion any time," he said. "If we move the rifle company too late, or put it so far away that it cannot be supported by the guns, then the supply problem can whip us. Such a risk can only be offset by getting in a lot of claymore mines, with defensive wire, and getting everybody to dig deep.

"As for a platoon, you cannot shore it up by itself, even with the use of artillery. The position is too small, the front too narrow. If hit by a larger force—or hit with surprise by another platoon on flank or rear—it practically has to move. Then getting in artillery to help it becomes a large problem.

"Finally, I figure that we can operate in rugged terrain better than the VC or NVA. This, I know. As individuals, we are bigger, stronger, healthier, and less inclined to do stupid things."

In the southwest sector of the zone that Walker's forces worked over during the first two weeks, the country is lower and flatter than elsewhere in the Central Highlands, being under 800 feet above sea level. The average rainfall in May is eleven inches. The May, 1966, monsoon blew in twenty-two inches, the most generous sprinkle of record. The land became a bog. No road stayed trafficable. Flats became lakes and creeks turned into rivers. Helicopters could not take the air until 1100, so consistently were the LZs socked-in morning after morning. When the medium armor backed away before it became ditched wholly, the central column was withdrawn to Oasis.

That left the two infantry battalions in line, the 1/35th screening in the south and the 1/14th screening in the north. Walker had held back 2/35th at Oasis as his reserve reaction force. During daylight hours the battalion screened to the north and northeast to further base security. As a rule, Task Force Walker leaves a stay-behind unit on each LZ when moving a column in either direction. It is the habit of the Viet Cong to throng back to an LZ when a seeming evacuation has taken place; they make the same mistakes over and again. Both the VC and the NVA in the Oasis region are given to the use of Montagnards as slave laborers. Some of the mountain men are guerrilla-oriented and go along willingly enough. The greater numbers are simply press-ganged.

The surveillance line run by the 1/14th in the north reached the Cambodian border on 15 May. It had not proved highly profitable. A few small packs of Viet Cong had been rubbed out. But most of the time the walk was a waste of matériel, energy and patience. Then when the weather turned sour, Walker pulled the column back to Oasis.

Alone, the column of 1/35th continued to plug westward. By the evening of 28 May its most forward element, Bravo Company, was ten kilometers to the west of Duc Co. The rest of the battalion was in perimeter near the outpost's air base.

Just before sunset Battalion got a call for help from Bravo Company but couldn't answer. The battalion had come under attack all around the perimeter just before the call came through.

Walker got Alpha, 2/35th, loaded on Hueys at Oasis to respond to the fire alarm. Maj. Wallace S. Tyson, the battalion executive officer, went along to take command during the emergency.

Though the emergency, while it lasted, was real enough, at the cost of much blood and sweat to Bravo Company, and to Alpha that served as the fire brigade, it generated the only ludicrous exchange in General Walker's running bout with the monsoon weather, all along billed as the natural ally of the elusive enemy.

Particularly because of the weather, Walker's tactics had been methodically prudent. And at last, because of this weather, his only remaining spearhead was about to win the daily double for him by being almost extravagantly careless. In truth, Bravo Company had been punching in air too long to continue keeping its guard covering its button.

So without prior reconnaissance it took a Huey hop westward to what had once been a U.S. air strip and was still designated as LZ Ten Alpha. The clouds grew bigger and the rain beat down harder as Bravo's choppers splashed to earth. The strip was under six inches of water. In the gun pits around the field the flood was more than a foot deep. And the guns were there, five of them, five 12.7's, set to clean the skies of just such birds as these.

Bravo had flown into the perfect deadfall—perfect, except for the absence of people. The NVA crews had quit their guns to get out of the wet. Bravo's people hopped to the guns and went into perimeter around the air strip.

That night the company was hit hard by a battalion of North Vietnamese, the same battalion that had been caught flat-footed by the arrival of Bravo in impossible weather and was now making a desperate bid to recover its guns. The fight raged through the night of 29 May and with the aid of the other battalion of 35th flown from Oasis ended as a smash victory for TF Walker. It was not easy; the influx of 35th casualties taxed the capacity of the base hospital at Qui Nhon.

The fight paid off in more than enough ways to offset its costs. Here was a prime example of stupidity and military slackness in an enemy whose military character is too frequently overrated. It made less painful the brooding within the American camp over our own blunders. Let it never again be said by historians that only the Chinese of yore had an army of such soluble stuff that it would quit the field rather than stand against a sod-soaker.

Coupled with Emerson's success at Bn Gia Map, the Ten Alpha affair drew the strategic gaze increasingly toward the possibilities of the troubled zone short of the Cambodian border. Quite apart from the desire to plug the hole-in-the-wall, there were reasons for this turning. The American military in Vietnam are deeply conscious that the presence of large U.S. troop bodies near main population centers in Vietnam creates frictions and is blamed for pricing consumer goods almost beyond reach of the average Vietnamese family. Some commanders argue that the mass of U.S. Army strength would be better off concentrated toward the western frontier, for this, if no other, reason. Very few Vietnamese stray west of the Pleiku-Kontum line. Were it not for Montagnards, that belt would be unpeopled.

Several more battalions were brigaded with the Oasis force as June opened. General Westmoreland tentatively scheduled a main effort by major forces in that area, to be known as Operation Hooker One, but called it off when an unexpected opportunity opened a few miles inland from the east coast port of Tuy Hoa, which blossomed as Operation Nathan Hale.

Not a few of Westmoreland's subordinates favored making the western Central Highlands, meaning Pleiku, Kontum and beyond, the area of principal U.S. concentration. Hardly any Vietnamese live there; but for the Montagnards it would be practically unpopulated. Nothing was more certain than that, as the war continued, the region would increasingly command the attention of the American planners and strategists, and Paul Revere would ride again.

So it happened that, following my return to the United States and during the month of August, General Jack Norton and the main body of the First Cavalry Division fought a main battle in the extreme far west of the Central Highlands which is remarkable for many more reasons than that it failed to capture any major headlines in the United States.

For months the division had been campaigning on ground much closer to the great base at An Khe. On the Bon Song plain next to the sea, in the foothills inland from the port of Tuy Hoa and among the high mountains directly northeast of Camp Radcliff, its brigades had taken on major forces of the enemy to exterminate the larger fractions and drive the rest from the field.

Then, as August opened, the great body of the division was lifted and committed more than sixty miles to the westward, beyond Plei Me and next to the Cambodian border, in a countryside dominated by rugged peaks, covered with dense jungle and rain forest, and running numerous streams. The switch of scene and action was accomplished in less than twelve hours. For speed and distance, there is no mass movement of troops to compare with it in history.

In this way was begun Operation Paul Revere Two, a show that lasted through the month. Before the end, fourteen battalions, six of them his own, had been fed into the battle lines by Norton.

The statistics of this campaign are amazing; it was the real whopper of the summer. The actual body count of enemy dead was 861, which under the conditions of the jungle warfare, with the enemy risking fanatically to extract his slain, betokens that probably twice that number was destroyed. Two hundred and two prisoners were captured, as were more than three hundred weapons, many of them crew-served. Confirmed as engaging on the other side were nine North Vietnamese battalions, which for brevity's sake will not be listed in this account, though I have the numbers at hand.

So we have here in aggregate a battle much larger than San Juan Hill and El Caney put together in the size of forces engaged, bigger and more impressive than Pork Chop Hill by any measure one chooses to use, and lasting as long as Belleau Wood.

And of these dimensions the nation heard and read almost nothing. Those who little noted, if at all, were entitled to the notion that the cavalrymen seemed to be off on another wild goose chase into the boonies which might result in some slight shedding of blood.

The Relief of Toumorong

On 17 May, in early morning, a mortar round exploded within a pen at an insignificant outpost in the western Central Highlands and killed several chickens.

The name of the place is Toumorong. Thereafter, for the next several days, more mortar rounds were lobbed casually toward the same target, some hitting the bunkers, others breaking outside the wire barricades, with none doing any direct hurt to humanity.

The daily reports still were ominous enough to add to the sufficient worries of at least two generals of note.

One was Maj. Gen. Vinh Loc, the Vietnamese commander of the II Corps Zone. Of royal blood (Vinh means Prince), age forty and something of a poet, Loc communicates even when his mouth stays closed. No one living has a more mobile face; his every thought is to be read there. Loc's headquarters is at Pleiku. From there a chopper can get to Toumorong in less than one-half hour.

The other was Maj. Gen. H. W. O. Kinnard, who had taken over as American commander in the II Corps Zone while Maj. Gen. "Swede" Larsen was on a thirty-day holiday in the United States.

Though the two opposite numbers were thinking along parallel lines, for several days both remained unaware of it.

Kinnard, who at Nha Trang was much farther away from the scene, had first taken note of the outpost when reading a report on 22 May. It said that three *ralliers,* who had surrendered at Dak To, were certain that an all-out enemy attack was brewing against either that hamlet or against Toumorong. Kinnard, however, was far from certain that Loc would go along with his idea of what had to be done.

So on 28 May a full-dress conference was held at Kontum. In attendance were Kinnard and Loc, Brig. Gen. Willard Pearson, Commander of First Brigade, 101st Division, Colonel Phouc, commander of the Kontum special military district, and Lieut. Col. Donald A. Seibert, his U.S. adviser.

Kinnard opened the discussion by saying that, as he saw it, continuing with Toumorong was "like hanging bait on the end of a limb."

Phouc said he thought that the threat against the outpost was "very real indeed. The mortars are getting closer every hour. They are right at the gate of the outpost."

Loc laughed at him and said, "Nonsense."

Kinnard then discussed the situation in general terms. According to the intelligence estimates the 24th and 88th Viet Cong regiments were thought to be somewhere in the Toumorong area. As for enemy intentions, the light attack then in progress against the outpost was the only indication, and it could be a feint.

He then asked Loc the blunt question, "Is Toumorong important to you?"

The grin on Loc's face was a sufficient answer, but he punctuated it with these words in English: "I couldn't care less, and frankly, I would rather not have that worry on my mind during the monsoon season."

Then Colonel Patch, Loc's U.S. adviser, spoke up, "To abandon Toumorong might have a bad psychological effect both in Vietnam and in the United States."

Said Kinnard, "It will be worse if we lose it."

The debate continued along these lines, though since it is clear that the two voices that really counted were as one, and the decision would go that way, the remainder of the conference notes can be dispensed with, the better to take a close-up view of the object under discussion.

Toumorong outpost is spectacularly set above the world, and were it not for the ugly bunkers and concertinas scattered about, would be the perfect retreat for anyone trying to escape its cares.

It is a summit, set not so much on top the clouds as within them. From the brim of Toumorong, on the natural flat top of this elevation with a name that delights the Western ear, one could look down to the silver lines where creeks threaded the several valleys; or one could try to follow the red trace where a dirt road corkscrewed up the eastern face of the mountain to enter the outpost, there to be lost to sight a few yards beyond the wire barricade where it dropped to the next valley. The road itself counted for little; it was there only to service the outpost.

In all directions high mountain ranges of an ever-brightening green defined Toumorong's horizon, and nothing short of that far distance, be it a trail crossing, a creek bed, or a Montagnard village built around a Happy House, could be called safe. Except for the outpost, everything was enemy country, which fact left the people of the outpost guarding nothing really important except their own lives. They were maintained through air resupply.

About their extreme isolation they did not complain; nor were they particularly harassed by the sniper and mortar fire that day by day through mid-May came closer as the enemy weapons moved slowly up the tree-covered slope of the mountain's northern face. The more precipitate eastern slope was peculiarly barren of jungle growth. The northern slope they thought they could handle. Either the VC coming up the slope were markedly reluctant to come to grips or the occasional air strikes against the northern slope were doing better than anyone knew. It was no siege. The pace of life atop the mountain was normal. Babies were born. Patrols went forth. The women kept the place policed.

But tactical doubts and issues aside, the Toumorong garrison with its fighters, camp followers, children and supernumeraries counted more than 150 bodies that together constituted a stake that Generals Kinnard and Vinh Loc were equally loath to forfeit.

Concern for humanity—yes, that was part of it, though not all. There was the still larger consideration, call it prestige, the psychological factor, or the importance of propaganda impact in wartime. Five outposts, of more consequence than Toumorong, had been dramatically over-run by the enemy during the 1965 monsoon, and with that the cry arose that the war was almost lost. No one wanted any such thing again. What should be held would be held. But it would be plain foolhardy to cling tenaciously to any position that had no real strategic value and in the end might become lost anyway from lack of tactical leverage. No outpost was of practical value as a baited hook unless its re-enforcement could be swift and sure. Toumorong was too often closed in by weather to qualify.

Kinnard and Vinh Loc were mutually surprised that they had no basis for argument, being of one mind. Their decision made, there remained only the details of how and when to bring off the relief of Toumorong, which problem, though calling for solution at the earliest moment, was not to be worked out at their level. Kinnard had already talked over the problem with General Westmoreland, who readily approved abandoning the position.

That evening the American half of the task of evacuating the Trongson (local militia) force from Toumorong, and trying to strike a few blows against the Viet Cong of the countryside while so doing, was confided to General Pearson and his brigade, then based in main at Cheo Reo. Colonel Phouc and his staff would work out the plan for the commitment of ARVN forces. Pearson's orders read simply that he was to move into northern Kontum Province and proceed to relieve the Toumorong garrison. He picked Dak To for his base because it was the one place closest to the heart of the countryside to be worked over and would therefore cut down time for all aircraft and ease the logistical strain.

Colonel Phouc and his retinue followed Pearson to Dak To, one of the outposts that had been overrun in 1965.

Together they established a joint headquarters, and ultimately the order was published by the Special Tactical Zone (Phouc's organization), though most of the concept and plan were of Pearson's doing. There is a minor footnote on how these things are done in Vietnam. They start with a joint flag-raising ceremony, Americans raising the yellow and red of Vietnam, the Vietnamese lofting the red, white and blue. But there are no speeches.

Pearson thought big. He proposed sending more than four battalions of infantry, supported by two batteries of artillery, forth to "rescue" one half-trained company of homeguard that was not pressed by any present and palpable peril. The battalions would start far apart and sweep from four corners toward Toumorong. Only one would be American, the 2/327th of Pearson's brigade. The ARVN 2/42nd and one C.I.D.G. company would move from the southwest. The ARVN Ranger 2/21st would be carried by choppers to a landing zone ten kilometers northwest of the outpost and would sweep south from there. Another company of C.I.D.G. and one company of the ARVN 403rd would march north, starting from the hamlet of Tan Cann.

As a plan to relieve Toumorong, this was like rolling out the railway artillery to shoot at a clay pigeon, as everyone well understood. The evacuation of the garrison was only a convenient excuse for beating out the wilderness all around it in a guerrilla hunt. Colonel Phouc altogether favored the scheme, though much of the burden of the plan called "Operation Hawthorne One" was on his forces.

They jumped off 3 June on what was reckoned to be a three-day sweep toward the common goal, which would terminate when the garrison marched out, unless one of the columns bumped against major force in converging toward the others. That was their highest hope, and as time wore on, and they got closer together, it was dashed. By midafternoon on 5 June—a Saturday—the whole thing had turned sour. Theirs had been a particularly bloodless outing. Maj. David H. Hackworth's battalion of the 327th was bumping the base of the mountain and about to climb to the outpost. It had drawn a blank. The ARVN Ranger Battalion was on its last hill, where it could be covered by the fires of Bravo Battery 1/30th Artillery. Its score was zero. The column of the 403rd ARVN, with the C.I.D.G. company coming after, had reached its destination in the north, and its bag was empty. The column of Montagnards atop Toumorong had its bags packed in preparation for departure.

Then a funny thing happened to the column of the ARVN 42nd on its way to the four of them. The hour was about 1630, and it would not be dark until around 1930. The day was fair, the dirt road they traveled was solid underfoot. Another 3,000 meters farther on lay their destination, the last hill where the guns could cover them, well within reach. The battalion approached a three-pronged ridge, no part of which rose more than twenty meters above the valley floor. That was on its right hand. The closest and farthest prongs nosed right down to the shoulder of the road; the center prong fell thirty meters short of it. At the other end of this ridge front there was a bridge where the road passed over a small creek, the Dak Djram, before turning northeast to continue along the valley floor.

To any unseen viewer from atop the ridge, taking note of both the column and the clock, it would have seemed a normal expectation that at this hour the battalion would keep marching, cross the creek, turn the ridge and continue up the valley. The ridge was not a practical position for night defense. There was some small bush and tree cover around its stubby ends and along the western base where the creek wound. Otherwise it was remarkably barren of bush, tree growth, or rock cover.

The battalion did nothing of the kind. It marched up the nose of the nearest prong and prepared to bivouac along the crest, thereby conforming to plan.

At the base camp in Dak To there was hasty preparation for a movement no less unexpected by those who witnessed it. General Pearson was having last-minute doubts about the security of Hackworth's battalion (1/327th) which was getting ready a perimeter for night defense near the base of Toumorong mountain. Landing Zone Jenny, as the position was called, could not be covered by fires by any of the guns already within the area. Pearson did not want the battalion to be that vulnerable on the night prior to its link-up with the people in the outpost.

At 1600 Bravo Battery, 2/30th Artillery, under command of Capt. Donald P. Whalen, a very young gunner with a professional look and manner, was alerted to move north at once to support Hackworth. Whalen hoped that he could get into LZ Jenny, possibly to help the battalion with point-blank fires (on which subject he was shortly to become an expert). But a quick reconnaissance by Huey showed that Jenny was too small and, at that moment, too muddy, to accommodate artillery. On the ride back in the Huey, Whalen saw what looked like the right spot for his guns. Right next Dak Djram creek five kilometers southwest of Toumorong was a gently rising and open shelf, so evenly graded that when seen from the air it looked flat. The peak of Hill 872 lay directly north, dominating it. Whalen picked it personally, and it was pure accident that the place of his choice was just around the ridge from where the ARVNs had turned off the road in preparation for bivouac. His guns would be within 300 meters of the bridge. But he did not see the ARVN battalion when he flew over; and they had not been informed of his coming.

No trouble whatever was expected where this accidental convergence was about to take place. An otherwise flat countryside with clear fields, it was considered well removed from the rugged highlands where the enemy had been hunted unsuccessfully. But where guns are deployed, and in particular where they are approachable from any angle, it is considered the better part of valor to send along infantry to cover and comfort them. While Whalen had been off on his reconnaissance, Capt. W. Ronald Brown had been told to alert Alpha Company, 2/502nd, for "quick movement to an LZ somewhere to secure a seat for an artillery battery." The man and the unit having been met before in this chronicle, there is no need to extoll either. Brown has a face like an English bulldog and is as warmly congenial as any citizen I know. The unit had many new faces since Bn Gia Map. By now they were all old hands at fighting guerrillas; they had done it for all of ten days, or played at doing it, which was enough to make them members of the club.

Twenty minutes after the alert, Brown had 170 men on the air strip at Dak To ready to go. They carried 500 rounds of M-16 ammunition each, one fragmentation grenade and one smoke grenade apiece, and 1200 rounds only for six M-60 machine guns. There were also with the company twenty-one M-79 grenade launchers, with thirty rounds per weapon. All in all, it was a somewhat unbalanced load, contrived in haste.

They were given fifteen Hueys, and ninety men flew north to the gentle slope alongside the creek on the first lift. So speedy was the take-off that no one had thought to pick a name for the LZ, so it was redundantly called LZ Lima Zulu. Whalen, who was meeting Brown for the first time, asked that he and his RTO be allowed to go in on the first of the Hueys, which was all right with Brown, who needed to be sure of hitting the right spot.

Men out of the first five Hueys to touch down dashed off to start the expanding circle to secure the general area. It was SOP; there had been no report of any violence close at hand. The landings had been made on a flat, red-clay trail running at a right angle into the road. It looked as innocent as a Central Park bridle path. Six pungi stick pits were spaced evenly under its surface and the clay covering was not less even. Running men fell into three of these traps. They arose unhurt. The traps were old. The sticks were rotten. It was reason to think the Viet Cong had lost interest in these parts. Squads from the first five Hueys formed the arc at 1200. Men from the second five filled in at 1500, and they kept going that way until the circle was complete.

Brown next sent two squads 200 meters farther upgrade beyond the LZ and toward Hill 872 where they were pretty much on line with the one platoon that deployed to secure the battery site next the roadway. Their function was to wait in readiness to provide a covering fire when the Chinooks came in carrying the artillery. This done, he sent another squad eastward: it would cross the road and the creek and go on 200 meters to the top of the small ridge directly confronting the landing zone. Its task was observation with a special instruction to "look for the ARVN battalion." Brown had heard about the ARVN's presence just before leaving Dak To and was told that the battalion would "throw out yellow smoke" to mark its location. But he had seen no yellow smoke when his Huey came over.

With the dispatch of this squad things began to slip a little. Brown thought of it as a simple reconnaissance, with no real combat implications. The ARVN battalion was, in fact, on the far projection of this same ridge, less than 600 meters distant, and at the moment was being hotly engaged. Of this Brown was getting no word, and the incessant roar from the rotors of the Hueys, followed by the Chinooks, landing and leaving, drowned out all sounds of the fire.

Whalen was standing by to receive his guns. There were four Chinooks and it took thirteen sorties to move the whole battery—tubes, men and 860 rounds of ammunition. Whalen was not thinking of how the battery might have to serve Brown or the ARVN battalion. Providing them with supporting fires was the task of Bravo of the 1/30th, lower down in the valley.

The gunner captain's jeep and command trailer arrived on the first Chinook. That enabled him to make a quick recon of the hamlet just beyond the battery site. With the second Chinook came Sgt. Charles Loveland and the advance party, followed at once by the delivery of the base piece, the point piece and a sling with enough ammunition to start a registration fire in support of Hackworth's distant battalion. Within five minutes the first guns were set and throwing shells in that direction. Whalen was paying no attention to Brown and his problems. With Brown was a forward observer, Lieut. Harvey Snowden, of Bravo 1/30th, and he was supposed to take care of local force needs.

In these same minutes Brown's attention became turned just as radically in the other direction, away from the simple mission of securing the battery site.

There came a sudden call from the ARVN commander of 1/42nd Regiment. The message was about like this: "We are under heavy mortar attack. There are at least two 81s firing on us. They are so close to us that we can hear the rounds going down the tubes.''

He concluded by giving the coordinates of his position.

Colonel Emerson was monitoring this conversation from the base camp at Dak To. The information shocked him. He asked himself, ''What is the minimum range of an eighty-one?'' but could not remember. Then he said to Brown, ''It sounds like they're in trouble.'' (This was on the RT.)

Said Brown, ''Yes, but how much trouble?''

Said Emerson, ''Anyway, you better try to help them.''

Brown got on radio to Lieut. James E. Tucker, American adviser to the ARVN battalion, asking, ''What's your situation, your disposition?''

Tucker said, ''I think we're engaged with a VC battalion from directly in front of our position.''

This was Brown's first warning of an infantry fight going on right next door. The words as given conveyed the impression that the battalion, while on the road, had run into an ambush, become stopped, was forced to deploy, and was fighting back. And that impression was totally wrong. Coloring the whole fight, and influencing the course of operations for the next week, it came of the fault that on neither end was sufficient information passed along. It was a glaring failure in communications.

The ARVN battalion had, in fact, made its bivouac on top of the first ridge prong, and for more than one hour the camp had stayed unmolested. Then at 1800 it was attacked from *the rear of the ridge* by an enemy force estimated at two companies. This fight was still going on when Tucker talked to Brown. It cost the battalion four dead and nineteen wounded. Nineteen enemy bodies were strewn around outside the ARVN perimeter when the close-joined fight quieted, and six more were found later buried in a shallow grave.

But little or none of the details of this small picture came through then to Brown or was passed along later to the brigade. Had it been done, intelligence and the command could hardly have failed to reach wholly different conclusions about what the event signified as to major enemy force being present between the small ridge and Toumorong.

Tucker said last to Brown, "Those rounds are coming in about eight per minute; our main concern is for you to get the mortar."

Brown said he would see what he could do.

Brown did not send a platoon to re-enforce the squad on the ridge back, though the mortar almost had to be somewhere in the median just beyond that prong.

Whalen did not turn his guns around to support whatever Brown saw fit to do; he kept firing north.

Neither the Americans nor the Vietnamese sent out liaison patrols via the wide, relatively bare and obviously unpeopled valley so that they might get the feel of each other's situation.

Yet there was no interdicting force in the way, daylight still lasted, and there was nothing to hold them back, except the failure to think about it.

A Piece of the Action

The Chinooks bearing the last half of Whalen's battery came in under fire.

There were bullets buzzing around the LZ and no one knew from where. A dozen rounds or so greeted each ship. They did more good than harm, giving the crews something to write home about.

The three last guns to close—they were M-102s, a new howitzer for air-borne artillery—were first pointed at the ridge just over the creek, Brown having told Whalen that there was trouble somewhere beyond it. But getting no order to fire, or request for same, Whalen repointed the pieces toward Toumorong. Once again, things had slipped a bit.

At the corner where the red-dirt track bounding the landing zone met the road there lay a handsome rosewood log, as if it had been dragged there and straightened to serve commuters. Brown sat down to think things over.

Having wrapped security forces around the LZ and the gun position, and having sent one squad to the ridge back, he still had the First and Third Platoons for disposal, forty-five men in one, forty-three in the other. Both platoons were marching down the path toward him as he worked out his plan.

The Third Platoon, under the Old Reliable, Sgt. Raymond Soto, would walk a little piece up the road toward Toumorong, pass the battery position, then cut sharply right along the base of the rear of the ridge. It was to "go like hell," locate the mortar, knock it out, and continue on the "1200 meters to the ARVN position." That was how Brown had worked out the distance, as a result of map error; it was only half that.

One squad of First Platoon under Sgt. Paul S. Wheeler, a replacement who had been in Vietnam only one week, would go on past the bridge and ascend the nose of the ridge just beyond it. This was the only portion of the ridge that was well covered with trees.

Brown said to Wheeler, "You will probably find a path there that follows the hump of the ridge."

The rest of First Platoon would follow along under Lieut. William Hookham, another newcomer. They would stand by along the road, awaiting whatever Wheeler's move might develop.

Brown thought of his deployments as having the nature of an envelopment. It took more than a little imagination.

It was about 1930 when they started. There was still a wisp of daylight for walking the 200 meters. The trail opening was quickly found and the slope of the ridge nose was not very steep. Within five or six minutes Wheeler was reporting that he was three-fourths of the way to the ridge top.

Came a long burst of automatic fire, startling Brown, startling Wheeler still more, for the bullets were right over his head, and the gun was only a few yards up the trail.

Brown recognized the AK47 rifle sound above that of the machine gun. Tracers were flicking out of the trees on the ridge nose.

He called Hookham to ask, "What's your situation?"

Hookham said, "We've bumped a hornet's nest; I'm getting all kinds of fire from the side of this hill."

Swiftly followed the sounds of grenades exploding on the ridge nose; they came in bunches, seeming like a dozen or more, sounding at that distance like cannon crackers.

The squad leader under Wheeler (he was the platoon leader), Sgt. Derrell Sharp, while ducking the grenades, had shot down two enemy riflemen with his M-16. Their bodies pitched down the trail and came to rest within ten feet of Wheeler, who was on the point of the squad.

Wheeler started crawling upward.

Sharp yelled, "You better hold it!"

Wheeler yelled back, "I'm going to get those weapons."

The two dead men, in falling, still clutched their AK47s.

In a few seconds Wheeler was up there, reaching out for the rifle that lay nearer, this eager newcomer following too literally what the training sergeant had told him: "Always go after their weapons."

Two grenades, thrown from both sides of the trail, sailed in on him, the fragments riddling his body, the force of the blast blowing all his equipment off.

Sharp crawled upward, bent on pulling him back. He was certain Wheeler was either dead or dying.

Sharp got to his body. A grenade came directly at him. He ducked and it exploded in the bush farther down the slope. But in the evading motion he had looked uptrail, and he saw the machine gun, only five feet above his head. The grenade had come from the same spot. He was so close that the gun could not depress to bear on him.

Sharp threw one grenade. It exploded on top of the gun, destroying the weapon and killing two crewmen.

Sharp backed away, dragging Wheeler down the trail.

Then he called Brown to say, "Wheeler's bleeding badly. I think it's critical. If we don't get him out, he's done for."

He added as an afterthought, "My one grenade didn't kill this Charley; grenades are rolling down all around us."

Brown talked to Hookham, told him to pull back the squad from the hill and return the platoon to the LZ at once.

So doing, he saved Wheeler's life.

Right after that he was called on the RT by Capt. Joe E. Jenkins, another adviser with the ARVN battalion.

Jenkins asked, "Where are your forces?"

Brown described his deployments.

Jenkins said, "Now that it is dark, and since those

mortars have stopped firing, I think you had better hold everything in place. I don't want a collision between the two forces in the darkness.''

Beyond doubt, Jenkins was righter than he knew. The ARVNs were only 600 meters away; Soto's platoon was proceeding on the assumption that they were at least 1200 meters away. So a collision was most likely.

Brown, not having any way of knowing that, disagreed emphatically with Jenkins. The thing to do was go after the mortar position. But while yessing Jenkins, he worked out in his own mind what he thought to be a reasonable compromise: He would extend both platoons. Soto would continue the move along the rear of the ridge. Hookham would work down the road along its front. The two parallel movements would close the vales at both ends of the central ridge prong and hold there. Should the enemy move before dawn, one platoon or the other would be able to ambush him. It was a reasonable expectation, since there was no thicket or bush to obscure the view within the two vales.

But when the enemy pulled out, at about 2115, his main force did so along the least-guarded and, therefore, most inviting route. The well-spread squad sent to do lookout duty from the height just beyond Brown's CP in the early evening was still there. It had played no part except to stand and wait, and now this pitifully scant line of pickets was getting a little sleepy.

The enemy force came with a rush in the darkness, from the low ground of the median, on the ends of which the two platoons had closed hopefully. Only one man stood directly in its path. He was Pvt. Denton W. Proctor of Buffalo, N.Y., who stood at dead center of the ridge top.

Proctor was not asleep. He heard something, fired quickly but not accurately enough, and was killed by four rifle bullets, two in the head and two in the chest.

Just as swiftly the enemy force vanished, running toward the northeast in the general direction of Toumorong. Sgt. Willy Leftwick saw the dark forms whip by and disappear before he had time to fire. He was running toward Proctor to see what had happened.

Leftwick called Brown to ask, "Shall I pursue?"

Brown said, "No." He was thinking that there might be more to come.

Emerson was listening in at Dak To. He called Brown and said, "You're right on that one; our job is to protect the artillery."

Thirty minutes later Soto called in. "Six VC walked straight into the middle of my ambush. We killed three, wounded one who is dying, and the others got away. One of my men got creased in the neck. He's nothing to worry about."

The rest of the night was quiet. Shortly after midnight Brown and his people around the LZ went on half alert, as did Whalen's men in the battery.

Somewhere along, information came to Whalen from the other Bravo battery that the "main VC force" was on "that high hill on the right of the valley"—and the finger was pointing in exactly the wrong direction. Whalen got cranked up for a big shoot at first light. When morning came, Brown told him that the enemy was either on the nose of the first ridge (the ridge of the night fight) to the left of the valley or was gone wholly. While that was hardly more enlightened than the earlier report, Whalen put thirty-six rounds on the ridge nose, 400 yards away. All gunners love to shoot.

The ARVNs, sizing up what had happened to them, concluded when morning came, according to Captain Jenkins, "that the enemy had managed to slip away to the eastward." So the guesses practically boxed the compass, except for the quadrant in which the enemy was seen fleeing. There is no more accounting for these differences than for the failure of the Vietnamese and Americans to exchange all relevant information.

By the time most of the American camp was awake, the ARVN column had gone on toward Toumorong. The Americans, thinking the Vietnamese had back-pedaled, griped about it, feeling more lonesome than was necessary, thinking they had been left in the lurch. No one had briefed them on the ARVN's mission, so they could not understand that the column was following plan.

So the little piece of action died on the same flat note with which it was begun. The two forces behaved like ships, not passing in the night, but drifting close together while incapable of setting a common course. The dimensions of their mutual need, and what benefits might derive from it, neither force understood because each was overconcerned with the small problem in its foreground. If they thought at all of themselves as a joined force at grips with a common enemy, they did not behave like it. Whose fault? No one had given them this grasp of their possible relationship to one another. No one at the base camp had perceived that any such need for a tactical concert would arise. That is not to say that they had failed one another or that their superiors had failed them. The confluence of their interests no one had been capable of imagining.

Fumbling and bumbling it was, but lovely, lovely. Had Whalen loosed his thunder against the nose of the ridge in early evening before Wheeler climbed it, or had ARVNs and Americans collaborated together to stage a faultless envelopment killing every enemy soldier, there probably would have been no Battle of Toumorong.

The Hypothesis

My billet during the night when Captain Brown and his warriors were having such a frustrating time was in the base camp at Dak To. I had flown there from An Khe to see an old friend, Col. Ted Mataxis, deputy to Pearson, and one of the better combat leaders of the Army. Also, there was more work to be done with Colonel Emerson and his battalion on the story of Austin Six, the fight at Bn Gia Map.

Mataxis' tent was large enough to enclose a two-man foxhole canopied with a mosquito bar, a touch of class missing from my rounds in earlier wars. It was not that the mortar rounds that occasionally ranged in on the camp were devilishly accurate. As Ted said, "I sometimes have nervous guests who object to running through the rain in their underwear to get to a bunker." Innate courtesy such as this has always distinguished him.

We heard a rather fragmentary description of the small fight near the battery position at the early-morning briefing. The terms of the discussion indicated it was not evaluated as other than a flash-in-the-pan, a slight collision on a side street, unrelated to the possibility that the sweep around Toumorong, now about to close out hollowly, might still prove worth all the trouble taken. What had happened was interpreted as another incidental brush with local VC and nothing more.

Some of the details stirred my curiosity. There are certain norms in combat operations, not excepting irregular warfare. Patterns repeat themselves. After one has worked through thousands of tactical situations, any marked deviation from the norm stands out like a red flare in a dark night. One may not at once sense its meaning; but one knows it is there.

So I asked that the schedule of work that had been arranged for me that Sunday be set aside and that as soon as the fog lifted from the Dak To airport, I would be flown to LZ Lima Zulu. The Huey and the weather were equally ready around noon. Col. Hank Emerson flew with me. In less than twenty-five minutes we were alongside the infantry position and within a stone's throw of the creek.

Through three hours that afternoon I sat with Brown, Emerson and Whalen on the comfortable rosewood log near the Dak Djram that Brown had warmed while cogitating the night before. The day was delightful; the camp was wholly relaxed. One or two patrols were out, but they were not roving very far; there was less tension in the atmosphere than if we had been sitting in a Turkish bath; troops acted with that added bit of nonchalance that outwardly expresses the inner thought: "Well, glad we're all through with that one; leave us now be of good cheer." The general silence and warlessness encouraged them to stretch and yawn, unthinking that the enemy might be looking on, there being literally nothing to chill his curiosity.

During those three hours we reconstructed the events of the prior night, as they were recalled by Brown, Whalen and the other principals at this end of the fight. (It was not until three days later that I dug the information on what had happened to the ARVN battalion.) Their candor was as winningly refreshing as was their hospitality. There was no need to ask prying questions. They came forth with everything they could remember, and there were no differences in view between them that had to be reconciled. The pieces of the story fitted together as do the parts of a jigsaw puzzle.

Brown said he thought the ARVNs had "lost about twenty people to the mortar fire."

Had he searched for the mortar? Yes, his people had searched the other side of the ridge spur right ahead of us, through the morning, but had found nothing. Did not the fact that the enemy had gone out running indicate that the tube might have been left behind? It was possible.

Inevitably most of my conversation was with Captain Brown since he had played the lead role.

But as we together talked on, all he told me but furthered my doubt that the individuals closest to the scene were putting two and two together. Something was getting badly fuzzed up.

Everything that had happened was tactically preposterous, unless the enemy were abysmally stupid, or had rigged a trap in conformity with a rigid plan, and then because of some unforeseen development had had the plan fall apart. The two possible explanations were not mutually exclusive, though how the enemy had come and what he had done were subject to but one interpretation by any person with a sense of ground, weapons, people, cover and timing—the factors in tactics.

No platoon should have waited on the partially wooded point of an otherwise almost barren ridge, evenly backed, in broad daylight, within 250 or so meters of an enemy rifle company and artillery battery set down right under its nose. To stay there, doing nothing, was to invite sudden death, the more so because the platoon still had time and terrain by which it could withdraw, via the draw leftward of the first finger.

Brown could have taken the enemy platoon whole, had he at once sent an assault platoon to the center of the ridge back that was so very close to him, with no difficult ground between; instead of posting to that point a squad told only to see what the ARVNs were doing and to look around for an enemy mortar, if possible. In sending a boy to do a man's job, Brown had made the common mistake of U.S. younger combat leaders in the Central Highlands—he had not proceeded as if the only dependable assumption was that the enemy was there. As Gen. Bill Dean wrote about our performance in Korea, that's how the American mind operates and no magic will change it. Brown had a better excuse than most—the landscape ahead of him had looked disarmingly innocent. Only a parcel of fools would fight there if there was any way to slip out of it.

The whole question was the significance of this markedly minor affair—minor in that little blood had been spilled and no one felt greatly alarmed. I remembered a saying by Gilbert Burck: "All the wrong decisions over the centuries from Darius' attack at Marathon to the birth of the Edsel have been at bottom the result of insufficient or inadequately processed knowledge." We seemed to be getting it.

Yet out of the talk had come a number of leads that together pointed in only one direction.

Obviously the enemy had not been waiting on that flange of the ridge lying next the creek with the object of ambushing a file of Americans. Brown and Whalen had been thrown onto LZ Lima Zulu at the last moment. Their arrival just off the enemy flank must have been a total surprise.

And speaking of flanks, there had, indeed, been two of them, the light one well forward where Wheeler and Proctor got hit, the heavy force on the farthest ridge spur where the ARVNs were attacked.

The split force had to be working toward one common object, carrying out one central design. What was it? There could be only one answer in logic, since the facts excluded any other hypothesis. The force had been set to ambush the ARVN column: the weaker element in front was to strike the head of the column when it came even; then when the battalion deployed, the main body was to hit it in the rear. When the ARVNs went into bivouac early, that plan became aborted, and so both flanks were left dangling.

The plan itself, when profiled against the terrain, was an index to the probable size of the force. The valley was open country, with little bush or other concealment on its flats. The creek banks were too low to offer any protection. The high ground had no cover favorably placed so that volume fire could beat upon the road from within it. These things put together, the enemy would hardly have sent less than a battalion out to trap another battalion. A company would not stretch far enough.

Last point: If the enemy was ready to throw a battalion block at one of the sweep columns just as the Toumorong operation was about to close out, there was reason to suspect that he wished to provoke battle, else he would have stayed in his hole. It was the first tangible reason for believing that he might have major force within the mountains north and east of the battery position.

What I have here written expands only slightly on the notes I put down when, after leaving Brown, I flew on through the clouds to Toumorong to see my old friend, David H. Hackworth, age thirty-five, home town, Memphis, Tennessee.

The word for Hackworth is merry. He has that kind of smile, accented more by the deep twinkle in his eye than the cracking of his face, and that rarer thing yet in a soldier—a merry gait; he rolls along like a sailor. Under high pressure he is utterly calm without having to be self-restrained, up till the moment when he must take the initiative, which he may do either with a laugh or with words that sting. Yet the words are never abusive. A thoroughly likable man, Hack, a stimulating companion who in conversation acquires force by deliberate understatement. And he is a fighter born, as well as being the kind of commander who sees beyond the skyline of immediate orders.

Spit and polish—no, not for him. There was a four-day beard on his face that added nothing to his age or beauty. I had last seen him when he was a platoon sergeant in Capt. Lew Millett's company in Korea, fifteen years before. It was the day his outfit staged the one great bayonet attack of that war. Lew got a Medal of Honor from it, Hack got a commission, and I got a wife. So the drinks should be on me. And this day Hack didn't look much older than in that long ago. Now, as we shook hands, Hack said, "If you wouldn't rather fight here than in Korea, I'm ready to argue." With Hackworth, wherever a fight is on at the moment is the best possible country. He had had three straight years of combat in the Korean show.

Toumorong was buzzing like a hive. The Montagnard families of the company being evacuated, having already gathered their few possessions together, were milling around restlessly. The males, wearing jungle suits, were pacing to and fro, either working the bolts of their weapons or doing else that might impress Hackworth, and the other officers, with their military attitude. The younger women, for the most part, were stripped to the waist, at least half of them packing infants in cradle boards. The smaller children ran about stark naked, though the air was a bit nippy, Toumorong being more than a mile above the sea. Hack and his battalion were scheduled to escort this crowd of wildlings down the mountain and to the nearest refugee camp at Dak To on the following morning unless the water of the streams in the bottomland was so high that the trucks could not get through.

Together we roamed about looking at the position. It was, indeed, pretty useless, and for one reason mainly. Beautifully perched with respect to all else, the redoubt was undone by an accident of ground just outside its back door, an outcropping thrust from the body of the mountain. A shoulder of this same ridge, thick with trees and bush and less than 200 meters away, rose twenty feet higher than the flat, almost bare floor over which we walked. One or two enemy machine guns there could wipe out the small garrison, and if the mountain happened to be cloud-bound, no force from outside could help a bit. No good as bait, Toumorong was a throw away.

As we walked, we talked.

I said, "Hack, my hunch is that this drag hunt around Toumorong is far from over. The foxes are still here; the pack just never got going."

Briefly I outlined what had happened in the valley position on the evening before.

Hack replied, "With me it's more than a hunch. I know it. Tell you something else. Charley never intended to take this place. He just wanted to make us think so. What's in it for him, making a fake pass, unless he is set to lower the boom somewhere right around here?"

He paused, reflecting, then said, "So I am not going to vacate the area with the rest of the columns. I'll see this crowd of people down the mountain tomorrow, if we don't get a flood. But someone else will take it from there. I'm going to beat out these woods, hill by hill, with the battalion."

He was way ahead of me.

Hack's eyes sparked in anticipation. One of the older Montagnards, who was also taller than most of them, walked past us. He wore lieutenant's insignia.

"That fellow," said Hack, "told me right where they are. I marked it on the map. Ought to get into the place by Tuesday. Call it curiosity. I want to see if he's right about it."

On that note I left him, both of us remarking that we would probably be together again before this show was over. About that we were wrong. When the fireworks started, the explosive part of the relief of Toumorong became labeled "Hawthorne 2," or sort of an annex to "Hawthorne 1." An electrical storm was coming on from the west when the Huey took off. The sheet lightning spread with a regularity not too soothing. We flew back via the pleasant little valley, because I wanted to get a bird's-eye view of the battery position on the red slope above the creek. As it receded from view, I felt certain I would be back there again—and soon.

It was in these same minutes—around 1700 on 5 June—that General Pearson arrived at Toumorong in his Huey to talk things out with Hackworth. His own estimate in that hour was that hardly enough enemy force remained in the vicinity to be worth seeking. The thing to do was evacuate the garrison from this eagle's nest, pull the columns out of the area, and try another sweep to the westward of Dak To.

Hackworth talked to Pearson with the earnestness of Willie Loman at the end of a blank month. One of the high qualities of this slender and sober-sided commander, who moved from civilian life as a reserve lieutenant when World

War II began, shortly to discover that battle was his cup of tea, is that he listens intently, particularly when he speaks to his subordinates. Pearson and the other field commanders in Vietnam are more receptive, in this particular, than any group of generals in the national history.

At the end Pearson said, "Hack, it's all yours. Do what you propose. If you make a contact and wish to hold on, do so, and call me when you need help. If not, you link up with Brown's company and the artillery battery in the valley. Then you will have a task force—your TF—and you march them out."

That's how it came about that on the following day all of the other columns were withdrawn to Dak To, while Hackworth's battalion, after escorting their charges down the mountain, began grinding away. Of Hackworth's persistence came the battle.

Between the self-made Regular commanding the battalion and the commanders of his rifle companies, all educated for the Army, two of them at West Point, there was a satisfying rapport, unmarred by difference in rank or any lack of frankness.

It was a relationship that strengthened under high pressure, and in that they were fortunate, as was the brigade.

Next day I flew in the Huey from Dak To to the cavalry division camp at An Khe, to talk briefly on Tuesday morning at a conference of combat intelligence people. Brig. Gen. Joseph A. McChristian, the G-2 of MAC-V, was the main speaker. My mind was full of the mystery that I had dealt with on Sunday, what I had learned while sitting on a log, along with some tentative conclusions, and I spoke of nothing else.

When the conference broke up, Sergeant Major Westervelt, who was my mentor on enemy weapons, was waiting outside the tent with a teletype message for me from the command in Dak To. It read:

"Come back at once. Unit you visited while with brigade on Sunday repulsed vicious NVA battalion attack early this morning killing 191 enemy."

By noontime I was back on the log.

Concerning his role and extraordinary prescience, however, Hackworth ever after declined to take credit, remarking with a grin, "I alone got all the breaks, being the only person permitted to approach the problem with a fresh mind."

Allowing for the reverse English, there is something in his statement. He had sat in on none of the tactical planning for Toumorong and did not know of the general concept until some time after the curtain went up. Being the Brigade Executive Officer, he had been at Cheo Reo throughout the preparatory period moving the Brigade to Dak To. He did not take command of 1/327th until 0915 on D Day and by 1030 that morning he was making his first helicopter assault with the battalion.

So there was no time for him to become dulled by planning talk around the table or to be influenced by what anyone else thought about the countryside around the outpost, whether it was enemy-infested or a sweetly innocent landscape.

"I had every reason to call the shots," he said with just a bit of a smile, "since all I had to do was read the signs on the ground."

If that does not make the story delightfully simple, call it at least delightful.

Rally of the Redlegs

The Screaming Eagles of 1966 in Vietnam, like those of the Old Breed around Bastogne and Carentan in 1944, are a joy to be with in the field.

They know they're good, they swagger a bit, are ever ready with a wisecrack, throw a salute as if they mean it and—something new—vocalize it.

In Hackworth's outfit, as the hand goes up, the soldier sounds off the motto: "Above the rest!" A bit startled on hearing this the first time, and not listening too well, I thought the man said, "Bugger the rest!" They straightened me out.

Any day with them, afield or in camp, adds zest to life. But if one had to take leave of them for twenty-four hours as they flattened the LZs and beat the trails around Toumorong, that Monday when I flew east was the right time for it.

Little or nothing worked out to anyone's satisfaction. All the other columns pulled back to Dak To, leaving only the 101st units in the zone of operations. Hackworth had the Trongson company on his hands and, having to play shepherd until they were safely delivered, couldn't get with the body of his battalion for most of the day.

Captain Brown had business in the Dak To camp that would keep him overnight. The battery position along the

Dak Djram was left in charge of his second, Lieut. Karl Beach. There was not too much concern over that piece of ground, the storm having come and passed. The infantry foxhole line lay mainly to the south along the low ground near the creek bed, so that it faced the ridge where the front of the enemy ambush party had waited on Saturday evening. There were no infantry positions north of the battery where the slope rose much more abruptly toward Hill 872, though no part of that mass had been worked over by patrols.

On their own, Hackworth's companies proceeded to sweep in the direction where he expected to find the enemy because of what one Montagnard had told him. The valley exit from the area lay southwest. They beat the trails running northwest toward the massive ridge line capped by Hills 1063 and 1073.

It was not a happy run for Capt. Benjamin L. Willis of Alpha Company and Bay Minette, Ala. USMA graduate, class of '61. He was having trouble all the way with his senior NCO, Sgt. James F. Long. Two weeks overdue for return to the United States, bitter about Willis's refusal to release him until a suitable replacement arrived, Long beefed loud and clear.

At 1400, near the hamlet of Dak Hanjro, two kilometers northwest of Toumorong, Alpha Company made contact. The lead platoon was checking out the area. The point saw a squad of soldiers in khaki 300 meters away, straight along the trail. Second Platoon went into perimeter and called for fire from Whalen's battery—fifty rounds. When the shelling ceased, the platoon, led by Sergeant Long, continued on to see what had happened. As it moved into the cratered area, fire came at it from the bush all around, and the men went flat. At the same time the troops to the rear under Captain Willis became hotly engaged by rifles and machine guns from their rear and one flank. They were already deployed in perimeter, with good cover.

The first hour of this fire fight made plain to Long, as to Willis, that they were both held and could not get to one another. Burning up much ammo, they were spinning their wheels. Willis called for the artillery again, only this time he asked Whalen's battery to split the guns and give simultaneous, but separate, fire, thus covering both groups. Two different azimuths were given. Something went wrong, either in the order or in its handling by the battery. This was at 1530. The shells delivered to Willis came in O.K. Those meant to help Long came right down on his platoon.

Willis knew about it when Long called on the RT. He said, "Now hold it steady, Captain. They got us bad. I've got five dead and five wounded here—by our artillery. I am reorganizing the platoon. We'll keep going, some way. But I'm dealing with a badly shocked group. We need help if we can get it."

So spoke Long, the disgruntled soldier, the man embittered against Willis, who had been beefing all day. Nothing counted now except that his friends were in trouble.

Hackworth got this message. He had already moved at 1500 to help the company. A tactical air strike came in on the heels of the jolt from the friendly guns. The 500-pound bombs, hitting between the two perimeters, stunned the enemy long enough that Third Platoon was able to get forward and re-enforce Long's position.

At 1600 Hackworth sent the Tigers to re-enforce the position as a whole. This is a Recondo platoon, with forty-five men, specialists in the rough-and-tumble of jungle warfare. The Tigers drew such heavy fire on the LZ that the Hueys shied off and a gunship strike had to be put on that ground before they could try again. Even so, they loaded and took off under fire. When they put down at Dak Hanjro, they drew fire again. Lieut. Norman Grunstadt, who was four days overdue for return to the United States, called in the report to Hackworth.

Hackworth said, "Set up an ambush just outside the hamlet and try to hold there."

A few minutes later Grunstadt had another report for him. "We have just run into a company-size base camp outside Dak Hanjro." That was at 1830, as the sun set. By then Hackworth was already up with Willis and company.

Ouchier than any of these people were Capt. Ernest W. Dill, of East Point, Ga., and Charley Company. They had

been held back through the day and didn't like it. Hackworth
had a very special mission for them. They were to fly as
quickly as possible after dawn to the battery position on the
Dak Djram. Then they were to sweep the high ground north
of it. The battery and Brown's company had been made a
part of Hackworth's TF and he felt a special responsibility
for their security. Dill would have gone there and started his
operation on this day had not the extraction of other battalions from the operations zone to Dak To kept all aircraft
overworked the whole time. A frustration, it was to prove
particularly ironic.

Around Willis and company the fight cooled as daylight
flickered out. The enemy was still there but did not fire
unless some American on the perimeter made himself too
conspicuous. Hackworth was content to lie low through the
night: working a squeeze play along the trails was difficult
enough in full daylight, and he was already convinced that
he was beginning to bump a main force.

At the battery position on the Dak Djram, Captain Whalen
said to his executive, Lieut. Larry Simpson, "We're a
mighty good target tonight; make sure of our noise and light
discipline." (Whalen's inclination toward soldiering started
when he was cradled on Missionary Ridge.) However, no
special arrangement was made with Lieutenant Beach, commanding Alpha Company, so that there would be effective
tactical unity in the night defense. Each unit proceeded as it
wished, as on the nights before.

Whalen turned in at midnight. At 0200 he was awakened
by mortar fire hitting his camp. Some of the rounds were
coming from the top of Hill 872 directly north of the gun
position, though in the excitement that followed no one
sensed it.

Beach's company was far overstretched as the attack
began. One platoon was on the ridge south of the Dak
Djram, 400 yards from the battery. Another was patrolling
the valley several hundred yards to the west. One squad was
covering—at unknown distance— to the north. The remainder of the company, and a squad of engineers, were in

fighting positions on the low ground near the bridge, which placed them about 300 meters from the guns.

A wholly injudicious deployment as to the infantry's main mission, it was to work out well in the long run, because of the more grotesque blunders made by the enemy.

In the two or three minutes required for Whalen to put on his pants and lace his boots, he counted twenty-one mortar rounds hitting close about. The battery was not firing in support of Hackworth in those moments, which fact made every explosion distinct. By the time he was outside, the enemy infantry attack, out of the northwest, was coming straight in on him. Only his one alert platoon stood ready to face it. The other gunners, rubbing sleep from their eyes, were crawling from the pup tents. Most of them were bootless.

The enemy thrust split around a brush-covered trench curving about the northwest angle, the main body of about forty men, firing rifles and throwing grenades, charging the No. 6 gun, a smaller party rushing the truck laager on the rear.

At No. 6 gun position Sgt. Jerry D. Carter was hit by a grenade that battered his head and ripped open his belly. He reeled backward a few steps and fell dead. Cpl. Robert Hemmes, hit by another grenade, badly wounded, was blown by the blast into a foxhole from which PFC Larry Cain was firing his M-16. Cain slung his weapon and dragged Hemmes back to where he could be shielded by gun No. 3. That was enough for the survivors in No. 6 position. They fell back on guns No. 3 and 5 and the enemy force went to ground around gun No. 6.

Enemy skirmishers swarmed around the trucks, guarded by a six-man outpost. Cpl. John Morgan stayed to make a fight of it, killed four of them with his M-16, and then, finding himself alone, with his weapon empty, fell back on the nearest gun position.

The fire fight had been going possibly ten minutes when Whalen backed to his FDC (fire direction center) with the intention of reporting: "I am heavily engaged and in close contact." None of his pieces had fired yet; restraining them was Whalen's fear that he might hit one of Beach's parties, whose exact locations he did not know.

As he approached the FDC, a 60 mm mortar round exploded at the entrance. Fragments hit Whalen, Lieut. Gerald Forest, the fire direction officer, and Spec. 5 Mike Walinski, the computer. Worse yet, the blast wrecked the FDC system.

Whalen told Forest and Walinski, "Stay where you are, keep listening, and try to prepare data so we can silence those mortars."

Then he said to Spec. 4 Streadback, "Put that PRC-25 on your back, follow me, stay right with me, don't lose me for a second." Streadback did exactly as told, coming through as one of the heroes of the night.

Via the portable radio, as he moved back to the guns, Whalen got through to the artillery operations officer at the Dak To camp. He was promised that ARVN artillery would quickly be firing in his support. Next he raised Lieut. Don Koumann, his own liaison at Hackworth's base on the LZ near Toumorong. He said, "We'll try to give you some fire with the eighty-one mortars."

All of this time Whalen was puzzling over what was happening to Beach's company. He could hear the infantry weapons firing but could not sense the direction. Then he had an inspiration: he would get his guns going anyway. Gauging liberally, he would shoot well over, west and east. It would be a waste of ammunition, except that working the guns would be like a shot in the arm to the gunners and would restore unity to the force.

Throughout the day Lieutenant Beach had felt a premonition that an attack would come that night. It had begun as he watched the other columns stream by, getting out of the area. So he caught a nap in the afternoon and resolved to stay up through the night. At 0015 he became certain that his hunch was not wrong. The leader of the squad on outpost to the north, Sgt. James G. Moffett, called on the RT to say, "We hear noises to our front—people moving. We're grenading toward them." Ten minutes passed and he reported another such incident. Beach did not alert Whalen. Moffett's men were now firing their rifles.

At 0205 Moffett called again, "I hear them moving past my front."

Beach said, "You go get 'em."

Beach started to move.

That quickly he found his squad rushing toward an enemy company coming on in a charge toward Whalen's guns.

There was nothing else for Moffett and his men to do but turn and run. They cleared away unhurt only because the enemy did not come on firing. Moffett headed for Beach's position, 350 meters away, on top the ridge where Sgt. Willy Leftwick's squad had had such ill luck on Saturday night. As he got there, shells exploded along the crest and the cry went up: "Mortar! Mortar!" The site was so close that the flattened men could hear the rounds leave the tube. This was the same mortar that had shelled the ARVN battalion on Saturday, which Brown had sought unsuccessfully on Sunday. The enemy had come back with a fresh supply of ammo. (The mortar was found next morning by Captain Dill's men.) After the sixth mortar round hit, small-arms fire ranged in on Beach from rearward along the ridge. His men became fully occupied in defending their ground. But Beach did not call Whalen and he had no real awareness of the deadly peril enveloping the battery. Both commanders were gripped by the problem next their elbows.

Sgt. Tyrone Adderly, leading First Squad, Third Platoon, was in the position directly north of the bridge and facing west. The enemy closed round him at the same time that Beach got hit. Beach had no way to re-enforce him because his group was pinned. Adderly could see dark forms moving off both flanks and across his rear. He whispered to his people, "Hug the dirt. Don't fire. They may miss us." It was the best policy. They survived the night unhurt. The First Platoon, echeloned to the left and rear of Adderly, fell back toward the artillery position and opened fire on the skirmishers among the trucks.

Was this then such a clever enemy? Look again at the deployment. Here was an NVA battalion in the attack.

Beyond doubt it had scouted the position and it knew just how the Americans were disposed, since all positions were hit at one time. Then that supreme advantage was thrown away when the battalion overextended in trying to devour everything at one time. Had it concentrated on enveloping the battery, then gone on to knock off the infantry, it could have had its way. The Americans had made the mistake of failing to stay collected, while delegating out-guarding to small posts and patrols. That faulty disposition tempted the enemy to make the one blunder that would redress the error; it was like throwing an ace on a hand already trumped.

Beach could look back over his shoulder and see mortar and grenade rounds exploding around the battery. The grenades told him that enemy infantry had closed on the guns.

Having taken gun No. 6, they thrust for gun No. 3. First came a grenade shower. Corporal Hemmes, who had taken a first wound at gun No. 6, jumped from a shallow foxhole to evade a grenade and got a bullet through the heart. One fragment hit Whalen on his right wrist and bounced off. Other grenades wounded badly five men, including First Sergeant Loveland, Sgt. Richmond Nail and Sgt. Malcolm Bentz, who, under Whalen's eyes, continued to "fight like tigers."

Largely because of the effectiveness of these gunners with infantry weapons, the charge against gun No. 3 was repulsed. As the enemy pulled back a little, Smokey the Bear came over and began dropping flares. The enemy came surging again in larger numbers than ever. Now it was like "shooting fish in a barrel." Every oncoming form stood out boldly in the glare. Whalen fired his M-16—a full clip—saw three men fall where he aimed. As that charge collapsed, led by Whalen, the Americans got back to gun No. 6, which was already wrecked beyond repair. They counted sixteen bodies right around the gun and picked up ten enemy automatic weapons.

The time was 0300. Shells from the ARVN artillery began falling on a ridge to the eastward, too far away to do any good. Whalen tried to readjust it by sound. The racket from grenade and mortar explosions right around him made it impossible. Came word that the 155s at the Dak To camp (Bravo, 1/30th) were displacing to where they could support him. About then Beach's First Platoon entered upon the battery position and Whalen settled-in its men next gun No. 5.

There came on an attack from the west—on a wholly new line—rifle and automatic fire in large volume, but with no direct assault follow-through.

A prolonged lull followed. Whalen called for a medevac ship, and the Huey put down directly next gun No. 3 without one shot being fired against it. Whalen figured the fight was over. The eight most critical cases were loaded aboard and flown to hospital at Dak To.

Gun No. 6—now just a relic, with the tube bearing the scars of more than 500 bullet hits—was held for all of thirty minutes. The enemy surged back at 0410. Sergeant Best fought for the ruined piece until he ran out of grenades. He and PFC Lonnie Bland were the last men off the gun.

At last Whalen and Beach were having a running dialogue and Whalen knew for the first time where all the riflemen were positioned. The enemy had bunched around gun No. 6. Whalen said to the crews on No. 3 and No. 5, "Turn those guns around and let them have it."

It was range twenty-five meters for No. 3, range fifty meters for No. 5. They fired high explosive, charge No. 1, wiped out the people around gun No. 6, then lifted fire a little to mash the skirmishers pressing forward toward them through the bamboo.

It wasn't quite all over. As the first light fulled, Puff the Magic Dragon came flying up the valley. This C-47 mounts three 7.62 mm mini-guns, today's high-polish edition of the old Gatling, each of which can pour out 5400 rounds per minute; it's a blast. The pilot, talking to Beach, said, "I've got 20,000 rounds." Beach replied, "Use every damned one of them."

Beach then turned to other things. With the growing light he could see a machine gun set up, downslope, within thirty-five meters of his CP. The gun wasn't firing, and it seemed to be pointing in the wrong direction.

Beach asked his RTO, PFC Russell Henderson, "Is he friendly or enemy?"

Henderson replied, "I'll be damned if I know."

From the gun position someone was yelling in perfect English, "Are you friendly? Are you friendly?"

Beach pondered, then realized that his own men wouldn't be raising the question. 1st Sgt. Kenneth Lamb, Spec. 4 Emmet Moneyhun and Beach all grenaded together. Their bombs blew the position apart, killing gun and crew.

Beach had lost two men killed and eleven wounded along the ridge during the night.

Puff had gone on to a good target. As the sun rose, Whalen could see large numbers of the enemy assembling along two low-lying ridges directly north of the battery. Some were firing machine guns toward him, but most of them were digging in.

Puff unloaded against the two hills. Lieutenant Snowden called in fire from the 155s against them. Then the gunships came on, followed by a napalm strike along the crest. The No. 2 gun of the battery was shifted a bit to shell the target line of sight. That was laying it on a trifle thick. Strangely none of this bombardment was laid on Hill 872.

Last, Beach's infantry deployed for attack. There was nothing left to hit. Atop the two ridges they counted 192 enemy dead and collected thirty-two individual weapons, five machine guns and five P-40 rocket launchers. So ended the repulse of a battalion-plus, with a loss rate around twenty to one in favor of the Americans.

General Pearson flew to the position on the Dak Djram at 0730. Hackworth arrived by Huey twenty minutes later. He had heard about the fight at 0400 and had sized it up right; he came with his CP, prepared to stay until some other prospect looked better. Pearson, after a brief run-down on the fight just ending, said to him, "Hack, I'll leave it in your hands and will be guided by your judgment."

This, then, was the pivot. The events of Monday had made little impression other than on Hackworth's men under the gun. It was the onslaught against the battery that convinced the brigade that the ground around Toumorong had to be beaten out all over again and that the task might engage the great part of its strength.

At Nha Trang, General Kinnard made a notation in his diary: "I today placed a string on one battalion, Second Brigade, First Cav. Div. It is now balled up somewhere around Oasis. [Brig. Gen. Glenn Walker's command post.] May have to send them to Dak To. Little action anywhere else."

General Pearson at Dak To, along with his brigade staff, reviewed that evening the day's developments and the operational problem confronting Hackworth. Pearson concluded that Hack was trying to bite more than any one battalion could chew. Brown's Alpha Company was already in the act. It was time to commit Col. Hank Emerson's battalion, 2/502nd, all the way. The companies would be flown north on the following morning.

The Hackers

Captain Dill and his company were landed at LZ Lima Zulu one hour later than Hackworth. After a quick briefing on the night fight, they started up the valley bound for the hamlet of Kon Honong, 1000 meters to the north. Getting there at 1000 on 8 June, they climbed the ridge to the westward, to overlook the valley road. Not one contact was made, though Dill was certain this was the route over which the NVA attack had moved against Whalen.

He started to swing the whole company to east of the road for a sweep in the opposite direction, then on a hunch split the command and sent Second Platoon right back over the same road. They moved 500 meters, and of a sudden both flanks were colliding with enemy stragglers. Second Platoon shot six men; all of them seemed dazed. Dill reported to Hackworth, who told him, "You get prisoners; I don't want bodies; I want information." They tried, but in trying they let half a dozen of these Charleys escape into the bush. Before getting back to the battery position, the flank on the east of the road killed another sixteen. At the last moment Dill grabbed a prisoner. He had been shot through the mouth and couldn't talk.

The most glittering performance in the neighborhood of the battery, however, was staged by Capt. John P. Hurling and Bravo Company. Hurling, a graduate of Scranton University, is from Auburn, N.Y. Beginning at 0800, his outfit swept the eastern fingers of Hill 872 and through the day worked over the upper heights with such thoroughness as to prove beyond doubt what all along should have been suspected—that from this dominant high ground had come the forces and some of the fire that had enfiladed the artillery camp.

The culminating discovery, high on the mountain, was a mortar base plate, the earth around it fresh with the litter and scars of usage within the last few hours. There was no doubt about it. The obvious had been overlooked only because it was too simple, though conducting the postmortem proved neither simple nor easy for Bravo Company.

Along the lower fingers the sweepers came upon bunkers, foxholes and machine-gun emplacements. They went on from that but did not get far. First Platoon, on the middle finger, came under the fire of two machine guns and half a dozen AK47s. It was then about fifty meters away from the two flanking platoons and higher up the ridge. 2nd Lieut. James McCoey called Hurling on his radio and said, "I'm up against at least a platoon, and I don't think I can handle it."

Hackworth asked, "How did the fight start?"

Said McCoey, "We saw a VC by a brook, with his feet in the water, cooling them. So we shot him. Then we got fire all along our line."

That first exchange had cost him six casualties, all of them wounded.

Hurling called Lieut. Peter Laizac, Second Platoon, on the right-hand finger, quickly briefed him on McCoey's situation, then said, "You move on up to where the fingers join, then swing left. [This would put Laizac on the enemy's rear.] I'll get some artillery on the upper slope to soften things up."

Hurling turned to his artillery FO, Lieut. David Drake, and told him to request the fire. That's where they hit a snag. Captain Dill called Hurling and said, "You can't fire; we are moving along the upper slope of this same ridge."

Dill was dead wrong about it. He was on the next ridge

north. But because of map error and the fact that one flange of the second ridge projected south along 872's flank, it was a pardonable mistake. But Dill's stricture left Hurling no choice; he had to proceed without calling on the artillery only 1200 meters away. By this time the 155 mm howitzers were displacing from Dak To to the position of Whalen's battery by the Dak Djram.

Hurling moved his Third Platoon over to the center finger, then with both platoons massing their fires, slugged it out. The advance was foot by foot, the fighting lasting from 1200 to 1350; all the time Hurling was under the illusion that he was driving the enemy into Dill's waiting arms. At the end the company was standing on the crest. The last of the enemy had slipped away through the bamboo on the left flank, carrying off as many of the dead and wounded as possible. Even so, eighteen NVA dead littered the path of the advance. The two platoons had bucked their way up the steep for 450 meters, and all the way the enemy had fallen back through prepared positions. The push had cost Hurling sixteen men, most of them lightly wounded. There was one KIA. Lieutenant Drake had been hit by bullets in both legs.

Atop the hill the company drew only a few rounds of sniper fire; Hurling did not pursue. His fundamental task was to protect the artillery position and it was time to get back there. Hurling called for two medevac ships to come in on one of the fingers where he had noted a flat, cleared space suitable for an LZ; an escort party was already helping the most serious cases down the mountain. They would be flying to hospital in one-quarter hour.

That gave him a few minutes to look about. He discovered the base plate for the 81 mm mortar, the indentations made by recent, repeated recoil. In the pockets under a brick-red earth bank he found the black plaster plugs, a fuse box and the canisters that went with the mortar. Almost satisfied, he started his descent. Where the trail to the southward began, he picked up a piece of enemy commo wire and decided to follow same. It led him right back to the artillery camp to within a few yards of his own sack. He figured that that just about wrapped up the case.

Willis and his people were in a fight before they could stir from the perimeter back at Dak Hanjro. The enemy came on firing. The men went flat and Willis called for artillery. That stilled resistance for a few minutes. They started moving. More fire came against the head of the column. Willis deployed two platoons in line and started a sweep. Second Platoon collided with three enemy skirmishers and, pursuing them, stumbled upon a strongly fortified bunker line. Its lines approached these works a little too incautiously, thinking them unoccupied, to be driven back and pinned down by a storm of fire. Second Platoon reported to Willis: "We are taking heavy casualties." Willis sent Third Platoon on along to ease the pressure. Third swung around Second and moved in against the far end of the bunker line, with the same result. The attempt to outflank had not gone wide enough; Third became pinned before it could help a bit. Willis asked the artillery to lay down some smoke to cover a withdrawal; his only reserve was the seventeen-man platoon that had been shot up by the artillery the day before.

Sgt. Ira Perkins, leading Second Platoon, moved around giving instructions so that his men would be set for the withdrawal. A bullet hit him through the heart. The others crawled away, dragging along twelve wounded. The enemy followed them right out, firing. Willis called Hackworth and said, "I need help." Hackworth sent him one of Brown's platoons from Alpha, 502nd. The paratroopers came in on a Chinook, to descend to earth via a rope ladder. Their arrival stabilized things a bit, though the fight wore on, with Willis, who is highly self-critical, saying to himself, "There must be a better way to do this."

The Tiger Platoon at Dak Hanjro had started breaking in a new skipper that morning, Capt. Lewis Higinbotham, of Houston, Texas, USMA '62, an old hand in Vietnam though new to the jungle-suited Tigers, a Long Boy with spectacles and a prominent Adam's apple, who looks like the mildest of men. Grunstadt was on his way back to the United States, a boon not yet granted to Sergeant Long because there were too many Charleys interfering.

Higinbotham did not regard himself as a fast mover; he liked to be sure as he went along that he was getting things wrapped up. It was his impression as he took over that he was on a hunt for stragglers, so he spent most of the day checkerboarding, while adding nothing to the bag. Shortly before dusk one of his patrols entered upon an unoccupied NVA battalion base camp. There were thirty-five spots where cooking fires had been set the night before. As he checked that out, one Charley walked into the camp, toting a machine gun on his shoulder. He was shot down. Dying, he threw a grenade that killed one of the Tigers, Spec. 4 Michael D. O'Guinn. Higinbotham reckoned that the base camp was the best possible spot for the night defense. It was dry; the works were solid. They settled in and for the next twelve hours were undisturbed. Their night ambushes snared nothing.

Next morning there was no place to go except into more mountains. They headed north, splashed through a deep creek, and within the hour ran into another base camp, complete with classrooms and also unoccupied. Still it "smelled of food and of bodies lately there."

They moved a few rods along the main trail. Higinbotham came to a sign in Vietnamese which he could read. The words said, "Friend Go Straight." But right there the trail split and there were two fingers on the sign, pointing in opposite directions. The ambiguity not only stopped Hig; it irritated him and he said under his breath, "Those smart-aleck SOBs."

Since they were about to start a steep climb and the day was hot, they dropped their rucksacks, and the pile was left under guard by PFC Johnny L. Johnson, Jr., Spec. 4 Rockford W. Goddard and PFC Edward F. Christie.

The main body split, one team under S/Sgt. Bryant Pellum, Jr., going up one branch, the second team, under S/Sgt. William D. Fowler, taking the other, with Higinbotham riding along. Both parties almost immediately made contact, came under fire, and took losses. The flank with Higinbotham saw three men jump up from an earth bank as if to duck into the bush. They were gunned down as they ran. Next they bumped an outpost of four men, who withdrew, shouting and shooting. If Higinbotham's men drew any blood, it was at a price. PFC Frank E. Wilt fell, critically wounded. Higinbotham felt that unless he could get medevac for him, he would likely die. The thought preoccupied him, though he could hear firing around the party on the other trail.

Nothing has been said of the bush through which they were moving. Such descriptions are necessarily somewhat repetitious. Even so, the environment in which men fight does influence the action and the outcome. They were in primary jungle, with a three-layer canopy. At ground level the most obstructive growth was bamboo. It grew in thick clusters, ten to fifteen meters through, altogether impenetrable. Then there were occasional open spaces of about the same dimension. At best, any man's horizon averaged about twelve meters.

The trails came together again. So the two teams formed together once more and started moving north along a ridge finger. Concerned about clearing the casualty, Higinbotham made an oblique move, turning toward a ridge saddle with about ten of his people. The party included one medic, PFC Farras Hamilton, his RTO, PFC Terry L. Gray, several men who had been wounded on the other flank, and a correspondent, Mr. Just, who was along because he had once been a paratrooper. Wilt, no longer conscious, was bleeding badly.

They were given just time enough to settle among the light bamboo in a small hollow, notching the saddle. Then they came under a crashing fire—a company-size fire—from both heights, north and south, directly above the saddle. Three machine guns and many rifles flailed the bamboo; they had blundered directly into the center of an NVA main position. The bullet swarm drove them to ground, blocked their escape route and effectively sealed them in the hollow, which is how they stayed for the next four hours, too pinned to make any worth-while reply.

In the shattering minute when the fire closed round them Higinbotham was called on the RT by Private First Class

Johnson, who had been left guarding the rucksacks. Johnson said, "I am the only man left here—the only man. Everywhere I look I see VC." Johnson sounded hysterical, but he was right about it. Goddard and Christie were both dead.

Higinbotham said, "I'll get someone to you."

Capt. Chris C. Vurlumis, commander of Headquarters Company, 1/327th, had come along that day because, like Mr. Just, he was curious about how the Tigers operated. He was with the main body, about sixty meters distant, up the ridge finger.

Higinbotham called him, asking, "Can you take five men and bring back the rucksack party?"

Vurlumis was quite willing. He called for five self-starters and they fell in willingly enough also. An enemy platoon had set up an ambush halfway down the slope to where the trail split: they walked right into it.

Vurlumis and PFC Thomas L. Yohn were killed instantly. Sgt. Clifford A. Carter, Sgt. Doublas V. Hicks, Spec. 4 Douglas J. Bazemore, and PFC David A. Brisco were wounded.

That wiped out the rescue party at one blow; some of the wounded came crawling back to the company position and reported a little of what had happened. It still left Johnson alive and alone somewhere near the rucksacks—Higinbotham hoped—and somewhat terrified—he suspected.

These things had taken much longer in the doing than in the telling. Fire from the knob to the north of Higinbotham, while keeping him pinned, was also beating against the main body, so that it could neither advance nor pull back through the hours of midafternoon. Spec. 4 Eladio R. Marroquin, Jr., was killing while trying to charge up the slope. Sgt. Emil Burmeister was critically wounded making the same effort. Spec. 4 Edwood R. Sturtz, the other medic, was hit while trying to doctor Burmeister. Sgts. Francis J. Donovan and Norman D. Bonaparte were struck by bullets early in the fray but kept going.

Getting these reports, Higinbotham knew that it was time to call on the lightning; until he could reconsolidate and count his casualties, he could not even be sure the platoon was in business. At 1420 he called in an air strike: the stuff struck too high on the ridge and did not markedly dampen the fires. So he requested artillery. The forward artillery observer had flown off because his Huey was running out of fuel. Directing the fires was taken over by Capt. Burton T. Miller, of Reno, Nevada. The novelty of the arrangement was that he was the forward air observer.

When the shells began hitting on the ridge, Higinbotham called for them "lower and closer," "lower and closer," until at last the almost inevitable happened—two rounds exploded too low, too close, in fact, within the main position on the finger.

Bonaparte and Donovan, already bullet-wounded, were stricken with shell fragments. Two privates, lying next them, were so shocked by the concussion that they were first speechless, then babbled like idiots—broken reeds, fit only for hospitalization—when they could get it. That was the "hell of it," for young Higinbotham, a new skipper having his first day. He said, "I had men killed, wounded, taken away—my men—and I did not even get to see their faces or know their names."

By noontime Hackworth had known Higinbotham was in straits and needed help, but he had no one left to send to the fire. Dill's platoons were already far spread out, checkerboarding the ridges lying east of Kon Honong. At 1200 the First Platoon was moving about 1000 meters to the west of Tiger Force; the Second was about 1500 meters to the southwest. They were bumping and killing small groups of enemy as they went along, but while moving in the right direction, their progress was too slow. Third Platoon was still farther to the rear, attached to Bravo Company. Around 1500 Hackworth told Dill, "You disengage and get your platoons up to re-enforce the Tigers as fast as you can."

By 1600 the Second Platoon, under 2nd Lieut. Kirby Young, closed on Higinbotham's position. By that same hour First Platoon, under Lieut. Peter Mitchell, was within 100 meters of it. The pinned men could hear Mitchell and his people yelling but could not see them, such was the thickness of the bush. They returned the shout with a will.

Here was a terrific morale booster that endured for all of ten seconds. An NVA platoon had sifted downslope and was waiting in ambush for Mitchell, between his ground and Higinbotham's men on the ridge finger. First Platoon lost two men killed and three WIA in the first minute. Spec. 4 James Kombs was the first to die, several bullets hitting him in the chest. The medic, Spec. 4 John Dollinger, not knowing he was dead, started pulling him to cover behind a tree a little way up the slope. Hit by several bullets, Dollinger died. Platoon Sgt. John Dixon, hit by bullets in five or six places, lingered on for a time but died in late evening. The platoon went into recoil. Mitchell called Higinbotham, saying, "I can't move." So they had been zapped twice the same way in one day—ambush within an ambush.

Higinbotham was still trying vainly to consolidate, worrying about Johnson at the rucksacks and the other wounded strung along the trail in the effort to succor him. Now that he had the two platoons from Dill, uncertainty about their flanks complicated his use of artillery. He knew that he didn't dare risk calling it in on the narrow salient which the enemy held between his ground and Mitchell's; the margins were too thin.

He decided to have Young and his platoon attack up the slope to the north. If they could knock out the machine guns on the bunker line, maybe with such strength as was left to the Tigers he could get to Mitchell, though he was down to eighteen effectives. So ran his thoughts.

Young and his men got to the enemy first line, found it held only by a thin line of riflemen, who resisted weakly and were easily gunned down. But these were no hasty positions. They were stout-walled bunkers with connecting foxholes—permanent works, built to last. Encouraged, they charged on to the second line and were there blown down by a grenade shower, "many, many" coming at them. One fragment tore out Young's left eye. Five other men were hit. The line didn't recoil, nor did Young withdraw. They dropped right there and began working their weapons. They did not overwhelm the bunkers. But they stayed all night, firing and so broke the pressure against Higinbotham's position.

By then Higinbotham knew that Captain Willis and his people were on their way to him. With the enemy bullet fire tapering off, he was able to walk about and get some of his wounded moved to better protection. The dead had to be left unattended for the time being. There were now eight KIA and eighteen WIAs on the hill belonging to Tiger Force. Higinbotham had been struck by several grenade fragments but after getting bandaged was feeling little worse for it.

He couldn't afford to be otherwise. There was only one way in and out and he well knew it. He was able to steer Willis so that he would come over the same unscorched groove by which Young had arrived. That was sometime around 1800. Counting himself, Higinbotham had sixteen men left in condition to fight. More than half of the company was dead or down.

Willis and company had begun their day badly, still pinned down by enemy fire in two different positions. By noontime, with the aid of the artillery, he was able to break that deadlock and reconsolidate the force without further loss, after a 700-meter march.

When at around 1600 Hackworth called him, saying that he wanted the company to go help Higinbotham, Willis objected.

"I haven't recovered Sergeant Perkins' body," he said, "and he died trying to save my pinned-down platoon."

Hackworth was sympathetic. He had known Perkins as an utterly fearless soldier. But right now his main concern was the living.

He said to Willis, "That will have to wait."

Willis' column approached Higinbotham's position from the south and attacked straight along the finger of the day's fight, going 200 meters with marching fire, seeing no enemy, stirring up nothing alarming along the heights, though a few bullets buzzed past.

However, Willis could hear the sounds of something "very hot" going on along the flank where Mitchell and his men were still flattened.

Willis talked it over with Higinbotham, saying, "I think the enemy is already withdrawing. Let me form the perimeter. I will enclose your force and you can go on clearing your own problems."

Then he talked to Mitchell, who said, "Every time any of my men move, we draw fire." (This was on the RT.)

Willis replied, "Then I think we'd better figure on waiting until first light to come to you. If we try now in the dark, we'll stir a lot of fire and get more men killed."

Mitchell agreed.

All night long the men on the hill and the two commanders were at work evacuating the casualties. It had to be done with HH43 Husky, the Air Force's ship for picking up downed crews; the ship stays air-borne; the body in the basket is winched aloft on a cable. The flare ship, Smokey the Bear, stayed over position to assist the operation.

Medical supply had become completely exhausted. Resupply, along with ammunition and rations, was flown in; the crews of the Hueys simply kicked the bundles overboard, and sufficient were retrieved to serve immediate needs.

As first light cracked around 0450, Willis and his men drove through to Mitchell. There had been a brief, brisk fire fight. One prisoner was seized, with a large part of one side of his face shot away. After he identified himself as a member of Fourth Battalion, 24th Regiment, he was flown to hospital with the last batch of American casualties.

At 1100 Willis got a call from Hackworth: "Go back to where you were yesterday. Recover Perkins' body and police that battlefield." Added Hackworth, "After that, you can attack north."

Higinbotham, from his position in the saddle, had been directing the policing of his own battlefield through the morning. The night before he had reported Spec. 4 Douglas Bazemore killed in action in the attempt to save the rucksack force. That report had to be corrected. He was found wounded, but still living, within five meters of an enemy machine gun, just setting up in a foxhole, as Higinbotham's cleanup squad moved down the hill. The gun had shot him, putting bullets through the calves of both legs, breaking one of the legs, and knocking him back into a foxhole. Trebly wounded as he was, he grenaded the gun, wrecked it, and killed or wounded some of the crew. The cleanup squad found the blasted metal and thick clots of blood all around the position.

It is an almost unbelievable example of human endurance, in view of what had already happened to this soldier. He had been shot through the side the afternoon before. Through the night he would have brief periods of consciousness and would then black out recurrently. Afraid to call for help—knowing that no help could come—in his conscious minutes, he played dead. All around him were enemy soldiers. He heard arms being worked, orders being given, enemy wounded crying for attention. He heard the medevac ship come in; he made note that the enemy soldiers chattered more loudly when it came but did not fire on it. The other American bodies were found stripped, possessions gone, as were the rucksacks. Enemy soldiers stood directly over Bazemore, then walked away from him. None had bothered to take his .45 Colt from his hand. The blast which had blown him into the foxhole had flung it far away.

All sorts of debris were found right around him by the cleanup squad—claymore mines which the enemy had left in his flight, a trioxine (fuel) bar with deeply imbedded toothmarks, a starlightscope cut in twain by an artillery shard.

Dill was still in business, despite the fact that two platoons had been moved from under him. With his Third and Fourth he was lifted that morning from Kon Honong, flown directly east two kilometers and set down next to the hamlet, Dak Hanjro, where the Tigers had begun their journey into the wilderness. Dill was told by Hackworth: "You will get ready to attack toward Hill 1073; that's where we'll find Charley in real strength."

Willis—and not just because of his feeling of obligation to the dead sergeant—was gratified to return to his stamping ground of Monday. He had made two real hot contacts there and anticipated making more. By 1615 he had moved on north of his former scene of engagement and was coming even with the western side of Hill 1073. Hackworth called him then and said, "Set up a base camp and start patrolling to the eastward. Tomorrow we'll go to town." Dill was in a good defensive position by then, on high ground, about one kilometer to the southwest of Willis. Nearby he had cut an LZ, with a nice clean approach for a chopper, free of menacing heights; it had been an easy task, a quick machete hacking through young and tender bamboo. Dill figured all he had to do was move the two platoons northeast along the creek bed and he would link up with Willis.

Willis completed the tying-in of his defensive perimeter. His patrols for the night ambushes were standing by and waiting for their marching orders. It was 1630. Willis was about to call Hackworth to tell him that the spadework essential to arraying the battalion for a full armed attack was done. A best-laid plan—right at the moment of being flushed down the hopper by a pull of one chain.

Hackworth called him. His message was: "Hold everything. You may have to move quickly to relieve Company C, Five O Deuce, heavily engaged and about to be overrun."

At 1750 Hackworth called again to say, "You're going. That company has a new commander, Captain Carpenter."

For the moment it didn't make much difference to Willis. He reflected out loud, "Whichever side of this mountain we fight on, it's just one more piece of the same porcupine."

The Hackers, II

Out of the whole battle of Toumorong the one famous incident is the epic of Captain Carpenter and the heroic company that escaped immolation by a distance not more than is required to raise a few shoots of bamboo.

Many American soldiers were killed during the campaign. None, according to the record, perished meanly. The great number met death courageously, going at the enemy.

The Carpenter story will be told over and over and in the telling, through the years, will become ever more enlarged and distorted. For that is the way with any classic in military history. The truth, which ever should be good enough, is never permitted to walk clear-eyed.

In this chronicle the Carpenter story is told separately. It must stand alone because the fight by men of the 327th never became joined with it. Hackworth had brought on the battle; until this day, except for Captain Brown's company, his men had fought the great part of it. Then came a call; they responded. The consequence to these worn troops for so doing is as poignant, as harrowing, as anything that can happen to men in war.

The start was a call from General Pearson to Hackworth, raising the question: "A Company from 502nd is about to be overrun; can you do anything to help?"

Hackworth replied, "I have a company a thousand meters south of the position you give. I'd like to estimate before I commit myself."

Hackworth then called Willis and asked his views. Willis said, "I can try, but I warn you, this one is going to be rough."

Hackworth called Pearson, told him that he thought in the circumstances control of Alpha Company should be passed to Colonel Emerson; then he gave Willis marching orders and on the RT advised Emerson on what axis the column would move toward Carpenter.

Willis called Emerson. From his view the whole conversation was unsatisfactory. He was given a coordinate but could not get an answer to the question: "Is that the enemy position or our position?" So he called the S-3, Maj. Arthur Taylor, who gave him a still different coordinate. The connection hummed with static and battle roar. At the end of twenty minutes of double talk, which only bred confusion, Willis said, "Oh, to hell with it!" and broke off. He decided to strike out on an azimuth due north. One of his aides, who had been monitoring another radio, said to him, "They say Carpenter has only twenty men left." Willis replied, "So we start right now."

Hackworth had been thinking things over. It looked to him as if Emerson's span of control was overstretched because of the far spreading of his companies. He would not be able to handle Alpha Company. He called Emerson and said, "Look, if it's all right, I'll sort of direct Ben, though I have passed him to you." Emerson replied, "O.K."

Willis marched in two columns, fifty meters apart, Second Platoon followed by Heavy Weapons, Third Platoon, followed by Headquarters elements, then First Platoon. They proceeded up the steepest slope they had yet encountered. Its tallest trees rose to 100 feet. There was not much bamboo; instead the jungle floor was heavily grown with matted thorn vine, lianas and banyan props. No trails ran through this forest; visibility at best was around thirty meters. That left no choice for Willis and his people but to hack their way through, with the point men wielding the machetes. That way they could move at a rate of 500 meters per hour, provided the point men were rotated every ten minutes. They cut their way across the first two ridge fingers—400 meters—in the first fifty minutes, after which they were fighting the dark as much as the forest.

They came to the third finger. On the radio the point reported back to Willis: "There are steps hollowed out in this bank as far up as we can see. We don't know what to make of it." Willis went forward to look. The steps looked new. The footholds were laid with bamboo. But a two-minute inspection did not lessen his perplexity; he knew that to cut his way out and around the end of the finger would take at least two extra hours. The uncertainty ended when he said aloud, "Oh hell, piss on it!" and led the column up the stairs. Though they made the top without contact, much to his relief, they found themselves amid a complex of bunkers, short trenches and spider holes, none of them occupied.

Right there Willis changed course twenty degrees, to get on a line which he thought would take him straight into Carpenter's position. He was confident now that he would get there. It was 250 meters to the next dip (it was hardly a ravine), the bush had thinned out, and they made it in fifteen minutes. The time was 1915 when they started up a small finger, about fifty meters high, that did not show on the map.

They got about halfway. The two columns were moving parallel, their fronts even. Machine-gun fire, AK47 fire, and grenades came against both of them. Tree snipers blazed away from the crotches of the banyans. The NVA line had waited until Willis' men closed to within twenty meters. Men fell—there was no way to determine how many—from that opening volley.

The fire fight went on twenty minutes. Reports from both platoon leaders were getting to Willis. "I'm taking heavy casualties." "How many?" "I don't know, but many; I have dead and wounded all over the place." "But how many?" "A lot." So it went, none of it helpful to him.

Willis knew that there was a bit of panic, and more than a little exaggeration, in what he heard.

At his own CP, Captain Dill was monitoring these conversations and relaying what he heard to Hackworth. Hack said to him, "It may not be long till you have to hit the road."

Willis felt certain that he could take the position—but at quite a cost—and his job was to get through and relieve Carpenter. So he backtracked with the idea of seeking a way around the position. The platoons crawled out of it, dragging their casualties—sixteen dead and wounded until that time—and moved back up the finger they had just crossed, with the object of regrouping for a fresh start. Only now the march order had become reversed with the change in direction. Willis reflected that he would leave one platoon—probably the Fourth—atop the finger to cover the casualties. Then he would take the other three, head north and "go like hell." That plan died aborning.

As they got to within thirty meters of the hump of jungle they had hacked their way through hardly forty minutes before, three machine guns and several score AK47s opened fire on both column fronts from thirty meters to their fore. Again, out of this still more bewildering surprise, they took heavy loss from the opening volley.

Regard the situation: There were now dead men and wounded men at front and rear of both columns, which condition superinduced total immobility in the entire company. It became tied by its own weight.

Willis, who was still in the center of what had been the right but was now the left column, called the leader of First Platoon, Lieut. Kenneth·Collins, to ask, "What's the skinny?" —the real dope.

What he didn't know yet was that Collins had had his left eye blown out by a grenade. He had picked the eyeball off the ground and was now carrying it around in his right hand, laughing about it. Nothing less funny than that ever made soldiers idolize their leader.

Saying nothing of the eye, Collins replied, "These bastards have too many machine guns and now the sons-of-bitches are rolling us with grenades. The platoon is becoming split, due to care-for-the-wounded pulling the able-bodied in opposite directions.''

Willis asked, ''Can you move an element either right or left to try to get those guns?''

Collins said, ''I'll try.''

He did. He tried it both ways. But the two probes were repulsed, and each probe cost the front squad two more men.

It had been raining for more than an hour. At 2100 the water came like a cloudburst. The steep red-clay slope became a toboggan. Prone men could stay in place only by clutching to vines and tree roots. The light kick of a weapon or the near explosion of a grenade would send them careening down the bank. Thereafter the company lost all sense of the passing of time. Watches became caked with the red clay beyond any chance of reading the dial. Willis continued to call Dill for the hour. He knew, he said later, that if the company was in the same position when dawn came, it would be annihilated. The rain and the pitch black, compounding its misery, were also saving it for the time being.

The only persons in the CP with Willis were his RTO's—Private First Class Wheeler, a new arrival, and Private First Class Corrao, an old hand. Both accepted the company plight so stoically that Willis felt bucked up.

Collins and Platoon Sergeant Woods, who led the other column, made answer to Willis' numerous calls as blithely as if the company were holding a picnic. Willis marveled at them. He said to Wheeler, ''I'll bet those guys don't know how bad this situation really is.''

The enemy guns continued firing. At 0200 Willis told himself that he was being ''a damned fool'' and had better call the whole thing off. Down in the draw on his rear, through which he had twice passed, he had noted a relatively flat and clear area that was about forty meters square; it was the only place around where he could possibly set and hold a defensive perimeter, though it had the slight flaw that it was dominated on three sides by high ground.

He passed around the word to the leaders: "Pull back to the draw. Dig in and prepare to fight it out down there."

The spot was about 220 meters to the rear of the most forward squads. There were now twenty-six wounded and six dead in the company. For some of them the movement downhill was little labored, for they could sit and skid down much of the slope. But the more critically wounded had to be carried, by teams of four men working in relays, once they were pulled into slope defilade. So the shift in position dragged out over three hours, and at 0500 some equipment was still being brought off the finger. The less desperately wounded were simply pulled down the slope. Willis heard one of them say to another, "Man, don't we look like a herd of water buffaloes?"

Collins' people were the hardest to get out because they were cheek to jowl with the enemy. They had to back away one man at a time, while the others covered them with fire. The men down the slope resorted to yelling and firing in the air to guide them. There persisted trouble and lack of direction. Collins had bled too much, shock was on him, and he was virtually in a coma. Willis sent a patrol formed of Platoon Sergeant Harrison, Spec. 4 Steve Schmidt and Private First Class Wheeler (the green hand) to take over and provide enough steady fire up the slope that Collins and the other survivors could be pulled out. It was successful. No end surprising in the modern history of war is the number of good soldiers named Wheeler. Wheelers are just not that common; in fact, far less common than dealers.

Because of faulty information, the short-circuiting of channels and the abnormal stresses of a grueling demand on the emotional resources of men, an unpleasantness had arisen.

At about 0300 Hackworth had talked to Sergeant Harrison on radio. He asked him, "How many of your WIA cases are critical?" Without referring to Willis, and making no effective resolve to tell him about it later, Harrison said, "At least seventeen." Though conditions were not really that bad, Hackworth took the report at face value. It gave him the belief that Willis' plight was utterly desperate.

Hack called Willis immediately afterward. Without quoting Harrison, he said, "Ben, I want to get Hueys into your perimeter at dawn for medevac."

Several pilots had at once volunteered for the run on hearing that there were seventeen men who might die if they could not be flown to hospital.

Willis stoutly protested. "Not on your life. I don't have a perimeter yet. We're still moving. I can't stand an assault till I get set up. I'm afraid of giving the whole thing away."

The exchange of view was going through Captain Dill, the relay, who was doing his best to take the sting out of the conversation between the two men. Hackworth hung up, retreating for the moment.

Quickly he called again and said to Willis, "I intend to send that medevac to get your wounded out. Now what have you got to lose?"

Willis replied, "I don't want to give this position away."

Said Hackworth, "That's BS, and you know it. The enemy is not fooled about where you are. I want to try these volunteer crews."

Willis remained unwilling.

Hackworth said to him, "Listen, if you don't want to do it, give over the company to your second-in-command and get him on the radio."

So there was an impasse, and a pregnant pause, as Willis said, "Give me one minute to think this thing out." He considered. Either he went along with Hackworth's idea or the command would go to Sergeant Harrison, since Collins by now could not function at all, which Hackworth did not know.

Willis said, "All right, I'll go along. But you hold off that Huey for one half hour. Give me that much time." Hack said, "O.K., I give you three zero."

Though Hack had firmly repeated the figure, right then he relented a little bit, and instead of rushing the ship forward, he gave Willis a full hour. The first Huey came over at 0430, to be greeted by a blaze of fire. While 300 feet up, the ship was hit by five bullets, and the pilot shied off, returning to base.

For the first time that night Willis had a good belly laugh.

He was entitled to it. Hackworth, the customarily firm guiding hand, had for once been wrong, though Willis still did not know why.

Dill, wide awake, still sat on the hill north of Dak Hanjro. At 0400 Hackworth had given him a warning order, "Be prepared to send out a patrol to find Willis."

Dill said, "I doubt the wisdom of that."

Willis heard him and said, "Relay to the battalion commander that I doubt it also."

Both captains figured that that was the one sure way to lose a patrol. Dill was down to ninety men and fifteen of them were out on an ambush.

At 0500 Hackworth called Dill, saying, "Take what you've got. Make contact with Willis and try to relieve the pressure on him." Dill moved at first light. Two hours later he was 1000 meters directly north of his jump-off point.

By then Willis had all of his men down the hill, though not all equipment. The WIAs and the KIAs were grouped in the center of the position. A check showed that about 80 per cent of the men had lost their packs, canteens, machetes and entrenching tools in sliding down the slope. That last deficit hurt worst. Willis established some priorities. "Take the few spades we got. Dig first the outer perimeter. Then dig to get the casualties under cover. Dig last the company CP." For two hours they toiled hard enough to banish fear and solitude.

Dill was following a trail well to the west of the line that Willis had taken. The column crossed a creek and started up what Dill figured would be the next to the last ridge. He remembered Hackworth's admonition: "Don't get yourself fully engaged; you're the last we've got." So he held up, to call for artillery to soften the way ahead; there was now plenty of fire available at the Dak Djram base. Then he changed his mind: if there were any overshoots of the enemy position, he would hit Willis. Instead, he decided to move up the finger lengthwise. So his headquarters people and the weapons platoon were held in the draw to keep open an escape route.

Their climb began at 1130. Third Platoon was leading

and Dill went with it. Second Platoon immediately followed. They got just twenty meters. Two machine guns opened fire on them. The lead man, Sgt. Isaac Steigelman, with only three weeks to go in Vietnam, caught one burst in the stomach. Dill heard the whack of bullets. Steigelman spun halfway round, crashed and folded. Private First Class Vasquez, the aid man, rushed to help him. Dill didn't see him go: he was flat now and peering through the bush, trying to get the outline of the enemy bunker, about fifteen meters away. The second burst got Vasquez right through the heart and his dead body pitched down the slope.

Dill called Hackworth and told him about it.

Hackworth asked, "Do you think you can get on?"

Dill said, "I'm going to have one more try."

Dill called Platoon Sgt. Barney Rasor on radio. Rasor is a Negro. He was not more than eight feet behind Dill, but Dill couldn't see him. Dill asked, "Do you think you can take the position?" Rasor answered, "Yes, sir, I think so." Twenty-three people with him, Rasor started sideslipping toward the right of the bunker. A third machine gun opened on them, with at least three tree snipers firing from roosts above the gun. Dill knew he was stuck. He personally had gone to earth in an abandoned enemy spiderhole and the bullets were now singing around it. Rasor's platoon was pinned and motionless.

Rasor called Dill and said, "Sir, I am coming the hell on back."

Dill said, "You come the hell on back if you can."

Dill scuttled out and led Rasor's men back to the draw. Second Platoon remained on the slope, twenty meters above where it had started. With this fallback, the enemy came surging down the hill right after Dill's men. Three of Rasor's were gunned down before they could turn about. Dill heard from Second Platoon, "They're coming around our flank," and next he saw the men of Second backing out of the position, not running, but on their hands and knees, and firing. Yet they had left their dead on the hill.

The fight had lasted until 1230. Moving them one squad at a time, Dill took his force to a knoll about 300 meters from the action and went into perimeter. He figured it was time to call on the artillery. The running of the shoot was turned over to the forward observer, Lieut. Lloyd Sack. The infantrymen turned to digging their foxholes. The engineer squad that had come along with Dill got busy with their chain saws and explosives, cutting out a landing zone.

For all of ten minutes the knoll was a little hive of industry. Then the NVA, having sneaked along the creek bed, came right up over the rim of it, charging. For ten minutes the duel went on at grenade range. Dill had two 60 mm mortars in his position that had been recaptured from the Viet Cong. While the fight went on around the rim, the mortars put forty rounds on the enemy bunker line. Slowly the attack eased off and then Dill called for a tactical air strike.

By 0730 Willis had managed to get all of his men in some kind of protective position, foxhole or other. The usual shuddering misty morning had yielded to bright sun. They stayed on defense. Off and on the enemy sprayed fire into their ground, but they did not bother to return it. Later the enemy "went fishing" with unobserved mortar fire, but all of the rounds were over. Several tear-gas grenades were rolled into the position; they all had a good cry together. By noon Willis realized that Dill would not get to him. He pondered, then sent a reconnaisance patrol 400 meters to the westward; it returned in an hour, having made no contact. Willis called in artillery and several air strikes. How to get the wounded out was still the main problem. Willis was told that Private Goodall, who'd been shot in the side, wished to see him.

When Willis went to him, Goodall said, "Ah, screw it, Captain. I know I'm going to die. So I want you to take off my boots."

One aid man, Spec. 4 Mengo, who was standing by, said, "Hey, he's not that bad hurt."

Another aid man, Private First Class Centenio, said, "That's right, he ain't."

As Willis paused for a moment in uncertainty, Goodall died. The eyes closed, the chin dropped, there was not a groan.

Mengo saying, "It wasn't your fault, Captain," didn't help Willis one bit. He was shaken and sore as hell at himself.

At 1530 Willis sent forth another patrol to check the escape route. This time it was discovered that the enemy had thrown a block across the creek bed that had been free in midmorning. That put them on all four sides. Willis called for artillery fire on the creek bed.

Hackworth by now was well aware that Emerson's battalion was no longer under unusual stress. Also he had gotten the word from General Pearson that all troops were to be withdrawn so that a B-52 strike could be thrown against the main enemy positions. (Twice, before Hackworth and Emerson had become deeply embroiled, Pearson had requested a B-52 strike against this same ground, only to be turned down.) Hackworth reckoned that Dill was in fairly good shape and holding a strong position; he figured that Dill should hold out there for a while, so that the NVA would not suspect the bomber strike was coming on. But he knew that Willis and the company had to be extracted, being in no condition to fight. So he attached two platoons from Alpha of the 17th Cavalry (organic to the division) to Higinbotham's cutback Tiger Force.

Higinbotham was to move from the saddle where he had his fight, to a position between Dill and Willis, there to establish a perimeter so that Willis could fall back through him for evacuation.

Hackworth called Willis and said, "You get ready to move right after dark."

Through the afternoon Dill was beating off attackers. Hackworth got up to him at 1330. His Huey was hit by five bullets while setting him down on the new landing zone. The enemy had renewed the direct assault. Hackworth jumped into a foxhole, already pulling the trigger of his M-16. The point of the attack came straight at him: he shot down five men.

Dill's men gaped in astonishment. One soldier yelled, "Look at the Major fight."—It was their first view of Hack and few of them even knew his name.

Most of the NV killed around Dill's perimeter—and there were many—did not die that way—in counterattack. They did not come on firing. They were trying to go past Dill, one way or the other. Some were coming forward, carrying rice bags and ammunition; the second stream moved in the other direction, carrying out wounded and dead. Even after they knew Dill was there, they made no attempt to deviate and continued to feed into the fire.

General Pearson flew into the position. He and Dill lay on the rim of the knoll and counted dead NVA bodies on the slope. There were twenty-three. One hour later all of those bodies were gone. (Here is a commentary on the worth of body count as the measure of relative success.) None of these bodies was included in the official count. Five NVA soldiers were killed while trying to pull back bodies from the hill; they were not counted either. Dill wanted the enemy weapons scattered along the slope. He sent two patrols to collect them. They both ran into fire before they had picked up one weapon. The first patrol lost four men wounded; the second lost two. That was too much for Dill. He said, "To hell with that, we will try no more." From where he directed the fight, he could see at least fifteen weapons on the slope. The company collected not one.

Every Huey flown into the position got him with bullets. But Dill had no other source of water for his troops. So the choppers had to keep coming.

The company lost only the two KIAs to the machine-gun fire. S/Sgt. John D. Caldwell, another Negro, took four slugs in his body and died two days later while being flown to Pleiku. The company lost another twelve men WIA during its two days of being a small U.S. island amid a moving tide of enemy. After completing the LZ, the engineer detachment fitted into the rifle line. At 1200 on 11 June Hackworth called Dill to say, "You've had about enough; come out of there at 2000." They moved out via another creek bed, with H & I artillery fires skipping along in front of them. They made it slick. By then Willis and company were long gone from the scene.

As his second evening came on, Willis knew that he

would either have to take a chance on medevac or move to blast his way out. He got word that Husky, the Air Force rescue ship, was being laid on for him. At the same time he sent a third patrol scouting along the creek the way the other two had gone. Forcing his decision, the men became not just restive but surly. Several came up to him and said, "What the hell is wrong? We can fight our way out of here." He called Hackworth and said, "Never mind Husky; we're going out under our own power." The patrol returned a few moments after that; it had gone 500 meters along the creek without drawing fire.

So at dark the company moved out, walking down the middle of the stream. The creek was between three and five meters across, according to where the channel narrowed, around eighteen inches deep, muddy, but breaking a great deal of foaming, noisy water over the rocks, flooded as it was by the heavy rains of the night before. On this thoroughfare they made 1200 meters in the nine hours between nightfall and sunup, wading along in a kind of tactile shuffle.

Only two of the wounded had to be carried out in poncho litters. They were up front. The other wounded hobbled along, helped by their comrades. They brought out only one body. That body had to be cached before they were far along the way; the whole column was sagging and slowing under the weight; it was recovered ten days later.

At first flare ships tried to help them along. But there was a heavy overcast and the lights were breaking above the clouds, doing them no good. It was just as well that the lights were discontinued.

Friendly shellfire walked along with them, plastering both sides of the valley. That helped drown out the noise of their movement; of greater help still was the incessant splashing of the boiling stream.

Around midnight Willis had reason to thank God for that. The scene and shadows along both banks swiftly changed, and it struck him like a blow in the face that the column was moving right through an enemy base camp. There was nothing to do but keep going.

Two bullets whistled over Willis' shoulder, fired from not more than ten feet away. He did not return the fire. The camp contained an enemy cadre and most of the men remained sleeping. One soldier had awakened and, hearing the sound of movement, had gotten off two quick shots, probably not even looking.

For the next few seconds the numbers of the forms passing him in the stream must have awed him somewhat.

Willis came abreast of him, his M-16 pointed at the man's chest. They stood not five feet apart. The soldier's AK47 was pointed straight at Willis.

The captain vigorously shook his head.

The NVA soldier shook his head just as vigorously.

It was a truce, cease-fire, gentleman's agreement or a deal, call it what you will. At least the understanding of the compact was mutual and complete.

"If you don't try to fire again and alarm the camp, nobody here will try to kill you."

The soldier sank back into darkness and Willis stumbled on. The biggest chill to come Willis' way, it was the company's narrowest squeak. The column was in no position or condition to fight. One machine gun could have wiped it out.

As the tail of the column got out of this gauntlet and Willis felt a little of the tension ease off, there came a call on the RT from First Sergeant Rutledge.

He said, "Unless we stop, one of these casualties is going to die."

Willis fairly exploded: "Hell, don't you realize that if we do stop everybody's going to die?"

The man didn't die. At 0445 the column linked up with Tiger Force, relieving Willis' worry of the last hour that he was coming out on the wrong creek.

At dawn the medevac Hueys came in and lifted out the wounded to the hospital at Dak To. The men who were still mobile marched the several miles to the artillery base on the Dak Djram.

Many of them had gone four nights without sleep.

By high noon they were all sleeping.

Still the battalion was not withdrawn. When I visited Hack on his last LZ, his people had been seventeen straight days in line. They had chopped the LZ out of the jungle the night before, and my Huey was the first or second to try it. The hole wasn't quite large enough. When the chopper sat down for an instant so that I could duck out, the rotor slashed through a clump of bamboo rearward and a five-inch tree trunk forward. Hack and his headquarters group had killed five Viet Cong on this same site the night before. The Huey had arrived in a downpour. Every man around Hack was soaked through; but a more cheerful group than his I have yet to meet in war.

Two days later they marched back to Dak To under their own power. Bearded, crummy, stinking, they still strutted.

By then the brigade staff had wrapped up the statistics proving that Hawthorne Two was considerable of a battle. They read:

	Enemy		Friendly	
KIA	459 (counted)	KIA		39
KIA	485 (add. est.)	WIA		196

As for the artillery, the lights had fired 15,250 rounds and the heavies 4,020 rounds.

The 10th Aviation Battalion could point with pride to its performance in support of the brigade. Its choppers had carried 8,657 people and 395 tons of cargo while flying 1,579 hours. Forty of its missions had been carried out under fire; fifteen of its choppers had been hit.

The Long Bite

By early morning of 7 June, General Pearson had realized it was time to commit such strength as was available from Emerson's battalion to lift some of the heat from Hackworth.

He also ordered up from Tuy Hoa Bravo Company of the 327th Battalion, which was working the ridges north of that port.

Brown's Alpha Company, after two nights of fighting at the battery position, was too beat-up and weary for immediate use.

The question was where to put Emerson. There is always a tendency, sometimes to be resisted, to go along with the made pattern. The ARVN Ranger Battalion, employed in the sweep by which Toumorong was relieved, had started from an LZ at the northwest corner of the zone of operations. That LZ still beckoned, and so it became the jump-off line for Emerson and his people.

Later Pearson chided himself that he had made a tactical mistake. He had launched Emerson on too long a bite; the force was too far from the already-seething center, ten kilometers distant.

Emerson found it to be that way. Moving southeast, his two companies beat the woods throughout 7 June, making no contact and finding no enemy works. The night was also without incident. Brown's company returned to the battalion in the morning of 8 June, still so much the worse for wear that Emerson put it in reserve.

Sill's Bravo Company was sent eastward right after dawn and was shortly contending against a washboarded terrain, with low-lying but steep-sided ridges, heavily wooded and running on almost endlessly.

The Recondo platoons moved out to checkerboard the countryside to the westward.

Charley Company walked a valley, roughly on a parallel to Bravo's line of march and pointing toward the high ground where Hackworth's companies were engaged. It was under a new skipper, Captain Carpenter, on his second tour in Vietnam, though better known to the public as the one-time Lonesome End of a football team on the Hudson.

It was Bravo Company that Emerson particularly worried about even before giving a thought to where he would establish his next command post. That would depend on operational developments. At 0800 he boarded his Huey and went looking for Sill and company.

Shortly he was directly above Bravo's column, or thought that such was the case, because of what Sill said on radio, though Emerson could not see the company, and Sill could not see the chopper.

The Huey dropped to 800 feet, to be greeted by a burst of .50 machine-gun fire. The first sensation was of tracers winking out a few feet from the aircraft. Then from the edge of a wood, perhaps 300 meters to his front, Emerson saw four guns firing.

He yelled, "Christ, look at that!"

The pilot, banking sharply left, said, giving the coordinate, "That's where I mark the position."

Emerson said, "So do I."

Sill cut in, "My God, that puts them within 200 meters of me."

Emerson told the pilot, "There's something wrong here. Let's make another pass and be sure."

So they barreled on back at 500 feet, again drew fire, and escaped unscathed. But they had been slightly wrong about the coordinates and Sill was mixed up on his location. He was 500 meters to the southwest of the guns and heading south. Emerson told him to reverse direction and go northeast. That should put him on a line toward the four guns.

Carpenter and his men continued on with their short march to the base of Hill 1073, on the far side of which Hackworth's companies had become embroiled. Gridline 39 had been set as the boundary between the two battalions, an allocation which decisively affected the day's startling developments, none of which was to highlight Sill and his company. Yet most signs pointed their way.

Having started well, and seemingly put on a hot trail, they walked and sweated and fumed through the rest of the morning but could not find the four-gun position. Very likely, after firing on Emerson, the guns had been moved elsewhere.

Yet it was Sill who concerned Emerson chiefly. When shortly before the noon hour Emerson set up his command post in a cozy nook within the jungle just off a pleasant glade suited by nature for chopper landings, his highest expectations still rode with Sill, who was about 2000 meters to the north of him.

Before the noon hour had gone, he was more certain than ever that he was right.

Sizzling news was coming in from Sill, but nothing important from Carpenter, who had been turned back from a feast.

Now heading south again, Sill "had come upon a main trail showing unmistakable signs of recent use."

Next from Sill: "We have just killed a VC on the trail; I am sure that he is a lieutenant."

Right on the heels of that news came this report: "We have come across commo wire running along the trail. I have sent a Recondo element [12 men] down the trail, with a machine gun, to follow the wire."

The CP leaned to these tidings. Brown and his people began to stir, figuring that a hurry call to re-enforce Sill might come at any moment. Emerson stayed glued to his radio at ground level, tense and eager for whatever word came next from Bravo Company. And all of this was to change dramatically within the hour, when the ball bounced in quite another direction.

Sill's Recondo patrol went 600 yards, then found that the trail and wire turned due north, which was reported to Battalion. Putting his Second Platoon in the lead, Sill followed after, the men moving on single file.

They were just barely under way when Lieut. James Apodaca, leader of the patrol, called on radio to say, "We have come under fire from a fifty-millimeter machine gun and several rifles, but we are not yet hurt." The patrol had not run into an ambush; the fire was coming from somewhere up the slope, and the positions could not be seen.

Sill said to him, "Move on up to the high ground and try to concentrate fire on their flank. I doubt they know you are there."

Sill relayed the news to Emerson, who told him, "Move all your people north and get with Apodaca; he may be bumping the real thing."

Within five minutes or less Emerson knew better; Carpenter began bumping "the real thing." It so wholly engrossed the CP that relatively little attention thereafter could be given to Sill's unsensational go.

Right after the start the Third Platoon got sidetracked onto a branch of the main trail, made 200 meters in the wrong direction, ran into three enemy skirmishers, killed them, captured two AK47s and a Mauser, discovered its mistake, and backtracked. The First Platoon, by then 600 meters away, was engaged by fire from the flank in the same minutes and lost five men, wounded. This was at the same spot where the Recondo patrol had been fired upon.

By the time Sill worked his way to the front of the main body, the .50 machine gun had gone quiet again and First Platoon had moved on uphill. The casualties were laid out alongside the trail in charge of the medic. He was working on Private First Class Thompson, who died soon afterward.

Sill called back for men from the Fourth Platoon to come forward to carry the wounded uphill. Heavy Weapons men in Vietnam often draw this backbreaking chore. The grade ahead was steep enough that the four-man lift for each casualty had to be changed every fifty meters. Sniper fire came in on this part of the column from the ridge slope at right angles to the way First Platoon had gone. Sill told Lieut. Dick Crockett to take some of his men and probe in that direction. There was a sudden volleying above them and the sniping ceased. Crockett returned, saying, "We killed one VC and the others ran away."

Sill pushed on for the high ground. He was now worrying more about getting a medevac ship in than about hunting the enemy, though the march still guided on the commo wire. Somewhere on the crest he might find bush less thick where he could hack out an LZ. For the next two hours there was no fire or any sighting worth report. The movement became torpid. In that time they gained the top, but they had not climbed more than 400 meters.

In late afternoon they started cutting the LZ and by twilight had cleared a pad large enough to receive one Huey. Most of the company had deployed in an irregular circle well out from where the work went on. The medevac chopper came on, started to descend; from a knob at least 600 meters away the .50 machine gun opened fire. The pilot shied off and was gone.

One of the wounded men was losing a great deal of blood. His plight, more than all else, concerned Sill.

He asked the senior aid man, Spec. 4 Joe de Lucas, "Give me your best judgment—can Wilcox live the night?"

De Lucas said, "I believe he can."

Sill's decision turned on that assurance. The company would go into perimeter right where it was and he would quit fretting about the casualties. Dark had fallen. An electrical storm was coming up. They would maintain a 50 per cent alert and hope that some of the men could get a little rest. An ambush would be set up on the trail, 200 meters from where they had cut the LZ. They would call for artillery fires frequently just to be on the safe side.

No stars hung over them that night, and they knew that they wore none. It had been a routine day, for Louis F. Sill, Jr., Class of '63 USMA, a hellishly dull day, and as it ended, he was not unhappy that the lightning was striking elsewhere than along the ridge top that was his bed.

The Case of the Unlonesome End

When Capt. William S. Carpenter, Jr., of Springfield, Pa., and of West Point football fame, led Charley Company forth at 0700 on the morning of 8 June, 1966, it was with the feeling that the day would yield nothing worth writing home about.

The battalion, 2/502nd Regiment, under Lieut. Col. Henry (Hank) Emerson, felt no less touchy and frustrated. Except for Able Company, its units had come a little late to the Battle of Toumorong (Operation Hawthorne), staged far to the west in the Central Highlands of South Vietnam. The laurels of the early action were with 1/327th, commanded by Maj. David H. Hackworth.

Then when it was committed, the battalion had been landed by Hueys at least four miles too far west and north, a tactical miscalculation which Brig. Gen. Willard Pearson later charged against himself, for the record. There followed a full day of futile bush-beating southward along the jungle trails, of which came nothing to troops except greater fatigue, a plague of tree leeches and a sense of missing the show.

Charley Company, taking the field for the first time under Carpenter's lead, though he was on his second tour in Vietnam, had maintained an ambush position throughout the night before. Missing most of its sleep, it had seen nothing worth noting and heard not one suspicious sound.

Now, in full daylight under a clear sky, it was returning approximately to the ground of its wearisome and profitless vigil. Emerson had told Carpenter to move only to the base, or thereabouts, of Hill 1073, a stride of only 500 meters from the ambush site. It seemed altogether unlikely that one more half mile would reverse poor fortune.

The company advanced in three platoon columns, the right and left flanks being separated by about 400 meters. The center column guided on a one-squad point which kept 200 meters to the fore. Just as the point squad reached the base of Hill 1073, an enemy soldier came out of a side trail equidistant between this scout element and the main body. Five men of the platoon fired and at least one dealt him a fatal bullet. He proved to be a medical laboratory technician laden with the equipment of his workshop.

No time was lost in speculating about his gadgets. Because the contact had taken place, First Platoon continued marching up the first finger of the great ridge for about 600 meters. Then and there it stopped, though not because it was confronted by a far-spread and seemingly unoccupied complex of enemy bunkers, lean-tos and trenches. According to the map, First Platoon was just about to go past the boundary with Hackworth's battalion, which in operations tight or loose is a very real trespass. Carpenter told the men to go into a defensive perimeter and hold steady. Of all that was happening to the battalion on the other side of the hill this morning these men knew nothing. They could hear no sounds of firing. For lack of knowledge, they felt very much alone.

Meanwhile Carpenter's headquarters people and the Fourth Platoon had converged along the bank of a broad creek curving around the base of Hill 1073. Then Third Platoon came abreast of the same creek, 350 meters from them. It was a refreshing setting for a fall-out lasting two minutes.

Three enemy soldiers popped out of a side trail several rods to the rear of where Fourth Platoon idled. One man— the Vietnamese interpreter—was looking in the right direction and, seeing them, cried warning. 1st Sgt. Sabalauski, probably the oldest fighter in the line in Vietnam, whirled, fired and killed the front man—range twenty meters. He also wounded the second man, who swiftly vanished uptrail. Sabalauski is somewhat heavy for sprinting. So Sgts. Nicholas R. Sorenberger and William E. Cummings took out after the quarry. He evaded. But fifty meters or so above the creek they ran into another Charley, walking toward them and carrying two water pails. They killed this Gungha Din.

Coincidentally (the time was exactly 1000) Carpenter got a call on the TR from Emerson. His message was this: "Hackworth requests that you back off a thousand meters to the north. There you will block any trails pointing to the east. Hack is about to call for a tac air strike against Hill one-oh-seven-three and he doesn't want any of your people to get hurt."

To troops not averse to being noticed, that signal was a heartbreaker. Carpenter read it as a portent that another day's hunting would be wasted. Emerson, too, rated it as a down for no gain and very unfeeling on Hackworth's part. Here they were just about to get their teeth into something worth biting, and the other battalion, for prudential reasons, was taking it away from them. On the other hand, there was the outside chance that the enemy force that had manned the bunker line might be trying for a getaway to the north and could be overtaken, a contingency seeming so remote that they felt no consolation. While field soldiers may not yearn for a fight, they positively abhor marching and countermarching to no positive end.

The company marched directly north from 1000 to 1430 with no contact, a four-and-one-half-hour haul which carried them considerably farther than one thousand meters. Most of the way the trail ran straight through a flat grown thick with elephant grass standing much higher than a man. It was a welcome respite from hard exertion, though the day was hot and the sun so bright that they did not damp their boots in crossing the green sea. They climbed the first finger of another great ridge walking the valley to the north. That leg proved to be a man-killer. Atop the first finger,

Carpenter, though in prime condition, felt so blown that he rested his men for twenty minutes. In the interval they saw and heard nothing suggesting the near presence of the enemy. From that point, continuing the march, Carpenter modified his order and bore directly southeast on the next leg for another seven hundred meters, simply so that the company could cross over the second ridge finger at a lower elevation and with less sweat.

A small decision when he made it, a minor digression from the instruction given him, it was to have vast consequence. There was reason enough for what he did: to exhaust a company prior to engagement is one certain way to lose it.

When the point of First Platoon passed the crest of the second finger and started downgrade, ahead of it about seventy meters a wide creek threaded the draw. It was a branch of the same stream, that twisting through the ridges, still lower down ran past Hackworth's position.

Sgt. Thomas Delemeter of Jackson, Mich., a wiry and highly articulate soldier, was playing lead scout for this front of the company column. Suddenly he halted and raised his hand. The squad stopped. First Platoon then closed up on the point. Delemeter said to Lieut. Bill Jordan, "I hear voices to my front—loud voices—maybe a platoon or more—speaking Vietnamese—I'd say two hundred meters away."

Jordan listened for a minute. He nodded to Delemeter.

Then he called Carpenter to say, "I've got Charley two hundred meters to my front. Shall I continue on the present azimuth or go for Charley?"

The question sounds like jabberwocky—as if he were contradicting himself. But the azimuth would take him straight toward the voices, though so going the column would risk the hazard of crossing the draw under observation. By the orthodoxy of tactics, if he was to attack, he would move up the finger on which he was standing to juncture with the third finger, then come down on the enemy.

Without hesitating, Carpenter said, "We'll go for Charley."

Carpenter next called Lieut. James Baker, leader of Third

Platoon, and said, "Get ready for a fight." The platoons would attack abreast up the ridge finger. Jordan's men, already standing in file on the right ground, had only to face left to be deployed correctly. Baker's platoon would close up and come in on Jordan's left flank if such an additional commitment became necessary.

Already there was enemy movement on the far side of the creek, and what chance there might have been for surprise by the Americans was dashed in the next few seconds.

Four enemy soldiers appeared on the other bank of the stream. Three had come with the obvious intention of washing the mess utensils and clothing. The fourth man's errand, if more urgent, was not less clear. In one hand he carried a roll of toilet paper—a fastidious touch in guerrilla warfare—and he already squatted with his back to the stream. Here was no scout party, no decoy, but the tokens of a force at ease and unalarmed.

Delemeter, who remained on the extreme right when the platoon faced left, took all of this in.

He said to Spec. 4 Walter Williams, "I don't like to bother anyone in that position, but that Charley shouldn't be fouling the stream. You try to get the others."

Delemeter killed his man—the soldier with one movement too many. The others, if they were hit at all, instantly scampered away into the bamboo. No fabled episode was ever begun on a less chivalrous note. Few attacks on an enemy rear have changed direction so quickly.

The same kind of thing had been done with impunity in the early morning. This time it was a mistake, though Delemeter was unaware of it and no one else had time to take note. Even as the sounds of the shooting died, First Platoon was in motion, advancing up the finger. Within five minutes thereafter, according to Delemeter, who is the most reliable witness on time intervals, its every man was flat on the ground, pinned by the fire of four automatic weapons which from the immediate right flank swept directly above the platoon line, virtually paralyzing it. That it came so quickly, unexpectedly and accurately compounded the shock.

Here is the most startling note in the story, more incredible than Carpenter's audacious action minutes later. There were no prepared enemy positions high on the finger; no force had been deployed in front of First Platoon. The NVA soldiers, having fallen out for a rest period, then becoming alerted by the few rounds fired at the four men along the creek, had whipped around the draw and begun their counterattack as if having inspired knowledge of how the Americans would try to develop the action.

Yet this was blind chance. 1st Sgt. Walter J. Sabalauski, the grizzled combat hand from Palm Beach, Fla., got a reading on reality immediately. It was a meeting engagement, pure and simple, and all the luck was running the other way. He said bitterly to Carpenter, "Damn it, we catch them flat-footed. They jump to it and start firing. They are not firing at us; we are walking into it." Now some instinct told him that things would keep going from bad to worse.

So far, however, their losses, if any, were trifling. Stalling or slacking all movement was the steady drone of bullets and the explosive crackling of the bamboo overhead. The thicket was so dense at ground level that once the men flattened, they saw little or nothing of one another. To wiggle directly forward was impossible, because of the clumps of snarled bamboo which they could only slither around, twisting sideways. Some few of them fired during the crawl and their aim had to be forward lest they shoot one another; yet the automatic weapons were flailing them from the right flank only. In the first five minutes, though they saw not one enemy soldier, they did not move more than five meters. Delemeter got a machine gun going on the right flank. Two grenades sailed in on him and exploded just beyond his right elbow. The corner of a clump of bamboo shielded his body from the blast. He thought this spot a little too hot and so he wiggled his way toward the left of the line.

Carpenter called Emerson on the RT to tell him, "First Platoon is in trouble and I'm about to commit Third Platoon."

Said the Gun Fighter, "Go right ahead. Be sure to police the field of all weapons when the fight is over."

There could not have been a more untimely admonition, though Emerson had no way of knowing it.

Carpenter replied, "Believe me, it's not a question of doing anything like that. We're under heavy fire, repeat, heavy fire."

Ten minutes after Jordan had attacked, Baker came in with Third Platoon on the left side of the ridge finger. One hundred extra meters of bush had given this unit insulation against all of the heat and most of the noise of the fight, and its members had no premonition of crisis. Neither did Emerson. At this stage he was much more worried about the situation surrounding Lieutenant Sill's Baker company, which through the day had been colliding with small enemy groups, than about Carpenter's problem. He figured this one as a side show, a small tangle quickly to be straightened out. It was no more apparent to him than to the driver that the chariot was skidding and about to career out of control.

Emerson held sway in what was essentially a foyer to nature and wildlife—an almost closed-off bower just inside the jungle marge. Almost triple the size of a middle-class living room, and with hardly more height, this chamber was devoid of hanging vines, flowering creepers and projecting limbs. The floor was hard-packed red earth almost barren of decaying vegetation. The walls and green roof were of such tightly intertwined foliage that, with the sun high, the bower was less than half-lighted. It was natural only in that nature was an auxiliary architect. The portal to a jungle trail that had been hacked out and kept that way by the Viet Cong, it was the work of years. Gnarled and knotted bamboo so hemmed it in that the air was stale and lifeless.

The trail ascended sharply and directly from the rear of the chamber and for the first thirty feet was terraced at three levels. Ferns in all sizes, some higher than a man, flanked the trail. There were also wild banana trees, coconut palms and breadfruit in this jungle. It might have been a good place for a picnic, on a cooler day.

Here was the right setting for the man now dominating it. The scene was lush and Emerson was flush. The Gun Fighter always runs a shooting contest in a mood of keen excitement. His voice is charged, his normally well-composed face lights up and reddens, still more so than when he is doing an after-combat critique, though he goes about both of these exercises with the fervor of a Deep South evangelist. Patient with subordinates, he sweats out a fight as moistly as any of his soldiers and he leans to the action so wholly that he stands on tiptoe when he talks things out on the radio.

The battalion CP was about 1400 meters from Carpenter and, except for the first finger of the same ridge mass where the fight went on, the way between was the already mentioned flat valley where the elephant grass stood as high as the beast for which it is named. Captain Brown was with Emerson, wondering if his Alpha Company was due for another fire call. Many of his men were also sprawled about the enclosure, sleeping, resting or engaging in small talk, hardly heeding the course of the fight. Their languor was in utter contrast to Emerson's tautness.

When Baker brought his men into line, Carpenter's position was slightly to the left of First Platoon and about twenty-five meters to the rear of Baker's closest flank. Still Carpenter could not see any one of his soldiers, owing to the thickness of the bush. Of a sudden, however, he could feel fire coming against his CP position from an entirely new direction. Off the third finger of the ridge rising from the creek bed where Delemeter had shot the squatting man, an automatic gun raked the ground all around him.

So far not one man had been killed in the company. Yet within the last few seconds every man in the headquarters element, except Carpenter, one RTO, Private First Class Ellman, and one medic, Spec. 4 Baldinger, had been wounded. Sergeant Sabalauski became so busy playing aid man and jockeying riflemen forward that he had no impression of how the fight was developing.

Carpenter told Lieut. Bryan Robbins, commanding Fourth Platoon (Heavy Weapons), "Move on over the creek and clean out that high ground." The platoon moved rightward all of fifteen meters. There it was beaten to earth by fire from two machine guns with crossing bands, one a .50, the other a .30 HMG.

Third Platoon, deploying at a right angle to Fourth Platoon's direction, got to a few yards beyond First's ragged line, where it was beaten down by automatic fire coming, this time, from the front. Sgt. Robert Hanna, its NCO leader, and a very rugged character, who was on right of the formation, couldn't take this embarrassment lying down.

He called to Sgt. James Young of Summersville, W. Va., leading Second Squad of First Platoon, "Get your asses on up here and we'll start moving again."

They crawled along, made five or six meters, then stopped once more when a swath of machine-gun bullets cut just above their heads. Lieutenant Baker was then at least two lengths ahead of any of his men.

Delemeter couldn't see Baker, but he thought he heard Baker call out something from not far behind him. It sounded like, "Move on."

Lieutenant Jordan called to Delemeter, "Move on! Get forward!"

Delemeter yelled back, "I can't. I'm already in front of Third Platoon."

Spec. 4 Williams called out, "Medic! Medic!" Williams also was to Delemeter's rear.

Delemeter yelled, "What for?"

From Williams, "They just shot Yracheta." (PFC Senen Yracheta was the Second Squad's grenadier.)

Delemeter yelled, "Then you stay with him, Big Will. He needs you."

By that time the fire fight had been going not more than fifteen minutes. There were no tall trees in this bush, and practically no canopy. A strong sunlight filtered down to them. They could have seen well enough had not their noses been so close to bush and earth. Delemeter looked at his watch occasionally. He was amazed that the seconds went so slowly.

Neither Carpenter nor Sabalauski was as yet aware of any crisis threatening Third Platoon, and till these moments there had been none. Emerson, out of respect for Carpenter's judgment and steadiness, was suddenly feeling more urgent about the company situation. He knew that "Ragged Scooper," the forward air controller, was up there above the ridge somewhere and that some of his ships were on tap, should there be a call for help. The lines—friend and enemy—were so close-joined that any such call seemed unlikely. He had given the word to Ragged Scooper: "Get over to these coordinates; I have an element in trouble."

The real thing came swiftly.

Sergeant Young heard a cry ring out from his left: "The platoon leader's hit!"

He did not know it was Sergeant Hanna who had yelled, and Young had not seen Baker fall, though neither man was more than twelve yards from him.

Hanna was on radio, talking to Carpenter, saying, "Lieutenant Baker has been killed by a machine-gun burst. Otherwise we're not being hurt too much by fire from our front. But they've now swung around us—in the draw on our left. Grenades are coming in."

Delemeter was close enough to get a third-man impression of these things. He had heard Hanna cry, "Check Lieutenant Baker!" Someone else shouted an answer: "He got it in the head." But he remembered also Hanna saying to Carpenter, "I think most of our platoon is done."

Then followed, in an instant or so, a great blast from the same direction as the voice he had just heard. Delemeter was certain it was a rocket exploding.

Young, who had propped himself up to look at Hanna, knew better. He saw it happen. Two grenades, bouncing right together, exploded next to Hanna as he turned to move away from the instrument; one blew off both of his legs, the other shattered his skull.

Young saw the body lifted by the blow, then fall, broken. Still he yelled, "Hanna, Hanna, get up!"

That was when Carpenter got a call over the Third Platoon radio, that had been shielded from the blast by Hanna's body. The voice did not identify itself. It screamed hysterically, "Hanna's dead. The lieutenant's dead. I'm the only live person left here. I can't see anybody. Grenades are coming in on me." The voice broke off before there was time for Carpenter to answer.

Carpenter did not know for days afterward who had called him. Young knew at once. He had seen Sgt. James Harding, already badly wounded through the right wrist and arm, drag himself to the radio and had heard him talk to Carpenter. But Young caught only a word here and there and had no idea of the impact on Carpenter.

Such was the spur-of-the-moment information that Carpenter acted upon. The anonymity of the call particularly disturbed him. But he also knew something of the situation right around himself and felt its pressure.

Senior Medic Schuyler was out of action, mortally wounded by three bullets. Aid Men Quattochi, Pickens and Baldinger had also been hit while dragging other wounded a little to the rear. Only Quattochi, shot through the shoulder, and Baldinger, with bullet wounds in both legs, continued to crawl from man to man, bandaging them and administering albumin.

Delemeter and Young had gone as flat as possible. No man any longer fired from either platoon. Grenades and bullets were breaking into the ground at too terrifying a rate. (The men who survived in the forward line bear witness that, whether the company was itself beaten at that clutch, at least they personally felt themselves doomed.)

Carpenter had been talking on and off to Battalion since the start of action. He now said to Emerson, "They're right in among us. We're being overrun. I've got to have napalm dropped right on my position." (The bravado tagline, "We'll take some of them with us," must have been a bit of embroidery added later by the press. Such stories do improve with age. Carpenter had no recollection of saying any such thing.)

Carpenter said, "I'll throw out yellow smoke," and fitted the action to his words.

From somewhere aloft Ragged Scooper said, "I see it."

What no one had reckoned on was the speed with which the napalm would be delivered. There was no time to warn either platoon of what was coming, which may have been just as well. The ship already was directly above them. Within one-half minute, given a few seconds either way, the fiery stuff splashed amid the bamboo tops, to become broken and diffused by it. Most of the napalm spilled forward into enemy-held ground in line with the forward motion of the carrier; some of it rebounded against the prone men in the company line.

More than half of the company still did not know that Carpenter had taken the desperate gamble or that there had been a napalm attack put on the finger. They heard a sharp crackling in the air as the green bamboo kept exploding from the flame; this they at first attributed to a sudden increase in the machine-gun fire.

Twelve of the Americans were burned. Only two became stretcher cases. PFC Edward Garcia later died. PFC Glenn W. Whitehead, of First Platoon, was ablaze all over, but the fire was so quickly beaten out by several comrades who jumped on him to smother the flame that his life was saved. Spec. 4 Charles Hampton and PFC Joe Hunter were the other more serious cases. Delemeter was burned on the right leg; Sabalauski was splashed on both hands (he did not at first know what had happened, not having heard Carpenter give the order). Sgt. Charles Harris was splashed badly on both arms. PFC Gerry Smith, already suffering from a gunshot wound, was blistered all along the back.

The immediate reaction of the men in the rifle line was a great sense of relief. They felt better even before they knew what had been done. The fire along their front died instantly and completely. Within a minute Young had arisen and walked back through the bamboo to where Carpenter was sitting. Delemeter had felt no shock when the stuff came down. He felt good when it was over. He "felt saved." As he arose and walked to the rear, he heard not one shot fired. And he, like all the others, had seen nothing of the enemy while in the forward ground.

Carpenter's immediate reaction was one almost of despair. He thought that at least half of the company had been wiped out, with part of it being done on his order. He said to Emerson, "I've stopped them, but I also hurt myself terribly."

Emerson's reply was, "I want you to know that I am putting you in for the Medal of Honor. You can be sure of that."

Since the pledge was made before Emerson really knew all of the circumstances, either as to whether Carpenter had been justified in what he did, or as to what had come of it, or how the men felt about it, that was rather indiscreet. But it was also spontaneous; and the words reverberated all the way to Washington, though Leon Daniel of UPI was the only correspondent hanging on them at the Gun Fighter's CP that afternoon. The Saigon press corps had snubbed the battle of Toumorong from the start.

Daniels' story made banner headlines in *The Washington Post* next morning. The President spoke in praise of Captain Carpenter at a press conference. The Pentagon cabled Saigon: "White House praises what Captain Carpenter did; what did he do?" The correspondents flew north like a swam of locusts. It is an object lesson in how history and heroes are made.

All that Emerson heard on radio during those next few minutes did not relieve his mind or make him feel Carpenter was taking too dim a view. Through a twenty-minute lull, the wounded were pulled out, and the able-bodied joined Delemeter, Young and the other early arrivals lower down on the finger, where Carpenter was holding forth. Some of the men were sent back to the burning wood in parties of two or three to gather equipment. Several of the radios and rucksacks were flaming so high that they had to be abandoned.

But where was Third Platoon? Sabalauski had counted noses, then made a swing forward through the bamboo, and had collected not more than a corporal's guard.

Sabalauski's first estimate, put through to Emerson, was that "about fifty have been killed." Emerson's subsequent actions premised that this was a proper reckoning. It signified that the great part of a three-platoon company had been wiped out, granting the usual ratio of dead to wounded.

Young and Delemeter would have named about the same

figure, had they been asked. Carpenter was too busy with other tasks to question it or to go forth and see. The main task was to get the company regrouped and established in a defensive perimeter right where they were.

On radio Emerson said to him, "Make that circle just as tight as possible. I'll ring the place with artillery. We'll have air strikes. I'll bring in Smokey the Bear. The Three-twenty-seventh [Hackworth] will be coming your way. I am starting Brown and Alpha."

In those minutes the Gun Fighter truly thought that Carpenter had bumped an NVA regiment. He, too, was having his bout with phantasmagoria.

Without a doubt, the desperation of the act, in the light of the information received at the CP, conveyed to him that the plight of the company remained no less desperate. Its Third Platoon was "up the pipe." Half of the company's strength must have been spent in a few minutes, and what was left of it remained cornered. Viewing through a glass, darkly, Emerson proceeded to take his extraordinary measures toward Carpenter's relief and extrication.

Captain Brown and Alpha Company were sent on their way through the sea of elephant grass to re-enforce the beleaguered perimeter.

Brigade was asked to put Hackworth and his battalion on a new axis, attacking from Hill 1073 straight toward Carpenter to ease the pressure against him. Though Hackworth and his companies were already worn down and hard beset, the change was made. Thus the whole operation was given a new focus.

A report of the fight, with the grimmest possible overtones, got all the way back to the brigade's rear base at Phan Rang. Emerson's executive, Maj. Donald Schroeder, chanced to be there. On his own, Schroeder organized a provisional company of sixty-five homeward-bound veterans of the battalion who had served their time and were awaiting a plane to the United States. They were not rarin' to go, but they fell in. This ill-armed, ragtag bunch flew for the scene in borrowed Chinooks. Emerson knew of it when they closed on his CP at 2130, and Schroeder, saluting, said,

"Sir, we are here!" as if speaking for the book. Emerson sent them along the way that Brown and company had gone.

On the ridge finger, the perimeter in which Carpenter's men settled, after pulling back from the burning bamboo, was a rough circle about forty-five meters in diameter. They had a thirty-minute respite in which to dig and they made the most of it; they dug deep—too deep, as things worked out. When the enemy resumed fire, First Platoon's sector, which faced toward the other finger, got the full treatment. Still the automatic fire, traversing up and down their slope, "made impossible" (Carpenter's words) any controlled sweep of where the Third Platoon had undergone its ordeal. The two wounded aid men continued to crawl about and administer such care as the other wounded received. There could be no medevac; there was no landing zone for it; there had been no opportunity to locate and clear one. They had entered upon the operation with food and ammo to last five days, expecting to stay that long.

Dark came, and with it an electrical storm, lightning in sheets, rain falling the same way. The foxholes filled. The men found it simpler (and also safer) to hunch down deeper into the holes, thereby to soak up more of the water or to push it over the brim, than to bail it out with helmets. There was too much of it for bailing.

The downpour slowed the march-up of Alpha Company, the men sliding and falling in the red clay of the trail.

Emerson besought help for Carpenter's people from Smokey the Bear. Illumination might be needed if a counterattack came on. Smokey replied, "I'd rather not fly in such weather." Emerson said, "You must do so," though he did not know the pilot and had no authority over him. Smokey said, "O.K., sir, I'll do it, crash or not."

There was need for Smokey. Brown's company, having started at 1700, made the first thousand meters across the valley flat almost at a lope. As they headed uptrail, where the big ridge began, they knew trouble. Rifle and automatic fire broke out against the lead squad. Its men hit the dirt. Working to the front of the column, Brown yelled at them, "Get up and push. We can't stop. We have to assault." But two men had been lightly wounded, so the others did not jump up and bound on.

The charge to the crest of the sub-ridge had to be slowly, carefully organized. Brown could not see the position above him, but he knew that if the men kept low they would be, most of the way, in defilade. Dark was coming and he wanted a little more of it. When at last they went, it was with a steady upcrawl, followed by a bound, with the front men firing. They thought they killed "at least ten VC," as they swept through the outpost, though no one stopped to count bodies.

Bedeviled by rain and dark as they began the descent to the draw, the column began to drift apart; an automatic rifle harassed them from the low ground ahead. Brown called for Smokey the Bear to come over. While the flare lasted they could see one another and converge again. In the dark interludes they once more became separated. So they went ahead jerkingly, at a pace no better than 150 meters per hour.

Approaching the ridge finger they had been seeking, Brown got Carpenter on the radio, saying, "Give me a cluster"—a green hand flare. He saw it only when Carpenter tried for the second time. The position lay directly ahead about 400 meters.

Off to their left, Brown's men could hear enemy voices. So they kept working to the right, away from the trail. Brown wanted no more fighting right then. He passed the word back: "If they come on, try to break contact." A mortar opened fire on them, but the shells went well over. Again the movement was drifting out of control.

Brown called Carpenter, saying, "Have your people fire in the other direction and we will guide on the sound."

Without knowing it, they had already closed to within voice range.

Carpenter's people yelled, "Strike Force!" as an experiment. Brown's returned the call, "Strike Force!"

Lifted by this cheerleading for the rest of the distance, they closed on the perimeter. Brown took one hour to fit his men into the position which "ran straight downhill" and had to be almost doubled in size to accommodate him.

He got ready to place his last man, PFC John Deisher. Right then an enemy group that had followed along the trail closed in. There was a heavy volley. Deisher was hit by eleven bullets through the back.

Brown, gone flat, felt crushed and miserable. The company had done so well until that moment. The sudden loss of Deisher was as if fate had mocked his best effort.

That happened at one-half hour past midnight.

More than one hour later, six wounded men from the Third Platoon who had been marked as "missing" came into the position. Their return moved Carpenter to make a more complete check of bodies—living and dead. He discovered, as so often happens in battle, that things were less black than he had thought. There were six KIA's within the position, sixteen members of Third Platoon remained unaccounted for, and twenty-five of the wounded were rated "gravely" so. No toll was taken of the lightly wounded. There had been no opportunity to count enemy dead, and none would come.

At 0200 Emerson was given the revised estimate on radio by Sabalauski, who said, "At worst, we have not more than fifteen killed, sixteen missing and twenty-five seriously wounded." He was still blowing things up a bit.

The added relief column formed of the sixty-five casuals from Phan Rang, re-enforced by the other platoon from Charley Company that had returned earlier in the day from a long patrol, having slogged forward under the command of Capt. Walter B. Wesley, Commander of Headquarters Company, did not make it to the top of the first ridge finger.

Emerson had intended to halt them there for the night, in any event. He was already feeling better about the situation. After Brown got to Carpenter, he ceased worrying that the position might be overrun. Besides, three companies of the 327th were pushing toward Carpenter and were only about 700 meters to the south of him. Emerson had no idea that Hackworth's forces were more heavily engaged through this night than were his own, and he would not learn of it until the following morning. Hack, on the other hand, did not get the word that Carpenter's plight looked less desperate.

This more sanguine outlook, further, did not bring about the halting of the provisional company. As the front of Wesley's column gained the brow of the first ridge finger, four enemy machine guns opened fire. Ten men of the Charley Company platoon fell wounded, including the leader, Lieut. James D. Olienyk, who was shot through the mouth. PFC Manuel Rodriguez kept crawling and, getting to the first gun, threw a grenade, killing the weapon and its crew. So did PFC Juan Sanchez, who knocked out the second gun. These were the work horses. Rodriguez and Sanchez then pulled back and dragged the wounded to cover.

Filled with admiration, Wesley concluded that he would have to fight onward with half a platoon—if at all. The casuals from Phan Rang showed no disposition to mix it. With orders in their pockets that would take them home, they lay there under fire but crawled no closer to its source. He scarcely blamed them. Who could?

Reserving to himself his doubts about the casuals, Wesley called Emerson on radio and gave him the ringsider's view of what he was up against.

Emerson said, "Withdraw down the slope until you get away from the fire. Then form a perimeter and hold. I'll get back to you after a while."

When daylight came to Carpenter's position, the rain, which had dropped to a drizzle around 0300, again fell in torrents and kept coming for hours. A low, clinging mist crept upward from the bottoms. These things, combined with the inability of other forces to get to them, the overload of casualties and the fire that buzzed around their flanks whenever they stirred, were enough to keep them penned for the second day. When dark came, Carpenter decided he must try to move; his wounded had been without skilled medical attention for thirty hours.

Litters—twenty of them—were dropped from a Huey at 2300. But there were twenty-six litter cases. The extras they tried carrying—six bearers for each body. It was a brave try, but still no go. An advance guard was put out to hack a path through the bamboo. With entrenching tools they cut steps in the oozy clay of the trail; the bearers still slipped and fell with the wounded. Begun at midnight, their march out by first light still had not gained 200 meters; the head of the column was only at the base of the finger on which they had fought. Carpenter halted them.

The day was hot and fair. The trails began to dry. Emerson called Captain Wesley and said, "You start hacking your way to them. Don't go over that first finger. Stay more with the low ground." The column veered a little too much to the left, promptly ran into automatic fire, then swung far right, and by luck bumped into a trail that wound toward Carpenter's position. With Brown's company leading, Carpenter's column got moving again. They met in midmorning, and by 1100 the wounded and dead were being flown out by Huey from the swale where Wesley's force had set up its perimeter.

It still took two hours to clear the casualties for Dak To. Carpenter and the men marked "duty" were taken out in three lifts from the LZ in front of Emerson's bower, beginning at 1730. They closed on the camp at Dak To at 1900 on 11 June.

The night before, Gen. Will Pearson had gotten together with Emerson, Hackworth and his other chief subordinates to talk over the situation. It was a brief huddle, made so by Pearson's opening statement: "I think it's time for us to back off and get some help from the air." They were all thinking the same way.

So Hackworth's battalion, like Emerson's, had been bent that day mainly on breaking contact with an enemy that, however badly battered, still hung on tenaciously.

Three days later the big B-52 strike was put on the enemy ground. Pearson had revised an earlier calculation that Carpenter must have collided with an NVA battalion on the move. He was now convinced that an enemy regiment was in permanent positions somewhere on the big ridge. But where? Both he and Emerson had thought deeply about the resistance that had recurred and strengthened atop the first ridge finger after Brown's initial and almost bloodless brush with it. Did it signify that this was the heart of the enemy's holdings in the region? They felt it did. That's why the B-52 strike was made on two different axes, with the lines crossing atop the first finger. A shot in the dark, it paid off handsomely. The battered bodies and strewn flesh, the shattered earthworks and information gained from the few prisoners indicated that the remnants of the enemy regiment were wiped out there by the bombers.

By 17 June, Emerson, Carpenter and the battalion had their tents pitched amid the craters along the first finger of that same nameless mountain. Its top was quite flat. Yet so close together were the craters that there was space only for a one-Huey landing zone.

Lieutenant Sill sat with them; both of his hands were wrapped in bandages because of jungle rot. He had been that way for two months but had refused evacuation for treatment.

Carpenter was reading a stack of fan mail from the folks back home. One letter enclosed a clipping from the New York *Daily News*, wearing the headline: GIS SAFELY OUT OF JUNGLE HELL. Passing it on to Delemeter, he said wryly, "Well, look about you. Now you know how it feels to be safely out of hell." More bored than amused with all the attention he was receiving, the one-time Lonesome End decidedly was not counting his blessings.

Emerson sat in the shade of his CP. It was a lean-to tent, roped to some broken bamboo, amid the churned-up earth nearest the largest of the craters. From this perch he could look across the valley floor to the bare spot that had been his LZ while the fight was on. Beyond it was as lovely a mountain vista as the eye is ever likely to behold. The hills and ridges rose in four terraces on the far side, and the tallest range of all would have seemed almost alpine had it been cloaked other than solidly in varying shades of green. On this cloudless afternoon a haze gathering around the summit helped create the illusion of the sky being brought down close. The only contrasting color was the red of the craters, which had baked dry. For almost a week the monsoon had brought forth faultless weather.

Emerson, if not touched by the bounty of nature, was somewhat more pensive than Carpenter.

"You know, Bill," he said, "it's a damned shame I didn't think to name this hill the OK Corral. We might have made it famous."

He said it dead-pan. Being the Gun Fighter, he is given to thoughts like that.

The Improbable Scholar

Following the spectacular B-52 strike that with unexampled precision unloaded its thunder at dead center of the red-clay ridge where gathered the last large remnant of Captain Carpenter's enemies, the first unit into the deeply cratered ground seemed hardly the right cast for the stage.

All witnesses outside the three-kilometer limiting line could attest that a mighty blow had taken place dead on the button, with the overlapping concentration precisely where it was supposed to be. There were, however, no experts present on the question of what such a wallop does to people round about, though not in position to blow up with the land. If weighed, the possibility that there might still be enemy skirmishers on the fringes of the erupted area who were in an ugly mood was not taken too seriously.

The bombers had completed their chore and were winging back to their Pacific rookery by 0840. At that, they almost outstayed the correspondents who, after interviewing Carpenter on life and love, had returned to Saigon en masse.

At 1230 Alpha Company, 326th Engineer Battalion Airborne, got orders to proceed at once to the scene of the morning party and sweep it up from the lower finger that the bombs had battered to the crest of the ridge.

Now tactical sweeping is hardly a combat engineer's

military occupational specialty, and a whole regiment of engineers with earth-movers couldn't have policed that man-made badland decently in the seventy-two hours they were to be out. But as it was put up to them, there were caves to be blown, tunnels to be explored, and earth to be leveled amid the craters so that choppers could come and go, all of which sounded like engineering tasks proper. So they went forth in the Hueys quite happily. They would have gone anyway, happy or not.

The focus here narrows to the Third Platoon and its day. It was commanded by 2nd Lieut. A. Isaacs, Jr., a twenty-two-year-old Reservist from Bakersfield, California, a slender stripling with a perpetual grin who bubbled with enthusiasm for his men. Wanting a piece of the fight, knowing that it was considered all over, Isaacs felt lifted not more by the Huey than by swollen expectations.

Their choppers put them down on a new LZ directly across the swale from where Colonel Emerson had held forth in his CP when the fray was hottest. The elephant grass rose almost to their ships' rotors. The ridge finger where the B-52's had dealt their heaviest blow was directly before them, its crown not more than 300 feet above the valley floor. They were atop it within one hour, carrying weapons, three days' rations and 240 pounds of ammonium nitrate. The surface by now resembled a monster egg container done in burnt umber. Some of the craters were interlocking, two or three bombs having hit approximately the same earth. The Pentagon term for it is overkill.

Seeing this, Isaacs' hopes drooped. The task of the platoon was to blow tunnels and caves within this one-time position while Alpha Company worked through the woods of the slopes above them. One look and Isaacs was convinced that had there been such, they would have collapsed under the impact of the bombs.

Amid the craters, it took them some time to figure out how they could organize a defensive perimeter that would be fairly snug, with satisfactory fields of fire. Dark was coming, and they were only thirty strong. Just off the thickly cratered ground—the top of the finger was rather flat—the bamboo still rose high enough to curtain off most of the slope below. Still they worked out their problem as well as infantry would have done. The night passed quietly, and other than a few sentries keeping watch, they slept.

Next morning, following breakfast, they found their token-size engineering task. There was just one tunnel left. And it they might have missed had it not been connected with the surface by a twenty-foot shaft.

By rope, S/Sgt. Joseph D. Morell was lowered into the hole. He was followed by Spec. 4 Wayne R. Loar and PFCs Russell A. Fabian and Timothy M. McGowan. Together the four set a forty-pound cratering charge, and together they blew the works. That was after they had been hauled up again. Morell had noted that the walls already were about to collapse.

Morell, of Rochester, Pa., is a Regular Army veteran, a congenial man with a fatherly interest in the young soldier. He said, "These kids were so eager about the job that I decided thereafter to stand aside and watch them go." It was a slight exaggeration, this thing about standing aside.

His mind on tunnels and the cratered area having no more such, Isaacs sent a patrol farther up the finger to where it joined the ridge mass, fifty feet above them. Soon they returned, having found no enemy works of any sort.

Then Sgt. William Wesley, Savannah, Ga., took off with four men, Spec. 4 John Sherrard and PFCs Gary L. Wilkins, Gerald Roche and Edward L. Wilkinson. Their task was to reconnoiter the lower slope along the still relatively intact foxhole line. They were to look for arms and equipment. They found much blood, hunks of flesh strewn about and two battered corpses, but apart from that, nothing of interest.

So they started down to the valley floor. The sun was high, their canteens were empty, and they were all mighty thirsty. Two hundred yards off to their right they saw a waterfall with a twenty-foot drop. At the moment it looked more lovely than Bridal Veil, and it drew them irresistibly.

They were halfway to it, still working carefully through the bamboo, when Wesley suddenly raised his hand, and they all halted in place. Twenty yards downslope, just walking out of the elephant grass, was an enemy soldier, to their eyes looking bodily sound.

"Try to take him prisoner," Wesley said to the others.

Forgotten was their thirst and the waterfall.

Saying nothing to them, Isaacs had come along behind.

They deployed in line and started downhill. But the bamboo was too noisy and the man below, hearing them, dove headlong into the bush.

Wesley yelled, "Fire!" and they did.

Back came a grenade which exploded between Sherrard and Wilkins.

By then Isaacs was with them, firing his M-16.

They moved on down the hill, working triggers as they moved. Another skirmisher jumped up in the elephant grass only a few yards from where they had seen the first man. He was aiming a rifle. All five men joined in gunning him down. By then Isaacs had doubled back up the hill to tell S/Sgt. James W. Shrump that he must send another squad on a sweep of the bottom of the ridge. Though he was unsure whether he had bumped a hornet's nest or was dealing with a few stunned stragglers, a certain pride drove him to complete the job with his own men.

Morell got the nod, and PFC Karlyle Wheeler moved out as the point. The second scout was PFC Robert Little, with Morell moving third, followed by the RTO, Fabian, then McGowan, and Loar at the rear. Trying to rush, the column more slid than crawled to the valley floor; the slope was both steep and wet and the red clay afforded no footing at all. They descended more or less evenly, only by clutching to the bamboo.

Come to the creek bed at the bottom, they formed a skirmish line and turned left from it, away from the waterfall and next the slope rising between them and the heavily cratered finger top.

They came to a long line of foxholes, only a few feet removed from the elephant grass. All along this cleared earth bank were scattered pieces of enemy and American equipment—weapons, packs and rice bowls.

For the moment they disregarded it and continued the

sweep. Fifty yards more—then fire came against them. Unhurt, they went flat and returned fire. The air quieted. McGowan crawled forward a few yards and pulled a dead NV soldier out of a foxhole.

They stood up and moved along. At the next hole, ten yards along, there was a machine gun pointing over the rim. Still the hole looked empty. With due caution, and with his rifle ready at port, Morell waddled toward it on his haunches, covered by the deep grass. Then with a bound he grabbed the gun and yanked it from the hole.

Next the hole was a large spar of green bamboo, twice as thick as his arm, neatly trimmed at the end. He hefted it and, puzzled at the weight, looked for the loading hole. Inside the bamboo were seventy-two sticks of U.S. dynamite.

They went on another thirty yards without incident, moving slowly, some of them staying with rifles at point while the others moved. Then they came to another small stream.

Loar, a slender blond with an immobile but youthful face, and McGowan were sent across it by Morell, who said, ''Be careful!''

McGowan saw a foxhole with a strange-looking bundle in it.

Whispering to Loar, ''Take it easy,'' he crawled closer.

But Loar was crawling faster and got ahead of him.

He saw two AK47s—the enemy rifle—standing straight in the hole.

It startled him: they had not been there an instant before.

As he gazed, they moved.

Loar poured twenty rounds into the hole from his M-16. His piece jammed after two bullets from the second clip.

Morell yelled, ''Did you get 'em?''

Loar answered, ''I know I got one right through the skull.''

McGowan asked, ''How about grenading?''

Loar said, ''And mess up both those weapons?''

Loar and McGowan had gone flat again. Morell and the others on the far side of the stream stood and poured more fire on the hole.

They moved along to a second hole, as the rear element came splashing through the water.

Within it something stirred. Both front men saw an arm suddenly flash and then disappear.

McGowan took a pamphlet from his blouse pocket, thumbed through a few pages, and to the utter astonishment of Loar yelled out, "B-o-o-ng, z-o-o-ng, zh-o-o-ng!"

Loar asked, "What in hell are you doing?"

"Trying to get prisoners," said McGowan. "That's their phrase meaning, 'Throw down your arms!' "

McGowan handed over the page. The words were "Buong, sung, xuong."

"I don't see any arms," Loar said blankly. The hole was in fact covered over by a laced bamboo platting. Again it lifted slightly to reveal an elbow and a flash of metal. So they both poured in fire, Loar having freed his weapon. They were in it now, well in it.

There were two dead Charleys and two sound rifles in the hole.

By this time McGowan was tired of all the shooting and had made up his mind to break off the killing if he could. Morell, on the other hand, was saying to the RTO, Fabian, "Call Isaacs and tell him this thing could go on all afternoon. We may need help."

McGowan looks and acts like an odd one, considering the bold part he played. A Bostonite, eighteen years old and a volunteer, he is small, slight of build, solemn-faced, and he wears thick-lensed glasses. A lover of literature, keen about writing, he had several days earlier asked for a place on public information staff, which was given him. These qualities rather set him apart but still made him a favorite in the platoon. Speaking of him as "The Scholar," they did it respectfully.

McGowan slung his weapon over his shoulder and took from his pouch a Kodak.

They moved on down the foot of the ridge with McGowan leading. Morell was standing back and keeping a careful eye on him.

Wheeler had moved up second to McGowan.

At the next foxhole a North Vietnam soldier stood waiting, a rifle in one hand. He held it rather uncertainly, perpendicularly to his body, the muzzle even with his shoulder.

McGowan had whipped out the camera with the idea of taking a picture of the next position.

Startled to see the man with the rifle, he walked to within six feet of the hole, pointed the camera directly toward him and said calmly, "You get out of there." Then he corrected himself: "You *come* out of there—you come out of there right now."

The man dropped the rifle in the hole.

Then he stooped, picked it up, and tossed it on the bank.

Wheeler pushed forward and tried to shunt McGowan aside, yelling, "You get out of my way; I'm gonna shoot him."

McGowan said, "You're not. We're going to take him. He looks like a very nice prisoner."

Wheeler dropped back, feeling abashed.

Morell was taking the play in, ready to intervene, but for the moment saying nothing.

The others stood around watching, holding their M-16s easy in hand.

Then to the amazement of them all the Vietnamese reached down into the hole thrice, each time coming up with another weapon. He threw the AK47 and two machine guns on the brim.

McGowan showed him how to put his hands on his head. He didn't get it. Little whipped around through the bamboo behind the foxhole, placed the man's hands locked on his pate. Then the POW stepped forth.

Loar, who hails from Iron Mountain, Mich., was fifteen feet from McGowan, side turned to him, eying along the ridge. He saw what looked like another hole a few feet beyond where Fabian was standing. But he couldn't be sure. Rushes and leaves were heaped there as if covering something.

He called to Fabian, "You check that spot!"

Fabian did and called back, "It's a hole, but it's empty."

Asked Fabian, "Then what is that popping up behind you?"

There was another NV soldier standing with his hands by his sides.

Loar made for him, grabbed him by the scruff of the neck and seat of the pants and hustled him over to the first POW.

A second soldier popped from the same hole and Loar gave him the same treatment.

Then he thought he'd better search it, though he wasn't sure it was now unmanned. Inside were two U.S. M-16s, one RPD machine gun, one SKS automatic rifle and one AK47, all in good firing condition.

Loar and McGowan decided the thing might be getting too big for both of them. Morell agreed and put it to Isaacs on radio that he had better send re-enforcements. But they didn't wait.

Little moved up to McGowan and handed him his M-16 and said, "You take it; I can do better without it."

They started to move along. McGowan chanced to look back. Five more enemy soldiers were coming out of the hole that had yielded the first prisoner.

They carried no arms and McGowan could see that two of them were wounded. He got out his first-aid pack and walked toward them.

Isaacs had sent posthaste Sgt. Donald J. Sunderland down the hill with a detail of ten men. They could see Morell's group working in the open before they were halfway down the slope and went straight for them. Not more curious than anxious, Isaacs decided to follow along.

The group of POWs had been stripped naked before he got there as a safety measure. McGowan was working on the wounded. One of the others had two red tabs in his hand that he had insisted on removing from his pocket. He rushed to Isaacs, shook him violently by the hand, and showed him the red tabs, anxious to establish that he was an officer. Little, startled by the rush, and not understanding the reason, was at the point of shooting him dead.

Isaacs called Sergeant Shrump on radio. He said, "You better get it to Colonel Emerson right now to send an interpreter and interrogation team up here. We have what everybody's been looking for.''

The worst wounded of the POWs they had to take turns carrying up the hill. So it was slow going. All were taken to the churned-up ground where they had laid out their perimeter.

They put them down in the bottom of the central crater, large enough and steep-banked enough that it looked blasted to order for the immediate purpose.

Isaacs collected enough spare cigarets to take care of the POWs' wants.

They were fed C rations.

Canteens were empty. So a carrying party was sent with plastic containers to replenish supply at the waterfall.

Then leaving a detail of three men to stand guard over the people in the crater, Isaacs told the rest of his gang to return to the valley and finish the task that had been started. They were to collect all weapons and equipment, prowl any more holes which had not been searched and blow any positions that might be turned to use again.

They took two more POWs. All of these soldiers were from the Fourth, Fifth and Sixth Battalions of the 24th NVA Regiment.

There were two more days on the position and at the end they had a modest inventory of loot—fifteen enemy weapons, two U.S. weapons, seventy-five packs, six mines, two bangalore torpedoes and twelve protective masks. All these trophies would be put on exhibit at the brigade headquarters to impress the visitors who regularly came in from Saigon.

Not to be so used were other, more chilling discoveries— thirteen enemy corpses and two dead Americans, earlier marked ''missing in action.''

But the play was the thing, and the live prisoners were what counted above all. Together, with no help from the outside, they had taken more enemy alive than any of the battalions engaged in Austin Six, Crazy Horse or Hawthorne Two, the three latest battles in the Central Highlands.

They had done it by a noteworthy exercise of patience on the part of them all.

But they owed what they had accomplished more particularly to the daring, imagination and willingness to try something new in two of their number. That pair had had their great day together probably because they rubbed off on one another very well.

Third Platoon was very proud of itself. It had high praises for Loar. But on their lips the name above all others was McGowan. The Improbable Scholar himself was happy to get back to his books and writing pad. Isaacs, with the approval of everyone around, was writing him up for a decoration. General Pearson and that durable fighting man, the perennial volunteer, his deputy, Col. Ted Mataxis, who all along had taken a fatherly interest in the boy lieutenant of engineers, were both happy about it. The paper would say something about how The Scholar had conducted himself with unusual courage and coolness under fire to the credit of the Screaming Eagle Brigade. McGowan knew better. Something of compassion deep within had stirred his action. Here had been tested whether he had an inherent will to kill; he knew now that he had no natural immunity to human suffering. About that discovery of himself, he was content.

Index

WARNER TAKES YOU TO THE FRONT LINES.

☐ **SOME SURVIVED** by Manny Lawton
(H34-934, $3.95, USA) (H34-935, $4.95, Canada)
A World War II veteran and prisoner of war recounts the true story of the Bataan Death March—a harrowing journey through dust, agony and death at the hands of the Japanese.

☐ **BIRD** by S. L. A. Marshall
(H35-314, $3.95, USA) (H35-315, $4.95, Canada)
The brilliant account of the First Air Cavalry's heroic defense of the strategic Vietnam landing zone called "Bird."

☐ **FOX TWO** by Randy Cunningham
with Jeff Ethell
(H35-458, $3.95, USA) (H35-459, $4.95, Canada)
A fighter pilot's birds-eye view of air combat in Vietnam, written by a decorated Navy jet commander.

Ⓦ **Warner Books P.O. Box 690
New York, NY 10019**

Please send me the books I have checked. I enclose a check or money order (not cash), plus 95¢ per order and 95¢ per copy to cover postage and handling.* (Allow 4-6 weeks for delivery.)

___Please send me your free mail order catalog. (If ordering only the catalog, include a large self-addressed, stamped envelope.)

Name _____

Address _____

City _____ State _____ Zip _____
*New York and California residents add applicable sales tax.   389